A His

MW00757286

PALGRAVE ESSENTIAL HISTORIES
General Editor: Jeremy Black

This series of compact, readable and informative national histories is designed to appeal to anyone wishing to gain a broad understanding of a country's history.

Published

A History of the Low Countries   *Paul Arblaster*
A History of Italy   *Claudia Baldoli*
A History of Russia   *Roger Bartlett*
A History of Spain (2nd edn)   *Simon Barton*
A History of the British Isles (2nd edn)   *Jeremy Black*
A History of Israel   *Ahron Bregman*
A History of Ireland   *Mike Cronin*
A History of Greece   *Nicholas Doumanis*
A History of the Pacific Islands   *Steven Roger Fischer*
A History of Korea   *Kyung Moon Hwang*
A History of the United States (3rd edn)   *Philip Jenkins*
A History of Denmark (2nd edn)   *Knud J.V. Jespersen*
A History of the Baltic States   *Andres Kasekamp*
A History of Australia   *Mark Peel and Christina Twomey*
A History of Poland (2nd edn)   *Anita J. Prazmowska*
A History of India (2nd edn)   *Peter Robb*
A History of China (3rd edn)   *J. A.G. Roberts*
A History of Germany   *Peter Wende*

Series Standing Order
ISBN 1–4039–3811–3 HB
ISBN 1–4039–3812–1 PB

If you would like to receive future titles in this series as they are published, you can make use of our standing order facility. To place a standing order please contact your bookseller or, in case of difficulty, write to us at the address below with your name and address and the name of the series. Please state with which title you wish to begin your standing order. (If you live outside the United Kingdom we may not have the rights for your area, in which case we will forward your order to the publisher concerned.)

Customer Services Department, Macmillan Distribution Ltd
Houndmills, Basingstoke, Hampshire RG21 6XS, England

A History of Korea

An Episodic Narrative

Kyung Moon Hwang

First published 2010 by
PALGRAVE MACMILLAN

Palgrave Macmillan in the UK is an imprint of Macmillan Publishers Limited, registered in England, company number 785998, of Houndmills, Basingstoke, Hampshire RG21 6XS.

Palgrave Macmillan in the US is a division of St Martin's Press LLC, 175 Fifth Avenue, New York, NY 10010.

Palgrave Macmillan is the global academic imprint of the above companies and has companies and representatives throughout the world.

Palgrave® and Macmillan® are registered trademarks in the United States, the United Kingdom, Europe and other countries.

ISBN 978–0–230–20545–1   hardback
ISBN 978–0–230–20546–8   paperback

This book is printed on paper suitable for recycling and made from fully managed and sustained forest sources. Logging, pulping and manufacturing processes are expected to conform to the environmental regulations of the country of origin.

A catalogue record for this book is available from the British Library.

A catalog record for this book is available from the Library of Congress.

Contents

CONTENTS

List of Images and Boxes

IMAGES

BOXES

Acknowledgments

Since the beginning of this project, I have benefited from the feedback of many colleagues and anonymous reviewers. I wish to start with heartfelt appreciation for Young-Hoon Rhee, John Duncan, Jennifer Jung-Kim, and Virginia Moon, who read the entire manuscript and offered much-needed criticisms and corrections. I would also like to thank Sunyoung Park, Gari Ledyard, Jihang Park, Christine Kim, Yumi Moon, and my Korean history students for offering helpful insights along the way. Colleagues at USC, in particular my friends at Parkside, East Asian Studies, and the History Department, were steadfast sources of comfort and encouragement. A special thanks goes to Jack Wills, whose work served as an inspiration for this book. The most endearing inspiration, of course, came from my wife and our son, as well as from family members both here in the US and in South Korea.

Finally, I wish to express my gratitude to the Palgrave Macmillan team, whose support, professionalism, and kindness made this book a reality: Kate Haines, Jenni Burnell, Felicity Noble and the team at Macmillan Publishing Solutions.

Kyung Moon Hwang

Note on Romanization

Korean terms will be Romanized with the McCune-Reischauer system, with the exception of the names of certain well-known individuals. The Romanization of Pyongyang and Seoul will use these more familiar forms instead of the McCune-Reischauer renderings.

Brief Chronology of Korean History

4th–7th centuries:	Three Kingdoms Period (Koguryŏ, Paekche, Silla)
668–918:	Unified Silla Kingdom
918–1392:	Koryŏ Dynasty
1170–1270:	Military Rule
1270–1356:	Mongol Overlord Period
1392–1910:	Chosŏn Dynasty
1446:	Promulgation of the Korean Alphabet
1592–98:	Japanese Invasions
1627–36:	Manchu Invasions
1894:	Tonghak Rebellion, Sino-Japanese War, Kabo Reforms
1897–1910:	Great Korean Empire (*Taehan cheguk*)
1905–10:	Japanese Protectorate
1910–45:	Japanese Colonial Rule
1910–19:	"Military Rule"
1919:	March First Uprisings
1920s:	"Cultural Rule"
1938–45:	Wartime Mobilization
1945:	Liberation and Occupation by Allied Forces
1948:	Establishment of the Republic of Korea (South) and Democratic People's Republic of Korea (North)
1950–3:	Korean War
1987:	Democratization in South Korea

Map of Korea

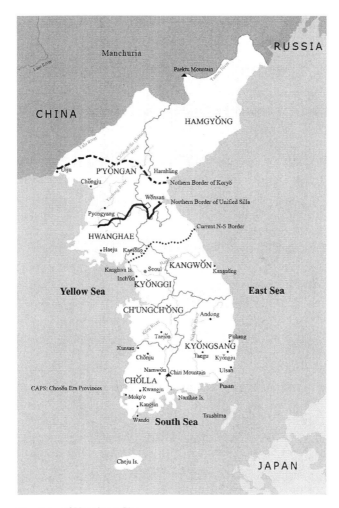

CHINA

RUSSIA

Manchuria

Paektu Mountain

HAMGYŎNG

Liao River

Yalu River

Ch'ŏngch'ŏn (Salsu) River

Uiju

P'YŎNGAN

Hamhŭng

Chŏngju

Nothern Border of Koryŏ

Taedong River

Wŏnsan

Northern Border of Unified Silla

Pyongyang

Current N-S Border

HWANGHAE

Haeju

Kaesŏng

Hangang River

Kanghwa Is.

Seoul

KANGWŎN

Kangnŭng

Inch'ŏn

KYŎNGGI

Yellow Sea

East Sea

CH'UNGCH'ŎNG

Andong

Kŭm River

Naktong River

Taejŏn

P'ohang

Kunsan

KYŎNGSANG

Chŏnju

Taegu

Kyŏngju

Namwŏn

Chiri Mountain

Ulsan

CHŎLLA

Pusan

CAPS: Chosŏn Era Provinces

Kwangju

Mokp'o

Kangjin

Namhae Is.

Wando

Tsushima

South Sea

Cheju Is.

JAPAN

Courtesy of Yongjoon Cho.

Introduction

This book assumes no prior knowledge of Korean history, but it does ask that the reader remain open to an uncommon narrative structure for presenting the richness and distinctiveness, as well as the universality, of one of the world's oldest cultures. The sweep of Korean civilization, furthermore, is matched by the scope of its modern transformation. This book attempts to make this complex history more accessible by dividing its coverage into short chapters, each of which uses a representative event, or "episode," as a window into the chapter's broader topic and themes. The order of the chapters is chronological as well as thematic. Not everything important that happened in Korean history is highlighted, but the hope is that a focus on particular events, people, and patterns will provide the reader a full understanding of the major historical connections and issues.

This is, then, a somewhat personal, idiosyncratic narrative. Some historians of Korea will undoubtedly find major topics either being neglected or given short shrift, while others will disagree with the author's choices. This book contains, for example, relatively little coverage of the mythological era of ancient Korea, King Yŏngjo's reign in the eighteenth century, independence movements during the Japanese colonial period of the early twentieth century, or the current North Korean leadership. The rationale for these decisions will either be explained or strongly implied in the respective chapters. Still other observers will of course object to the author's own biases, however veiled, in interpretation, analysis, and even periodization. This book remains mindful of the significance of legendary accounts of earlier times, for example, but its coverage of Korean history starts much later—with the Koguryŏ kingdom around the fourth century CE—than in most narratives.

Approximately half of the book is devoted to the premodern era, and half to the modern, with Chapter 14, covering the events of 1894, functioning as a narrative fulcrum just as the year 1894 acted as a historical turning point.

The reader will also wonder how to make sense of all this information, particularly about a culture that for many will be completely unfamiliar. The following themes can act as narrative anchors that ground the information to a comprehensible structure: Korean character and identity; forms of political authority; religion; economy and daily life; gender and family; social hierarchy; and external relations. The themes will allow the reader to draw connections over vast temporal distances through the perception of recurrent patterns, such as Korea's complicated relationship with China and Japan, the ties between social hierarchy and political power, or the bursts of momentous change inspired by religion. Some chapters will tackle multiple themes, some just one or two, but all the information is designed to illuminate either a theme or a specific argument. No content is presented just for the sake of transmitting information. Interpretative statements infuse every chapter, with the hope that these claims will spur further thinking and exploration from the reader. For this purpose a list of English-language sources and further readings is provided at the end of the book. Many of the primary texts from a given historical period that are referenced in this book are, in fact, available in English translation.

Historiography, or the study and method of historical inquiry, is thus featured prominently, with most chapters alluding to a historiographical debate, usually by connecting the topic at hand to larger perspectives on Korean history. Each chapter acts, then, as an intervention, of varying degrees, in these considerations of historical meaning. The historiographical issues are also critical because they reflect contemporary circumstances in Korea. While always a point of contention (and control), the historical consciousness of Koreans is key to understanding Korea today; in both the North and the South, Koreans are fully aware that they are the products of their past, from the ancient to most recent times. This book attempts to demonstrate why.

I
....
Koguryŏ and Ancient Korea

CHRONOLOGY

108 BCE	Establishment of Han dynasty commanderies on Korean Peninsula
1st c. BCE	Founding of Koguryŏ
3rd–4th c. CE	Emergence of Paekche and Silla kingdoms
581	Founding of the Sui dynasty in China
598	First Sui invasion of Koguryŏ
612	Sui dynasty campaign of 1 million soldiers against Koguryŏ
618	Fall of Sui, founding of Tang dynasty in China
668	Defeat of Koguryŏ at hands of joint Silla-Tang forces

THE GREAT BATTLE OF SALSU RIVER, 612

In the first half of the year 612, China attempted to conquer a pesky kingdom on its northeastern border and threw at this effort the full might of its resources and skill. The decisive battle in this campaign took place in what has come to be known in Korea as the "Great Battle of Salsu River," when the outmanned defenders of the Koguryŏ kingdom maneuvered the invading army into a death trap that left barely 3000 Chinese survivors out of an initial force of over 1 million soldiers. The utter failure that the Chinese Sui dynasty experienced in what should have been an easy victory does not enjoy major coverage in China's long historical lore, but in Korea this event has been considered the break-through for a nascent civilization, when it withstood the first of many major threats to its existence from the continent.

The Koguryŏ kingdom (first century BCE to seventh century CE), the earliest political entity on the Korean peninsula supported by substantial and reliable historical records, ruled territory extending from the middle of the peninsula to Manchuria at the height of its powers in the late sixth century. This geographical dominion, together with historical evidence of its military prowess, its cultural achievements, and its forms of political and religious authority, has led to the widespread and official perception of this kingdom (in both North and, interestingly, South Korea) as the great representative of early Korean civilization. This identification of Korea with Koguryŏ (from which the name "Korea" itself is derived) has grown even more acute recently as a backlash against recent Chinese efforts to insert this kingdom into China's own historical trajectory. Such an uneasy relationship with China, which undergirds a panoply of issues regarding Korean history and identity, has characterized Korea's existence since the very beginning, a beginning that Koreans believe even pre-dated Koguryŏ. The earliest years of Korean civilization are shrouded in sacred myths that invoke familiar themes (progenitor from heavenly descent, early trials and tribulations, etc.) but also speak to distinctive features of Korean identity, especially in relation to the dominant civilization on the continent, China.

ANCIENT KOREA AND KOGURYŎ

Koguryŏ as a coherent political entity appears to have materialized out of the consolidation of proto-states and statelets in the first century BCE, long after the purported foundation of Korean civilization itself, according to official and conventional histories. Indeed the Korean people supposedly began with the mythical progenitor, Tan'gun, born through the mating of the son of the presiding god over the universe who had taken human form, and a bear transformed into a woman. This legend, the earliest extant version of which dates to the thirteenth century, relates that Tan'gun established the state of "Chosŏn" in the northern reaches of the peninsula and extending well into Manchuria. The curious precision of the date of this founding, 2333 BCE (Tan'gun is credited with a reign over Chosŏn lasting over 1500 years), has given license to round up the age of Korean civilization in today's common parlance to 5000 years. Chosŏn, or "Old Chosŏn" as it is

2

referred to today, supposedly gave way to smaller states that developed more features of higher civilization on the peninsula. Needless to say, there is very little historical documentation confirming these early states except for the occasional mention in ancient Chinese histories, which, with a few exceptions, acknowledged these polities as little more than barbarian tribes. The faint historical support for these legends should lead us to doubt their accuracy, but they should not lead us to dismiss the value of these foundation myths themselves.

For one, these stories tell us much about the folk religion on the peninsula and its place in the formation of these societies. The most common element to the foundation myths of all of these early states on the peninsula, including that of Koguryŏ, is the birth of the founder from an animalistic element, such as a bear or an egg. Mythologists detect in such features the power of the native religion of Shamanism, which perceives the natural world as infused with spirits that affect human life and can be appeased only through a priestly *shaman*, the liaison to the spirit world. As in many other early civilizations, the priest who claimed access to the spirits (or gods) enjoyed political power as well, and this appears to be reflected in the mythologies of these early states. Tan'gun, with his parentage in the spirit world, can be considered the embodiment of the first Great Shaman, and the same could be said for Chumong, the mythical progenitor of Koguryŏ, who is said to have hatched from an egg.

The foundation myths also suggest a strong consciousness of the well-established civilization on the continent, that of China. The best-known version of the Tan'gun myth, for example, recites that Tan'gun introduced administrative capacities to govern his realm. This suggests the need to legitimate this civilization as worthy of both Chinese-derived recognition, on the one hand, and autonomy from China on the other. Indeed, Korea's ability to resist absorption into China while benefiting from the Middle Kingdom's cultural influence has been central to Korea's existence since the earliest times. This theme was exemplified by the well-known story, eventually integrated into the "Old Chosŏn" narrative, that Tan'gun was succeeded by a sage named Kija, a refugee from Chou dynasty China, in the centuries before Koguryŏ came into being. Kija represented the authenticating presence of Chinese civilization, and until the twentieth century Koreans commonly believed that Tan'gun bestowed upon Korea its people and basic culture, while Kija gave Korea its high culture—and, presumably, standing as a legitimate civilization. Nationalist sentiment in the modern era has diminished Kija's place today to the point of near extinction, but unquestionably, whether Kija was real or fictitious, he symbolized the powerful self-consciousness vis-à-vis China from the earliest times of Korean civilization.

More historically tenable is the struggle Koguryŏ waged, in its formative years, against the Chinese military presence on the Korean peninsula. In the corridor between the peninsula and northeast China, the Chinese Han dynasty established four "commanderies" that ruled over parts of the peninsula and Manchuria, much as modern imperial powers governed their colonies. Like their contemporary Roman counterparts, these Chinese colonies transmitted the fruits of a more advanced culture and technology to the "barbarians," but they also had an uneasy relationship with these tribes, whom they both nominally ruled and kept a wary distance from. Eventually the Lelang (Korean: Nangnang) Commandery, centered around present-day Pyongyang, would establish itself as the most stable and enduring of China's colonial administrations on the peninsula. And the kingdom of Koguryŏ constituted the Korean counterpart providing the most consistent challenge to Chinese dominion. While the Lelang Commandery survived the fall of the Han dynasty itself, in the early fourth century Koguryŏ overran it. Soon Koguryŏ had to contend with competing kingdoms on the peninsula that had undergone much the same process of consolidation from tribal confederations. All these early kingdoms, from their adoption of Buddhism and Chinese writing to their mimicking of Confucian administrative patterns, reflected the blend of Chinese cultural influence and longstanding peninsular cultural behaviors. Among them, Koguryŏ, thanks to its geographical proximity to China, remained the most wary of, even hostile to, Chinese influence.

THE RISE AND FALL OF KOGURYŎ

Koguryŏ seems not to have taken well to the notion of "Eastern Barbarians," the original Chinese moniker for the peoples of the peninsula that eventually became a self-deprecating term of prestige for Koreans, who considered themselves "first among seconds" in relation to other peoples surrounding China. After the fall of the Han dynasty in the early third century, China itself underwent four centuries of fragmentation, and Koguryŏ took advantage of this situation to grow increasingly powerful in northeast Asia and dominant on the peninsula. The martial vigor, economic vitality, and cultural advancement of this kingdom, so visible in the numerous tomb paintings still extant, gives a good inkling of the impressive political and military power that Koguryŏ amassed. The other major polities on the peninsula—Paekche, Kaya, and Silla (see next chapter)—were much younger and, until the latter part of the sixth century, left to fight among themselves for the southern half of the peninsula, while Koguryŏ's dominion extended all the way to the far reaches of Manchuria. An early peak of Koguryŏ power was achieved at the turn of the fifth century under the reign of King Kwanggaet'o, whose exploits in pushing the boundaries of Koguryŏ's dominion in all directions befit his name, which means "extender of territory." Koguryŏ, however, did not seek conquest of the entire peninsula, despite the perpetual condition of competition and struggle among the kingdoms. At times it offered aid, such as to Silla when invaders from the Japanese archipelago harassed the southeastern region. At other times the Koguryŏ court sent its own cultural missionaries—to a nascent kingdom in Japan, for example—to transmit Buddhism, the arts, architecture, and other fruits of high culture. Koguryŏ was, in short, the great power on the peninsula, indeed of the entire northeast Asian region, and this was to last until the latter half of the sixth century, when developments both on the peninsula and in China threatened this status.

Koguryŏ's contestation for power achieved some notable gains, and in fact the cessation of ongoing hostilities with the people on the mainland allowed Koguryŏ to turn its attention to expanding its reach into the peninsula. This transition was apparent in the early fifth century, when the capital was moved from a locale in Manchuria to Pyongyang, former site of the headquarters of the Han commandery of Lelang and subsequently one of the regional capitals of Koguryŏ. Henceforth Pyongyang would cement its standing as a center of Korean civilization, even when it no longer functioned as the capital in subsequent dynasties. (North Korea's claim of Pyongyang as the proper locale of Korea's capital, then, is strongly supported by history.) Koguryŏ did not trample across the peninsula, however, and the balance of power was maintained when Paekche and Silla, by now the other two remaining kingdoms, entered into a semi-formal alliance in the fifth century to check Koguryŏ. Henceforth the borders between these three ebbed and flowed. Even Paekche, better known for its cultural achievements than for its martial prowess, managed to gain territorial victories. It was the prickly, relatively late-blooming kingdom of Silla, however, that began to enjoy advances in this tripartite rivalry by the middle of the sixth century, which would not have endangered Koguryŏ had it not been for the simultaneously threatening circumstances brewing in China.

In the year 581, after nearly four centuries of fragmentation, China was reunified by the Sui dynasty. Soon thereafter the Sui turned to one of the most nettlesome matters that had plagued Chinese polities, namely, what to do about the feisty kingdom to its northeast, Koguryŏ. The early years of the Sui witnessed an effort on both sides to establish a working relationship, but soon the age-old mistrust, coupled with internal developments within Koguryŏ, fueled a downward spiral in relations. As with its drives to extend the Grand Canal and to fortify the Great Wall, the Sui dynasty took a heavy-handed approach to the Korea question. And as with these other campaigns, the efforts to conquer Koguryŏ would contribute to the short life span of the Sui polity itself. In response to Koguryŏ's advances into the western banks of the Liao River, the first Chinese invasion attempt came in 598, amassing a force of 300,000 naval and ground soldiers that became bogged down in bad weather and worse luck on their way to the peninsula.

The heavy losses suffered by the Sui forces in 598 would pale in comparison to the calamities of the next major invasion attempt in 612, which would end with defeat at the Battle of Salsu River.

The Chinese force mobilized for this campaign in the early part of the year was staggering in scale: 1,133,800 in soldiers alone, not counting the accompanying forces to move and feed them. The historical records recount that the original six divisions of fighters marching together stretched for thirty miles. These armies managed eventually to overcome the Koguryŏ forces in crossing the Liao River and penetrating the Koguryŏ foothold in the Liaodong region of Manchuria. The Chinese, however, suffered enormous casualties and other losses (through, for example, sickness and runaways), enabling Koguryŏ not only to stave off conquest but also to inflict severe damage to the attackers. In its siege of the Koguryŏ capital of Pyongyang, the Sui forces, severely weakened in morale and supplies, penetrated the outer walls of the city, but the Koguryŏ defenders held off the attackers long enough to negotiate a peace settlement. This agreement would ostensibly bring about Koguryŏ's capitulation and entrance into a subordinate tributary relationship with the Sui emperor, in return for Chinese withdrawal from the peninsula.

The Koguryŏ commander assigned to relay this message to the Sui forces, Ŭlchi Mundŏk, would go down in Korean historical lore as one of its most heroic figures, not for negotiating a surrender to the Chinese—for this was but a ploy—but for destroying the Sui army during its slow retreat back to China. As it trod northward along the northwestern coast of the peninsula and found its way to the Salsu River (known as the Ch'ŏngch'ŏn River today), Ŭlchi readied his troops. As the Sui soldiers crossed the river, the Koguryŏ forces unleashed a barrage of attacks that utterly destroyed the Chinese army. Among the strategies deployed was the releasing of dammed water up-river that overwhelmed many of the Chinese soldiers. The Korean historical records note that the Sui army, which had begun with over 300,000 soldiers laying siege to Pyongyang, numbered a mere 2700 when it reached Liaodong several weeks later. It would go down as one of the monumental defeats in world history; rarely had such an enormous force—beginning with over a million soldiers—suffered such a devastating defeat from a severely outmanned counterpart. For the Koguryŏ, and for Koreans looking back on their history of constant suffering at the hands of foreign invaders, this episode constituted a victory of epic proportions.

The stupendous scale of this defeat did not deter the Sui emperor, however, from launching another invasion the next year, and yet another in 614. Both subsequent efforts also failed to conquer Koguryŏ, but the kingdom was undoubtedly weakened by these campaigns. The Sui dynasty, though, also paid a price; it began to collapse shortly thereafter, partly because of the enormous cost of these conquest attempts. The succeeding unified Chinese dynasty, the Tang, followed up with campaigns of its own in the 640s, but these, too, met with failure due to fierce resistance under the direction of the military dictator of Koguryŏ, Yŏn Kaesomun. It was evident that the Chinese would not be able to destroy Koguryŏ on their own, and indeed it took an alliance with the peninsular kingdom of Silla, which had chafed at Koguryŏ's imposing presence, for this to take place. The political unification of the Korean peninsula would finally come in 668 through the destruction of Koguryŏ at the hands of the joint Silla-Tang forces.

The wall paintings of the Koguryŏ tombs

The relative dearth of written documentation about Koguryŏ is compensated by the wondrously vivid details of the wall paintings found in more than a hundred tombs around the major Koguryŏ settlements, in particular the Liaodong area and the capitals of Pyongyang and Kungnaesŏng, on the banks of the upper Yalu River. These extraordinary paintings visually expound upon what the textual evidence hints at: a vigorous, sophisticated, and advanced civilization.

That these paintings exist at all tells us that Koguryŏ was a highly stratified society with a powerful and wealthy aristocracy, the highest members of whom, along with the royal families, left this world encased in elaborately decorated tombs. The paintings on the tomb walls usually depict the buried person

⫸

himself (or herself), accompanied by attendees drawn to smaller size but equally colorful in their dress. Other scenes testify to a ruling order that was not only glamorous but martial in orientation, with depictions of muscled strongmen that celebrate vigor and strength, battle scenes of elaborately clad warriors, and hunting scenes with immaculately dressed warriors on horseback aiming their bows and arrows at leaping deer and tigers. Great skill in archery and horseback riding, indeed, would constitute signal features of Korean military culture thereafter.

The wall paintings also provide a strong indication of how the Koguryŏ people, or at least its ruling class, viewed the greater cosmos, and how sophisticatedly the arts and architecture reflected this cosmology. Wondrous spirits abound, including the "four guardian deities" (*sasin*) of ancient East Asian folklore. There are also depictions of human-like figures in flowing robes representing the gods of the earth, moon, sun, and fire. Buddhist paintings tell us that this imported, systematic, and textual religion was making its presence felt in the religious order, likely melding with native folk practices and boasting an understanding of the movement of the heavens, as represented in the star charts painted onto the walls. Art was not limited just to the service of Koguryŏ cosmology, though, as we see in the depictions of musical and dance performances and other scenes of a sophisticated aristocratic sensibility.

Depictions of the daily lives of the people, however, are equally revealing. We are treated to scenes of an ancient form of "ssirŭm," or Korean wrestling, women going about their weaving activities, and people in the fields and marketplaces dressed in polka-dotted clothing. We also get a strong sense of the economic advancement of Koguryŏ civilization, for amidst the displays of agricultural and handicraft goods are numerous appearances of wagons. Indeed, there is even a depiction of what appears to be a "wagon goddess" wielding an oversized wheel like a magic wand. Based on the lack of such visual

⫸

depictions and the general condition of Korean roads thereafter, which were designed for walking—both by humans
and horses—wagons seem to have diminished considerably
subsequently in Korea's socioeconomic order until the twentieth century. Indeed, these extraordinary wall paintings suggest
that economic technologies might have been just one of many
aspects of Korean civilization for which Koguryŏ had achieved
an early peak.

KOGURYŎ AND KOREAN HISTORY

Until the twentieth century, the Silla unification enjoyed the
stamp of legitimacy in the prevailing Korean historical perspective, for each succeeding dynastic order traced its lineage ultimately to this seventh-century event. In the modern era, however,
nationalist history gradually deemed the Silla unification more a
betrayal of the nation than a resolution of centuries of peninsular
balkanization. Silla's misstep was said to be twofold. First, it turned
to the Chinese for solving an internal Korean issue and thereby set
a precedent of dependence that would inflict the entirety of Korean
history thereafter—a pervasive cultural dependence that robbed
the Koreans of their sense of identity, and a military and political dependence that would reappear repeatedly, indeed well into
the twentieth century. Second, the Silla-Tang alliance destroyed
what many modern nationalists consider the true representative of
Korea's ancient civilization, Koguryŏ. It was Koguryŏ that appears
to have had the most vibrant and advanced political, military, and
cultural order, and, perhaps most importantly, Koguryŏ was the
one ancient kingdom that refused to budge in the face of threats
to peninsular autonomy. Koguryŏ's relentless resistance to the
Chinese could not have stood in starker contrast to Silla's behavior of turning to the Chinese to solve a dispute between Korean
polities.

   The problem with this revisionist perspective, which is now
orthodoxy in North Korea and widely accepted in South Korea,

10

is that—aside from overlooking the many examples of Koguryŏ's close ties to China and exaggerating the dependence of Silla or Paekche on outside forces—it imposes a modern nation-centered perspective on the history of the fourth to seventh centuries. In this era of the "Three Kingdoms" (Koguryŏ, Paekche, Silla), the people of these kingdoms likely did not perceive a common bond. In fact, the reordering of history to make it appear as such began with the subsequent Unified Silla kingdom itself in order to legitimate its dominion over the peninsula. The official historians of the Koryŏ dynasty (918–1392), whose name purposefully evoked the glories of Koguryŏ, further cemented the notion of a "Three Kingdoms" era and bestowed upon the Unified Silla kingdom the status of national unifier. Ironically, their successors in the twentieth century would turn this imagined unity into an insistence on the centrality not of Silla, but rather of Koguryŏ.

Indeed, so widely accepted has this historical perspective become on the Korean peninsula today, that to consider Koguryŏ an independent kingdom based partly in the Korean peninsula and partly in Manchuria is to provoke outrage. What contemporary Chinese historians have done, apparently with the blessings of the Chinese government, is to go one step further and imply that Koguryŏ was actually an actor in *Chinese* history: just as China today is one country with many ethnicities, China in the past was one country with many groups, including the people of Koguryŏ. From the Koreans' perspective, this amounts to robbing them of their own history, the history of the very kingdom on which the name of "Korea" itself is based! Lying beneath the surface, however, is the latent Korean belief, of which the Chinese are aware, that Koguryŏ can provide a great lesson on how Koreans—eventually reunified, as warranted by the official national imperative—should deal with a resurgent, dominant China: at arm's length, and with an assertiveness of Korea's autonomy and interests. Such is the power of history, even the history of ancient times, in Korea today.

2

....

Queen Sŏndŏk and Silla's Unification of Korea

CHRONOLOGY

SILLA'S DISPATCH OF A TRIBUTE EMBASSY TO CHINA, 643

Feeling besieged, the monarch of the kingdom of Silla sent a tributary embassy to the emperor of Tang dynasty China in 643 with an urgent request for Chinese assistance in fending off the unrelenting incursions from the other two peninsular powers, Koguryŏ and Paekche. The Chinese emperor, sensing another opportunity to strike Koguryŏ, vowed to attack the two adversaries and even offered thousands of Chinese army uniforms so that Silla soldiers could intimidate their opponents on the battlefield. The emperor's third suggestion, though, was startling: Silla should accept a Chinese prince as its interim ruler, whose presence would put an end to Silla's misfortune—a misfortune that, according to the emperor, was due to its monarch. It was not the Silla ruler's actions or policies that were objectionable, but rather the ruler's gender: Silla's monarch was Queen Sŏndŏk, the first of three female rulers of Silla.

Significantly for the subsequent history of Korea, this brazen push to reestablish a Chinese foothold on the peninsula was (respectfully) resisted by Silla, despite the Tang emperor's support for the anti-Sŏndŏk elements within the Silla ruling order. Queen Sŏndŏk managed to weather this storm, and during her reign from 632 to 647, Silla proceeded not only to survive but to thrive. It further centralized state rule, sponsored the continuing growth of Buddhism, nurtured the flowering of science and culture, and solidified the Silla state and military power through the cultivation of skillful people who eventually were to lead the country to peninsular supremacy. Tang China would be Silla's indispensable partner in the wars of unification, but as shown by the pressures exerted upon Queen Sŏndŏk's rule, Silla had to remain wary of ultimate Chinese designs. The Sillan leaders' capacity to walk this diplomatic tightrope between assistance and autonomy would prove instrumental in securing the peninsula's unification under Silla domination. That this process would begin during the reign of a female monarch also reveals a great deal about distinctive cultural patterns inscribed onto the peninsula by not only Silla but all of the ancient civilizations on the peninsula. Indeed, Queen Sŏndŏk herself would embody many of these qualities, including the tantalizing signs that, in regard to the role and status of females, Silla might have been ahead of its time.

BUDDHISM AND POWER

Queen Sŏndŏk's most notable accomplishment might have been to achieve an early peak in the relationship between Korean political and social power, on the one hand, and royal sponsorship of the Buddhist establishment on the other. Buddhism, a religion preaching the path of overcoming human suffering through ritual, action, study, and meditation—just as its founder, Siddhartha Gautama (the Buddha), had done in the sixth century BCE—had by the fourth century CE traversed its way eastward through northern India, Tibet, China, and the Korean peninsula, on its way eventually toward Japan. Through this process this religion gained a tremendous following, usually first among learned elites, who developed different approaches and perspectives in line with their specific cultural heritage. They then disseminated the modified forms to the laity and usually persuaded the ruling groups to embrace this powerfully spiritual and systematic set of teachings. The political rulers, in turn, found Buddhism, in particular the Buddhist clergy, a useful ally in further consolidating their domination and in heightening the aura of their authority. Eventually, political domination went hand-in-hand with patronage of Buddhism.

The authoritative twelfth-century Korean historical source, *History of the Three Kingdoms (Samguk sagi)*, relates that an especially large number of Buddhist temples was erected during Sŏndŏk's reign, firmly establishing a defining pattern of Korean history until the fourteenth century. Not coincidentally, some of the oldest surviving artifacts of Korean civilization are stone pagodas that dot the countryside and Buddhist temples, some dating back to the ancient era even if the wooden buildings that surround them do not. Queen Sŏndŏk, like other monarchs on the peninsula, appears to have benefited from this association with the religious order, for it provided support for her claims to monarchical authority. In fact, the "Mirŭk" or Maitreya sect of Buddhism that prevailed on the peninsula considered the monarch the embodiment of the Buddha himself. The ancient Korean rulers, even those of systematic, sophisticated states like Silla, basked in this religious eminence, which accompanied the increasing centralization of state authority visible in all three kingdoms.

For some leaders, like Sŏndŏk, the historical perception of their rule appears to have been firmly wedded to their spiritual mystique. The *Tales of the Three Kingdoms (Samguk yusa)*, a work dating from the thirteenth century that mostly recounts the often legendary history of Buddhism in ancient Korea, provides glimpses of this relationship. Sŏndŏk is said to have issued three prophecies during her reign, all coming true: one concerning a cryptic gift from the Chinese emperor, another suspecting an imminent Paekche attack, and finally a prediction of the manner of her own death. The content of these prophecies reflects important issues that surrounded her reign, as we will see below. But the overarching impression left behind by these stories is of a skillful, sagacious monarch whose glories were reflected in her mystical powers. It was if she was indeed a reincarnation of the Buddha, or at least the embodiment of the blending of Buddhist teachings and native shamanistic practices.

Buddhism exerted its influence also through the great standing that China enjoyed as the perceived center of high culture. The Three Kingdoms each sent students and scholars to the Middle Kingdom to gain exposure to advanced Buddhist learning. The most prominent and gifted scholar-monk of Silla was a younger contemporary of Queen Sŏndŏk, Wŏnhyo (617–86). Indeed Wŏnhyo is still the most celebrated figure in Korean Buddhist history, so influential was his attempt to synthesize Buddhist teachings into a more comprehensible form. He could be characterized as the first great Korean popularizer of this foreign religion, and his influence extended all the way to Japan, which became a depository of continental civilization as filtered largely through the kingdoms of the Korean peninsula. Such activity was not limited to Buddhism, however; other aspects of Chinese culture were eagerly absorbed (and transmitted), including the complicated but impressively ordered set of teachings about government and politics that we know as Confucianism. According to legend, Wŏnhyo's own son, Sŏl Ch'ong (660–730), established himself as one of the early great Confucian scholars and has traditionally been credited with developing the Korean writing system known as *idu*. Together this father–son tandem symbolized the momentous transitions in Korean civilization during their life spans, in particular the unification of the peninsula under Silla rule.

LEGENDS OF THE UNIFICATION

Queen Sŏndŏk's reign is often credited with the commencement of the inexorable unification process, which ended in the 670s when Silla, having conquered the other two peninsular states, established a working peace with its main ally-turned-rival in the unification wars, Tang dynasty China. As noted in Chapter 1, until the twentieth-century Korean historical orthodoxy had considered this a legitimate and inevitable step in the historical trajectory of Korean civilization. Queen Sŏndŏk stood as a central character in the unification saga, but the best-known figures were two officials who came of age under her reign, Kim Ch'unch'u and Kim Yusin.

In the 630s, when Queen Sŏndŏk ascended to the throne, Silla did not stand in a strong position to emerge as the eventual victor on the peninsula. It was under constant attack from both of its rivals and losing territory, especially to Paekche. As the *History of the Three Kingdoms* recounts, when Kim Ch'unch'u, a nephew of Queen Sŏndŏk, lost one of his daughters in a Paekche attack in 641, he turned his grief into a raging pursuit of vengeance. He received Sŏndŏk's permission to take a small delegation to Koguryŏ to ask for its assistance in the struggle against Paekche. The Koguryŏ monarch demanded in return promises from Silla to return some of Koguryŏ's former territory that Silla had seized earlier. When Kim rejected this demand, the Koguryŏ king immediately incarcerated him. Word reached the Silla court, and soon Queen Sŏndŏk had a talented military official, Kim Yusin, mobilize 10,000 crack troops to attack Koguryŏ. Before fighting ensued, this daring move appeared sufficient to earn Kim Ch'unch'u's release, and the legend of the two Kims was born, eventually to climax in their respective roles in the unification wars.

Kim Ch'unch'u would gain fame as the ambitious enabler of Silla's unification. He laid the diplomatic groundwork, through his trips to China as Silla's royal envoy, for the indispensable alliance with the Tang dynasty. For this, he would also be eventually excoriated by some modern historians for setting a precedent of subservience. Later, after being enthroned as King Muyŏl in 654, Ch'unch'u cemented this relationship with China, which paid off when, in early 660, the Tang emperor sent 130,000 Chinese troops to the western coast in order to join Silla in its attack on Paekche forces. Paekche would fall that summer in the famous Battle of Hwangsanbŏl. Ch'unch'u died the following year, and it would be his son, the next Silla king, who would oversee the completion of the unification project under the direction of Kim Yusin.

If Kim Ch'unch'u has faced a mixed reception among modern historians, Kim Yusin has continued to enjoy a positive assessment.

The military hero of the unification wars, Kim Yusin's popular standing has as much to do with the many legendary stories of his exploits as with his historically verifiable accomplishments, which were spectacular to begin with. First, he played a central role, as Kim Ch'unch'u's brother-in-law, in providing the political and military support for Ch'unch'u to ascend to the throne in the first place. He served thereafter as Ch'unch'u's right-hand man in efforts to solidify the alliance with Tang China, consolidate and strengthen monarchical control, and carry out the military campaigns against Paekche. As the leader of Silla's forces, Kim Yusin is credited with defeating and eventually conquering Paekche, and with mapping out the plan to conquer Koguryŏ. The defeat of Koguryŏ, again in partnership with the Tang forces, came finally in 668, but not without the threat of Silla itself becoming absorbed by the Chinese ally. When Tang forces remained in Korea to enforce the Chinese emperor's claims to dominion over the peninsula as a whole, Kim Yusin led the resistance in what has come to be known as the Silla–Tang War of the 670s. Kim's eventual success in driving out the Chinese from the peninsula was tempered by the compromise reached for the sake of peace, namely the limitation of Silla's advance into Koguryŏ's old territory. While modern historians would lament this outcome, Kim Yusin's heroic status remains untainted. In fact it has spawned a modern romanticization of Kim and especially of the troupe of young men that had trained him, the *Hwarang*.

The *Hwarang*, literally the "Flower Youth" Corps, appears to have risen to prominence during the reign of Queen Sŏndŏk's father, King Chinp'yŏng. The *History of the Three Kingdoms*, which seems to have used as a reference a work called the *Chronicles of the Hwarang* (*Hwarang segi*), includes a few passages that portray the *Hwarang* as a youth group that inculcated the spirit of camaraderie, learning, and service. Kim Yusin was the most famous *Hwarang* graduate, but prominent also were his son, Wŏnsul, and Kwanch'ang, a brave youth who died in the decisive battle against Paekche in 660. The legendary standing of these three, and the relative absence of *Hwarang* actions in the records after the seventh century, point again to the appropriation of people, events, and legends for the historical legitimation of the Silla unification. Such an exercise was not limited to the Silla unification, however. Even before, but particularly after, the controversial discovery of a manuscript of *The Chronicles of the Hwarang* in the late 1980s, political and cultural leaders in South Korea pointed to this troupe as a model for traditional values, patriotism, national service, and even the martial arts.

Paekche, the Third Kingdom

The debate about the national legitimacy of Silla's unification of the Three Kingdoms is itself based on the notion of the Three Kingdoms being somehow "Korean" because what later became Korea occupied the same geographical territory as the Three Kingdoms. Such a structuring of the past according to what happened later—what historians call the fallacy of *teleology*—overlooks the political as well as nationalistic motivations for devising such narratives of legitimation and primordial national character. Furthermore, this premise tends to downgrade other important elements of ancient history on the peninsula, in particular the "third kingdom" of Paekche. In addition to being a major political and cultural entity, Paekche best reflected the complex, close ties between the peninsular polities and those in the islands to the east that, around the same time as the Silla unification, formed what we now call Japan.

At one time Paekche might have been the most dynamic and powerful of the three kingdoms. It enjoyed the economic advantages of occupying the peninsula's fertile south-central and southwestern regions, which also provided easier access to China for trade and cultural exchange. Although the mythologies of this kingdom date its founding to the first century BCE by migrants from the north, historical records more soundly place its emergence in the fourth century CE. The early

IIII➡

Paekche state, however, was driven from its original position around present-day Seoul further southward, and for the last two centuries of its existence until 660, Paekche territory commanded the southwestern portion of the peninsula. There it developed a sophisticated political and economic system, but achieved its most impressive advances in religion and culture. Indeed Buddhism's paramount position in Paekche civilization appears to have inspired the most outstanding examples of religious artifacts from the ancient era.

Paekche transmitted many of these cultural advances, including technologies in metallurgy and architecture, to the polities that began forming simultaneously across the strait in the Japanese islands. The archaeological and historical evidence, including from ancient Japanese sources, of consistent, active interaction between the archipelago and the states on the peninsula is overwhelming. So strong were the ties between the early Japanese state and Paekche, in particular, that when Paekche battled Silla in the unification wars, aid arrived from the islands, and after Paekche's defeat in 660, many of its rulers fled to Japan. These developments reinforced a connection that likely dated back several centuries. But how close was this connection? Did, for example, Paekche rulers contribute to establishing the Japanese royal line, and if so, to what extent? In 2001 the Japanese emperor himself acknowledged the Paekche contributions to his ancestry, which further complicated the historical claims on both sides. But the larger lesson is that there were no such things as Korea and Japan before the seventh century, and that these two countries began as political constructs rather than as primordial civilizations.

SILLA'S "WINNING" FEATURES

The modern appropriation of the *Hwarang* myths served as a capstone to the centuries-long drive to see something spectacular in Silla's conquest of the other two kingdoms. But it can be argued that these attempts to incorporate the unification struggle into a grand narrative of national unity did a disservice. In Chapter 1 we noted that this traditional perspective faced a backlash from many modern observers, especially those who considered Koguryŏ to have been a truer representative of ancient Korean civilization. A further historical disservice lay in the fact that the glorification of Silla's unification heroics tended to overshadow other intriguing features of this kingdom. Two overlooked facets of Silla in particular and, by extension, of ancient Korea as a whole, come to mind, both highlighted by their association with Queen Sŏndŏk.

The first theme is the impressive technological and cultural advancement of the ancient societies on the peninsula. We have noted already the Koguryŏ achievements in this regard, and Paekche also demonstrated these advances, particularly in the realms of architecture and metallurgy. Silla, too, reached notable heights, with stunning examples still readily visible today in the "museum without walls," the city of Kyŏngju, Silla's capital. These include enormous and immaculate bronze bells, the pagodas in the showcase Buddhist temple of "Pulguksa," the intricately crafted stone carvings of ancient spirits and legends that grace the numerous tombs and other artifacts, and the extraordinary "Sŏkkuram" Buddhist grotto that achieved perfection in the unity of art and spirituality. Perhaps the most stunning remnant of ancient Kyŏngju is the eight-meter high "Chŏmsŏngdae" astronomical observatory that visitors encounter literally on the side of the road. This observatory's precise date of origin is unclear, but all of the historical accounts about it, beginning with the *History of the Three Kingdoms*, point toward the reign of Queen Sŏndŏk. In addition to the historical records, another feature of this observatory also seems to support this perspective: it is comprised of twenty seven layers of stone, and Queen Sŏndŏk was the twenty-seventh monarch of Silla. Before dismissing this as a coincidence, one has to consider the precision in the construction of this observatory. The twenty seven layers are divided by a square-shaped entrance mid-way up the structure, which takes up three layers. That leaves twelve layers above and below the entrance, in reference to the twelve months of the lunar year. Even the number of stones is roughly 365, the number of days in the year. Given its role in setting the agricultural calendar, forecasting the weather, and, presumably, predicting natural disasters, astronomy (or astrology) occupied a central place in the economic life of the people and, hence, also in maintaining the aura of legitimacy surrounding ancient monarchs.

Another notable feature of the observatory's construction is its shape (see image 2), which is very different from other astronomical observatories in traditional Korea. While one could easily regard this shape as that of a vase, one could also argue that, because it was built during the reign of Queen Sŏndŏk and may have even stood as an altar to her, the observatory actually is shaped to resemble a female body. Whether this is true or not, the possibility leads us to the other feature of Silla and ancient

Image 2 The Ch'ŏmsŏngdae Observatory, Kyŏngju, South Korea. (Author's photo.)

Korea evoked by Queen Sŏndŏk, and that is the surprisingly high status of females. Textual and archaeological sources point toward practices, such as uxorilocalism, or the custom of the husband living in his bride's household, suggesting a relatively high standing of females in the ancient kingdoms. The Koguryŏ tomb paintings discussed in Chapter 1 also feature prominent females in a way never seen again in later Korean eras. Perhaps the most convincing sign of high female standing, however, are Silla's three female monarchs, starting with Sŏndŏk, then with her successor, Chindŏk, and finally Queen Chinsŏng, who reigned in the late ninth century toward the end of the Unified Silla kingdom. A female ruler of Korea would not reappear thereafter.

There remain competing interpretations about the background of Sŏndŏk's ascent to the throne, which laid the foundation for the other two female monarchs, but the important point is that Sŏndŏk was almost certainly much more than a figurehead, and that indeed she elicited fierce pride and loyalty. The legends surrounding her mystical powers, described above, point to this, but a more convincing source is the *History of the Three Kingdoms*, which notes that, even before her reign, she had proven herself "generous, benevolent, wise, and smart." This source reveals that, upon ascension to the throne, she undertook a major relief campaign on behalf of frail commoners in the countryside, and later she coordinated efforts to find a solution to the constant barrage of attacks from the other two peninsular kingdoms. The most memorable episode came in 643, when she dispatched a diplomatic mission to the Tang emperor of China, only to be ridiculed for being a female monarch in the first place! The Tang emperor, it is recorded, put forth three proposals in response to the Silla ambassador's pleas. First, he would attack Liaodong in order to divert the attention of Koguryŏ, China's longtime nemesis, and carry out a naval campaign on the western coast of the peninsula to preoccupy Paekche. Second, the Tang emperor would provide thousands of Tang uniforms and Tang army flags in order to help Silla soldiers disguise themselves as fearsome Chinese troops. Finally, the emperor would send a Tang prince to serve as the new monarch of Silla, for Silla, according to the emperor, faced constant siege because its enemies were

emboldened by Silla's female monarch. The unsettling implications of this final proposal could not have escaped the Silla
ambassador, who is recorded as having simply but respectfully
acknowledged the emperor's proposals. This only invited more
scorn from the Tang emperor, who wondered about the fitness of
such a man as a diplomatic envoy.

What is equally remarkable about this historical account is that
the twelfth-century compiler of the *History of the Three Kingdoms*,
Kim Pusik, was a Confucian scholar-official who disdained the idea
of a female ruler. In addition to other details suggesting that the Tang
emperor's proposals provoked political intrigue among Sŏndŏk's
opponents in the Silla elite, the *History of the Three Kingdoms*'
account of Queen Sŏndŏk's reign concludes with commentary that
support the Tang emperor's proposal: "According to heavenly principles, the *yang* [male] is hard while the *yin* [female] is soft; and
people know that men are to be revered and women are subordinate.
So how could Silla have allowed an old maid to leave her inner
sanctum in order to govern the country's affairs? Silla allowed her
to ascend to become the king, and sure enough chaos ensued. How
fortunate that the country did not get destroyed!"

Not only did the country avoid destruction, but it might have been
Sŏndŏk's accomplishments, including her patronage of science
and technology as well as her savvy in cultivating Sillan statecraft,
that saved the kingdom in the face of its imminent demise. That
this might even have contributed to Silla's ultimate triumph on the
peninsula is an irony that seems to have escaped Kim Pusik, himself
a descendant of the Silla aristocracy, in his Confucian critique.
But these tantalizing signs of Sŏndŏk's prowess, however scarce
the reliable historical details, have worked in a way that reverses
the traditional historical perspective. Today Queen Sŏndŏk, like the
Silla unification, Kim Yusin, and other venerable relics of ancient
Korea, is being reevaluated and freely appropriated by Koreans in
reconsidering their identity and heritage. In reimaginings reflected
in popular culture, Queen Sŏndŏk today often serves as a paragon
of female virtue, a great symbol of a time when Korea, unsullied
by Chinese and other external influences, stayed true to itself and
held (some) women in high esteem.

3

The Unified Silla Kingdom

CHRONOLOGY

THE ASSASSINATION OF CHANG POGO, 846

The mid-ninth century witnessed the peak of the powers of Chang Pogo, the local strongman of the southwestern coast of Silla who dominated the profitable trading networks that linked the peninsula to Japan and China. But despite Chang's tremendous economic and military authority, a wily assassin was able to penetrate the defenses surrounding him and end an ongoing struggle between Chang and the central elites of the Unified Silla kingdom. Chang's death at the hands of this assassin demonstrated that, for all his powers, he could not evade the intrigues of court politics 200 miles away in the Silla capital of Kyŏngju—indeed, Chang had willfully engaged in them, even going so far as to arrange a marriage between his daughter and a Silla monarch. When this effort turned powerful aristocrats against him, he met his fate.

As it turned out, Chang's demise would mark the beginning of the end of the Unified Silla era. This appears fitting, for Chang's successes and travails also symbolized key facets of Silla society, from his social background and his growth as a local warlord to his activities beyond the Korean peninsula. That Chang would go down in historical lore primarily as the man most responsible for Korea's brief standing at the heart of the northeast Asian trading system points also to the revival of interest in him in contemporary times, when (South) Korea is seeking to reinvigorate its regional standing. This interest in Chang's exploits from 1200 years ago harkens back to an era, swathed in mythical overtones, when Korea lay in the center of northeast Asia.

CHANG POGO, CH'OE CH'IWŎN, AND UNIFIED SILLA SOCIETY

The scattered sources of information regarding Chang Pogo's early life hardly suggest a future as a historically important figure. He appears to have made his way to the Shandong Peninsula in China as a young man, where he became a local military officer and later gained experience in seafaring and trading activities as a member of the Silla expatriate community. He is also credited with establishing a Buddhist temple for the Sillans, *Pŏphwawŏn*, which served also as a kind of consulate, a base for not only religious worship and ceremonies but economic and diplomatic activities. Chang's return to his homeland is the next entrance in his sketchy biography. However, it is uncertain whether he was driven by a determination to thwart the pirates who regularly plied the shores of Korea, snatching Korean captives to sell as slaves in China, or if he became conscious of this issue upon his return. In any case in 828 Chang was able to convince the Silla government to put him in charge of a large naval fortress off the peninsula's southwest coast near the island of Wando. This fort became known as "Ch'ŏnghaejin," or Ch'ŏnghae Fortress, and it boasted a 10,000-man garrison. From this base, Chang not only put a stop to the pirates, but he applied his Shandong formula of combining military with economic pursuits to establish himself as the dominant figure in the tri-lateral maritime trade between Korea, Japan, and China.

Chang soon became enmeshed in the politics of the Silla central court, if not by his own initiative, then certainly because his prominence made him a ready target for those court figures looking for support. In 836, Kim Ujing, loser in the latest battle over royal succession, made his way across the southern coast and pleaded for Chang's protection, and within two years Chang found himself raising a private military force to battle the court's army on Kim's behalf. When victory allowed Kim to ascend the throne, he showered Chang with gifts and the greatly elevated title of Grand General of Ch'ŏnghae. Chang, flush with success in his interventions in capital politics, maneuvered in 845 to marry off his daughter as the monarch's second queen (which might have been a condition for helping Kim Ujing in the first place). This appears to have gone too far, for the aristocratic elite in Kyŏngju, apparently aghast at Chang's brazen move to insert himself into royal politics, sent the assassin, Yŏmjang, to finish off Chang in 846.

While there is no explicit evidence, the common perception among historians is that resistance to Chang's involvement in the highest circles of politics and society likely had something to do with his social status. This in turn leads us to consider the Silla social hierarchy as well as why Chang might have faced difficulties. For Silla deployed an early form of the stout social status system that came to characterize premodern Korea as a whole. Known commonly as the "bone rank" (*kolp'um*) system, the Silla method assigned a "bone rank" to people, based on their parentage, that determined their social status and, in turn, their spheres and manner of social interaction, marriage possibilities, tax and service obligations, and eligibility for bureaucratic office (or even royalty).

Especially striking is the interesting correspondence between economic activity and social status, on the one hand, and the limitations of economic activity in generating social mobility, on the other. For social status, as it would be throughout the premodern era in Korea, was first and foremost determined by birth. One's occupation or primary economic activity also flowed from one's birth status. Although the evidence is sketchy, there likely was a substantial group of people born into servitude. Above them were the majority of the population, the commoners, most of whom

were engaged in agriculture, while some earned their livelihoods through artisanal crafts, fishing and hunting, or trade. The
category of "merchants" in reference to the latter group included
those whose scope of trading activity ranged from inter-village
exchange to international trade, as was the case with Chang Pogo.
Like Chang, merchants could amass wealth and in turn sociopolitical prestige, but this wealth ultimately could not gain entry
into the highest "bone ranks" occupied by people who lived off
the masses through rent and bound labor, or through government
office. In the Silla system, even those eligible to live off the taxes
collected by the state were distributed into an intricate hierarchy,
again according to birth.

By the time of the Unified Silla kingdom, the original highest
rank of Hallowed Bone had dissipated, and the monarchy and top
officials came from the True Bone ranks. Those in Head Rank Six
to Head Rank Four (presumably the head ranks reached down all
the way to one) comprised the hereditary elites and could attain
government office, but they encountered limitations in gaining
the highest posts. Chang appears not to have fit into any of these
upper head ranks, and so his attempts to ingratiate himself into the
governing order likely generated gasps of shock at such a violation of social norms. He was, in other words, a prime example of
both the flexibility and rigidity of the Silla social hierarchy—able
to rise to prominence as a local strongman engaged in maritime
commerce, but unable to overcome the barriers to social and political power at the center.

Probably the best known example of the constraints to talent
imposed by the Silla social hierarchy was Ch'oe Ch'iwŏn, the
most prominent intellectual figure of the era and archetype of the
Confucian scholar-official in traditional Korea. Ch'oe, born into
Head Rank Six a decade after Chang Pogo's death, traveled to
China to study at the age of twelve, likely following the example
of many precocious Sillans of the age. Ch'oe's talents, however,
were exceptional. He passed the Tang civil service examination,
a remarkable feat on its own, and before he turned twenty had
already achieved renown, particularly as the scribe and advisor
to the Tang official in charge of putting down a major rebellion.

(This uprising would eventually lead to the fall of the Tang dynasty itself.) Ch'oe managed to return home to Silla in his late-twenties and took high office. He appears soon, however, to have chafed at the barriers, in both promotion possibilities and policy implementation, put up by the Silla sociopolitical hierarchy, and withdrew from the capital to take provincial posts and eventually to retire to the haven of a Buddhist temple. His works—including a famous "Ten-Point Policy Recommendation" to the final female Silla monarch, Queen Chinsŏng, as well as a chronicle of his observations while in the service of the Tang emperor—displayed the full range of his scholarly expertise, from Buddhism and Confucianism to poetry. Only a fraction of his voluminous writings remains today, but they were prized and rediscovered throughout the subsequent course of Korean history. Like those of Chang Pogo himself, Ch'oe Ch'iwŏn's life and times offer a window into the final phase of a golden age in ancient Korea, when Silla showed both its maturity and its old age.

SILLA AND NORTHEAST ASIA

That Ch'oe Ch'iwŏn and Chang Pogo both made their reputations and gained seminal experience in China before applying these lessons back in their homeland illuminates the vibrant connections that Silla enjoyed at the crossroads (or cross-straits) of the northeast Asian region. In fact, Chang Pogo's influence extended to Japan and likely beyond northeast Asia, and indeed there might not have been a Korean historical figure better-known outside northeast Asia until the twentieth century. Most of the sources upon which his biographical portrait has been constructed and embellished, in fact, are from China and Japan. Especially influential are the writings of the great Tang poet Du Mu, whose familiarity with Chang reflects Chang's considerable fame and what appear to be strong connections to the Chinese elite, and the chronicles of the Japanese Buddhist monk Ennin.

According to Ennin's fascinating "Account of Travels in Tang for the Purpose of Seeking the Law," the Sillans in Shandong constituted a thriving community that dominated the regional maritime trading system. Centered around the Korean Buddhist temples, the Sillans built homes away from home, carrying forth with their own ways of life and trading. Indeed Ennin witnessed a major Korean-Buddhist festival that endured for three days, another festival commemorating Silla's victory over Koguryŏ 150 years earlier (!), and other expressions of Silla's collective identity. Although Ennin never recounts meeting him, Chang Pogo, not the king of Silla, is the looming authority figure to whom this community answered. So moved was Ennin by the kind treatment and protection offered to him by Chang's surrogates in the Shandong Silla society that the monk wrote the great man a letter of gratitude. To Ennin, Chang was clearly the mastermind and dominant figure behind this intricately and efficiently designed network of merchants, monks, and others who plied back and forth from the Korean peninsula to the eastern coast of China.

From this base of operations Chang's agents in turn connected to a vast trading network that stretched all the way to eastern Africa and the Arabian peninsula, merchants from which, it appears, also visited Silla. The items that flowed through these passages in northeast Asia originally reflected the official commerce in tribute goods such as ginseng and silk, but by the time Chang achieved his dominant position based in Ch'ŏnghae Fortress, trade items also included animal products such as horns, falcons, and sealskins, and particularly ceramic goods. In fact, Chang appears to have facilitated significantly the process of not only circulating Chinese ceramics, among the best in the world, but also of applying Chinese ceramics technologies to further develop a native Korean ceramics industry on the southern coast of the peninsula. The prime locations connected with Korean ceramics, including Kangjin and Namhae Island, are usually associated with the subsequent Koryŏ era, but this development might have begun in Chang's time. Excavations of both ceramic factories and shipwrecks from the era have added to this impression that Korea's maritime power once served as a stimulus for economic activity in the country. Such a connection between Korea's seafaring potential and internal development has reached another peak over the past thirty years in South Korea, with its export-oriented industrial growth and the preeminent position of Korean companies in the global shipbuilding industry.

Indeed Chang Pogo's commanding influence over trade in northeast Asia tells us much about Silla's relationship to the region as a whole, and it stimulates further thinking about the standing of Silla in the longer trajectory of Korean history. In one sense, Chang Pogo's activities suggest that this period represented a peak in Korea's capacity to take advantage of its geography at the center of northeast Asia instead of being victimized by these circumstances, as it did repeatedly both before and after Chang. Furthermore, Chang's story shows that, in this particular era of Korean history at least, trade and commerce could indeed play a dominant role in the country's economy, enough to allow one particular merchant to use his wealth and power to play political mediator and, indeed, even kingmaker. Both tendencies—Korea's commercial prominence in northeast Asia and the force of economic activity in the realms of politics, society, and culture—are being pursued by Korean leaders in the early twenty-first century. Since the 1990s a steady stream of Chang-related developments has rekindled interest in, and furthered the mythologizing of, Chang Pogo: the establishment of tourist-oriented memorials and museums in Shandong, site of the temple complex that Chang established; and pop culture products in Korea such as the "God of the Seas" hit television series. These developments, however, also have the potential of contributing further to expansive visions of Korean identity and standing in the context of globalization and regional integration. Chang serves, then, as an embodiment of the dreams of Korean prominence in the region through regional integration. If it could be done before, so the thinking goes, it can be done again, with Koreans in the lead.

The reconsideration of Korea's regional position via a creative appropriation of Chang Pogo and his era also accompanies, ironically, a recent downgrading of Unified Silla in Korea's historical trajectory. A growing perspective in both popular and academic arenas has come to view "Unified Silla" as somewhat of a misnomer, given that Silla's vanquishing of Paekche and Koguryŏ in the seventh century left unincorporated the vast majority of former Koguryŏ territory. This territory was claimed by a thriving kingdom, Parhae, that stretched from the northern part of the peninsula well into Manchuria. Parhae's status in conventional Korean historiography has always been somewhat ambiguous, as only its ruling elite seem to have descended from Koguryŏ origins, while the masses came from a mish-mash of various ethnicities. More powerful in excluding Parhae were official histories compiled in subsequent periods instituting the notion of a "Three Kingdoms" era of ancient Korea that came to an end through Silla's unification. Partly due to nationalist sentiment over the course of the twentieth century and into the twenty-first century, the concept of a "Unified Silla" era has lost ground to a perception of this era as that of the "First North-South Division," with the strong implication that Parhae was a fully Korean historical entity. (In North Korea, for obvious reasons, this view is a matter of course.) Chang Pogo, then, is not the only artifact of the late first millennium to be mined for contemporary purposes; Parhae is grounds for claiming that Korea at this time was a central player in northeast Asia in more ways than one. However transparent the motives behind this revisionism, these issues draw beneficial attention to the significance of these long-ago eras even beyond their contemporary connections.

LOCAL STRONGMEN AND THE END OF SILLA

For all his utility as a symbol of Unified Silla's growth and achievements, in the end Chang tells us just as much about its demise. We have reason and documentation, in particular the remarkable fragments of village household registers discovered in the early twentieth century, to believe that the Unified Silla state had made great strides in extending central control—or at least taxation authority—following its conquest of Koguryŏ and Paekche. But there appear to have been limits to this integration effort. Indeed Chang's great power might have reflected not the Silla state's authority but rather its weakness in the outer provinces. And the court's decision to turn to Chang to command the southwest might have reflected the state's lack of control and revenue outside the original Silla territory of the southeastern part of the peninsula. Within half a century after Chang's death, the very region that had served as his base (and was likely his original home region)—the southwestern part of the country that used to belong to the kingdom of Paekche—would erupt in rebellion against the Silla state. This uprising was led by a local warlord, Kyŏn Hwŏn, who, while fanning the flames of Paekche resentment and calling his breakaway region "Paekche," likely envisioned himself a successor to Chang Pogo. Another local strongman, however, would prove even more effective in overturning Silla control, and he called his territory "Koguryŏ."

4

· · · · · · · ·

Founding of the Koryŏ Dynasty

CHRONOLOGY

Late 9th c.	Beginning of the Latter Three Kingdoms period
895	Wang Kŏn joins Kim Kungye's rebel movement against Silla
918	Founding of the Koryŏ by Wang Kŏn
935	Silla's surrender to Wang Kŏn, solidification of Koryŏ Rule
936	Final defeat of Latter Paekche by Wang Kŏn
943	Drafting of Wang's Ten Injunctions
958	Institution of the state examination system

THE ISSUANCE OF WANG KŎN'S "TEN INJUNCTIONS," 943

The founding of the Koryŏ dynasty constitutes a seminal event in Korean history in many ways. It pacified the peninsula after decades of civil war during what is commonly called the "Latter Three Kingdoms" period (late ninth–early tenth centuries), extended the territory of the country further northward by incorporating the southern edge of the Parhae kingdom, integrated the ruling groups of both the Parhae and Silla into a new aristocratic element that might have lasted into the twentieth century, and expressed a clear sense of national identity based on native religious and cultural elements. The apex figure in this process was Wang Kŏn, the founder of the Koryŏ dynasty, and the event that binds him to these significant trends is his issuance, just before his death, of the "Ten Injunctions" to his royal successors.

The Ten Injunctions has come down as one of the most influential documents in Korean history and a testament to the forces that shaped Koryŏ into an enduring political entity. This series of directives accentuated the significance of Korea's distinctive cultural identity, emphasized the centrality of both Buddhism and geomancy as well as Confucian statecraft, warned of the "barbarians" to the north, and institutionalized, some say, discrimination against the southwestern region of the peninsula. This last feature, specified in the eighth injunction, has aroused considerable interest lately because of its ostensible sanctioning of the bane of South Korean politics since democratization in 1987—namely, regionalism. Many scholars claim, in fact, that Injunction #8 proves that the Ten Injunctions were a forgery, that circumstantial evidence renders it highly unlikely if not impossible that Wang Kŏn himself actually issued such orders. The skepticism is well founded, but it does not deny the impact of this document in Koryŏ and Korean history. Indeed, that the Ten Injunctions remains an object of contention continues the long history of its service as a helpful lens into the significance of the Koryŏ founding on Korea's identity and culture.

"GREAT FOUNDER OF KOREA"

Wang himself was born and came of age as the idea of a single country began to fall apart in the final two decades of the tenth century. As noted in Chapter 3, the Silla kingdom experienced difficulties keeping the outlying parts of the peninsula under institutional control, and the local strongmen who arose in the peripheries, such as Chang Pogo, served as potentially dangerous challengers to Silla rule. Indeed the first major rebel leader, Kyŏn Hwŏn, was a high Silla military official assigned to the same southwestern coastal zone that had served as Chang's power base. Kyŏn Hwŏn fanned the flames of anti-Silla resentment and remnant Paekche loyalties to amass a territory that he called "Latter Paekche," which proved formidable enough at one time to ransack the Silla capital and install his own preferred monarch. His primary challenger, however, came not from the Silla court but rather from another rebel leader based in the central part of the peninsula, Kim Kungye, who referred to himself as the successor to the Koguryŏ monarchs. Like Kyŏn Hwŏn, Kungye had belonged to the upper tiers of Silla society—he was a prince, in fact. When he was cast off from his family (likely because he was an illegitimate son), he retreated to the countryside as a Buddhist monk. Before long, however, he joined the growing anti-Silla movement among local strongmen and displayed great skills in capturing territory in the peninsula's heartland. Kungye's battles against Kyŏn Hwŏn over peninsular supremacy at the turn of the tenth century rendered imminent the death of Silla, but this duel was not decided until Kungye was toppled, not by Kyŏn Hwŏn, but rather by one of his own lieutenants.

The person who took Kungye's place was Wang Kŏn, who had for some time been Kungye's most successful general in the struggles against other regional lords. Wang had entered Kungye's orbit in 895 when Wang's father, the court-sanctioned local leader in the west-central coastal city of Songak—today known as Kaesŏng—joined the monk's new kingdom, which by the year 911 had conquered a vast territory. When Kungye began to grow cruel and show disturbing signs of uncontrolled despotism, Kungye's top officers overthrew him and handed the crown to Wang Kŏn. In the official historical accounts from the Koryŏ dynasty, Wang is depicted as having displayed great reluctance to betray his loyalty to his superior, Kungye, but it is likely that Wang himself led the effort to take control. Kungye perished while being chased from the throne, and immediately Wang set his sights on overcoming the resistance of both Silla and Latter Paekche. His longtime nemesis, Kyŏn Hwŏn, who had meanwhile been overthrown himself by his own son, actually joined Wang's cause to defeat his former country. By 935, Wang had gained the peaceful submission of Silla's last monarch. Upon putting down the final bout of Paekche resistance in 936, Wang, known historically through his reign name of "T'aejo," or "Great Founder," accomplished the success-ful reunification of the country.

Given his own beginnings as the scion of a powerful merchant family in a far-off province of Silla, Wang knew well the poten-tial pitfalls presented by regional power holders. Hence his most daunting task in fortifying his rule was gaining the subjugation, or at least the consent, of the many local chiefs scattered around the peninsula. This issue would remain at the forefront of challenges faced by the Koryŏ monarchy for the rest of the five-century-long dynasty. Eventually the Koryŏ instituted a kind of cooperative "hostage" system, much like the one used later in Shogunal Japan, that required local chiefs to reside for stretches of time in the capital. For the moment, however, Wang Kŏn did what many rulers around the world in similar circumstances have done: use marriage alliances to consolidate political rule. Wang in fact went a step further; he himself did the marrying, and to the daughters of an astounding twenty eight different local rulers! Not all of the many sons produced from these alliances went on to become king or even play important political roles, but this step proved instrumental in securing a large pool of loyal descendants with a stake in maintaining the dynasty. To them, and more specifically to his eldest sons—three of whom would take turns in serving as the succeeding monarchs—Wang would leave behind a very specific blueprint for ruling the Koryŏ dynasty and a personal vision for what made Koryŏ Korea.

CONTENT OF THE TEN INJUNCTIONS

The country that Wang Kŏn envisioned reflected the many different strands of thought and religion, originating internally and externally, that had come to shape civilization on the peninsula. More impressive than the specific policy recommendations, which were significant in themselves, were the Ten Injunctions' expansive proclamations of the central currents of culture that defined Korea's past, present, and future. One specific civilizational strain, however, stood out as primary: "The success of every great undertaking in our country depends upon the blessings and protection of the Buddha," begins the first of the Ten Injunctions. Indeed, the significance of regulating well the Buddhist establishment, of building temples and other places of worship, and of sponsoring the major Buddhist festivals is emphasized in three separate injunctions. Little wonder, then, that the centrality of Buddhism to Korean civilization would reach unprecedented heights during the Koryŏ dynasty, reflecting the maturity, diversity, and even the decadence of Buddhism's near-millennium of dominance, especially in concert with political power. One could argue, in fact, that the state's patronage of Buddhism in the Koryŏ produced the peak of Korean civilization itself, given the extraordinary cultural advances that arose from this relationship.

Like Buddhism, Confucianism had entered the peninsula from China in the Three Kingdoms era. By Wang Kŏn's time, Confucian thought had pervaded the vocabulary of statecraft on the peninsula, and a critical mass of interested scholars and officials had emerged. Wang Kŏn himself appears in the Ten Injunctions as holding a keen awareness of the importance of Confucian precepts, and four of the injunctions allude to Confucian teachings in prescribing lessons for royal succession and the management of state affairs, including the acceptance of admonishment by the ruler. The numerous allusions to passages in the Confucian classics, in fact, might lead one to take Wang for a Confucian scholar himself.

Wang appears well versed in the great thought systems that had originated from abroad, but the pronounced tenor of the Ten Injunctions is actually a proto-nationalistic call for maintaining the distinctive ways of Korea in the face of foreign influences, including those from the Middle Kingdom. "In the past we have always had a deep attachment to the ways of China ... but our country occupies a different geographical location and our people's character is different from that of the Chinese," warns the fourth injunction. "Hence, there is no reason to strain ourselves unreasonably to copy the Chinese way." Buddhism, though, is considered a native cultural element, as stated explicitly in the sixth injunction, which insists that the great state-sponsored Buddhist festivals retain the worship of the shamanistic and geomantic spirits of primal Korean religion. Indeed in the fifth injunction Wang credits his great achievement of peninsular reunification to the combination of geomancy and shamanism, and he implores his descendants to remember the centrality of Pyŏngyang in Korean civilization. He designates this city the Western Capital, second in importance only to his home town, the Koryŏ capital of Kaegyŏng (formerly Songak, and later known as Kaesŏng). This dualism suggested by the Ten Injunctions—on the one hand, native, including Buddhist, ways, and on the other, "Chinese" Confucian learning—would rise to the level of considerable tension over the course of the Koryŏ dynasty.

The strong nativist impulse in the Ten Injunctions is reinforced by the explicit condemnation of the people lying to Koryŏ's north, the Khitan, who are referred to as "savage beasts" (more Confucian language). The periodic invasions and skirmishes from the north—a recurring theme throughout Korean history—was not lost on Wang. In his ninth injunction Wang instructs his followers to maintain a watchful eye on the northern frontier. This proved prescient, for Koryŏ would suffer major invasions from various northern peoples, beginning with the Khitan, and then the Jurchen, then finally the Mongols, who would conquer Korea in the thirteenth century and rule the country as semi-colonial overlords for almost a hundred years (Chapter 6).

The wariness of the northern part of the peninsula was understandably inscribed into the Ten Injunctions, but what of the wariness of the southern part, in particular the southwestern territory of the peninsula that had previously stood as the domain of Latter Paekche (and before then, Paekche)? In the infamous eighth injunction, Wang goes into detail about the negative geomantic and cultural features of this area as a prelude to the stunning instruction not to allow people from this region to become government officials. The recent history of straining to conquer Latter Paekche is unequivocally acknowledged as the source of Wang's suspicion of this region. Even so, as historians have pointed out, it is remarkable that Wang would put forth such a pronouncement, given his general policy of appeasement of local elites around the country (he married several women from this region), and given that one of his highest officials came from the southwest. Here we encounter, then, the doubts about the authenticity of the Ten Injunctions itself as originating with their purported author, Wang Kŏn. There are persuasive arguments that indeed, the Ten Injunctions date to the late tenth century, more than fifty years after Wang Kŏn's passing, and that they reflected the political circumstances and concerns of that subsequent period. The more important point, however, is that, regardless of the precise dating of this document, it exerted a great influence in the following four centuries of the Koryŏ as the blueprint for proper rule. In any case, the eighth injunction did not raise doubts about Wang's authorship of the Ten Injunctions until the latter part of the twentieth century, when regional hostilities, particularly on the part of the South Korean dictatorships toward this area, flared into a major detriment to South Korean political culture.

LEGACY

It is difficult to determine to what extent, if any, the eighth injunction had on Koryŏ history, especially given the prolonged periods of real sociopolitical power being held in the hands of military officials and Mongol clients. The other injunctions appear more effective in forecasting the tasks and concerns of the Koryŏ, especially in regard to the country's collective identity and cultural core. The founder's strenuous efforts to legitimize his family's dominion, for example, went far beyond his incorporation of local lords through marriage ties. He also placed the Koryŏ dynasty firmly in the historical lineage of the peninsula through the dynasty's name, which reinforced Koryŏ's claims as a successor to Koguryŏ, and through his acceptance of the former leaders of both Silla and Parhae into the country's aristocratic order. The significance of the Parhae connection, in fact, could have been the cause for the Ten Injunctions' vitriol against the northern "barbarians," especially the Khitan, who conquered Parhae around the same time that Silla itself came to an end. It was a matter of reinforcing Korea's distinctiveness from the peoples who surrounded Koryŏ. Subsequent periods in the Koryŏ era witnessed follow-up efforts, such as the compilation of official histories, to reinforce these historical ties. As noted above, perhaps the most notable feature of this consolidation of collective identity was, as seen in the Ten Injunctions, the insistence on the centrality of Buddhism as the country's dominant cultural element. Indeed, the rest of the Koryŏ era saw little divergence from this command.

Just as important but perhaps less notable were the substantial administrative advances that the Ten Injunctions appeared to endorse. The systematization of government, both institutionally and symbolically, constituted an urgent task for the early Koryŏ rulers, whose efforts turned toward overcoming the decades-long period of disintegration and local rivalries. The pervasiveness of Confucian language when describing the general approaches to proper government paved the way for major developments during the reigns of Wang's immediate descendants on the throne. These included the establishment of a provincial administration more closely tied to the central government and, in 958, under the reign of King Kwangjong (one of Wang Kŏn's sons), the implementation of that great institution for recruiting government officials in premodern Korea, the state examination system.

5

· · · · · · · ·

Religion and Regionalism in the Koryŏ Order

CHRONOLOGY

THE OUTBREAK OF THE MYOCH'ŎNG REBELLION, 1135

In early 1135 came news of an uprising in Pyongyang that had quickly spread throughout P'yŏngan province, and soon most of the north-western region of the country appeared under the control of a band of rebels under the leadership of a charismatic Buddhist monk. Before demonstrating his propensity for havoc, this monk, Myoch'ŏng, had set his powers of persuasion—the official histories called it something more akin to sorcery—on the king himself, convincing the monarch that the dynastic capital must be moved to Pyongyang in order to avoid national disaster. When the king, under great pressure from his highest officials, changed his mind, Myoch'ŏng and his cohorts in Pyongyang broke away. The leaders of this movement proclaimed a new, paradisiacal land, but to the Koryŏ court, of course, this action constituted nothing more than the latest rebellion.

It took over a year to quash the uprising, and the reverberations in this region and, indeed, in the country as a whole, would endure much longer. The Myoch'ŏng Rebellion shook the foundations of the country and encapsulated important social, political, and cultural developments in the Koryŏ dynasty both before and after the uprising itself. Myoch'ŏng's downfall also had significant repercussions for the structures of political and social power in Koryŏ, including the decline of the monk's home region, and reflected the ongoing influence and special character of Korean religion.

THE INSTITUTIONALIZED INFLUENCE OF THE BUDDHIST CLERGY

Following the religion's inception on the Korean peninsula around the fourth century, the Buddhist clergy and the sociopolitical elite developed a mutually beneficial relationship by incorporating each other into their respective realms of influence and claims to legitimacy. As the Ten Injunctions showed, this relationship had reached a peak by the early Koryŏ dynasty (Chapter 4). But Buddhism was not limited to the monarchy, for the centuries of steady propagation among the population had produced a culture suffused with Buddhist sentiment. Both the regional and central elites patronized the Buddhist establishment, whether through their support of local temples or sponsorship of nationwide Buddhist festivals. Surely the most visible example of the pervasiveness of Buddhism, especially among the aristocratic taste-setters, was the emergence of the remarkable style of blue-green "Koryŏ celadon," prized now (as then) even beyond Korea for its ethereal beauty. These ceramics' almost indescribable sheen itself seems to evoke Buddhist spirituality, as do the many inlaid graphical motifs that refer to well-known Buddhist themes.

The state took the lead in this patronage of Buddhism. The separate spheres of influence had long ago been settled: the spiritual realm, including rituals for the afterlife, for the Buddhist order; and the secular realm of political power for the state. But the state continued to incorporate Buddhist learning and the clergy by recruiting a special segment of the officialdom through a

The Buddhist printing advances of the Koryŏ

When asked to name their people's greatest cultural achievement, most Koreans likely would choose the invention of the native alphabet in the fifteenth century, but they might also list two products from the Buddhist-dominated civilization of the Koryŏ era: the remarkable celadon ceramics, and the great advances in printing developed by the Buddhist establishment. In fact, one could argue that, taken together, the most impressive accomplishments of premodern Korean civilization came in printing technologies, dating back to the Unified Silla era (668–918), when the oldest extant work of woodblock printing in the world was printed and stored in a Buddhist altar. Woodblock printing was invented by the Chinese, but this technique achieved new heights in Koryŏ dynasty Korea and, furthermore, these developments laid the groundwork for the next major breakthrough, that of moveable metal type printing, also invented by Koryŏ Buddhist clergy.

Most people in the West associate the invention of moveable metal type, the holy grail of premodern techniques because of the flexibility and durability it provided to enable mass printing, with Johannes Gutenberg of Germany. Gutenberg's invention in the mid-fifteenth century ushered in the era of widespread information dissemination in Europe, which had an immediately colossal impact through the pamphlets and other rapidly-produced written works that fueled the Renaissance and the Protestant Reformation. Very few people outside of Korea know that moveable metal type was actually invented two centuries earlier, around 1230, by Buddhist monks in a temple in south-central Korea. In fact the earliest extant book printed with moveable metal type, a Korean work of Buddhist scripture, dates to the 1370s, and is held in the French National Library in Paris. (How France managed to gain possession of this book is a matter of dispute.) In Korea, however, this breakthrough did not lead to significant social or religious change, even after the crafting of the Korean alphabet in the fifteenth century—a significant issue, given the impact of the printed vernacular on the rise of early modern Europe.

Around the same time as this invention, the storied *Tripitika Koreana*—wooden blocks on which were carved nearly the entirety of the East Asian Buddhist canon—was being destroyed by the Mongol invasions that began in the 1230s. Originally produced as a testament to Buddhist devotion amidst the Khitan invasions of the eleventh century, the *Tripitika's* destruction by the Mongols prompted the Koreans to reproduce it, again as a way of appealing to the Buddha for salvation amidst the

Image 5   Wooden blocks of the *Tripitika Koreana*, in Haeinsa Temple, near Taegu, South Korea. (Author's photo.)

carnage. The result was a project that took nearly two decades in the mid-thirteenth century to carve over 80,000 wooden blocks, which are now preserved in Haeinsa Temple near the southern city of Taegu. This extraordinary feat bespoke not only the cultural centrality of Buddhism at the time, but also the authority of the Koryŏ state and the Buddhist establishment in mobilizing the enormous human and material resources necessary for the project. It also testified to the high level of literacy and technology associated with Koryŏ Buddhism.

nationwide Buddhist examination system. The state also sponsored the erection of massive temple complexes throughout the country, which enjoyed tax and other benefits that allowed them to accumulate, and often abuse, extraordinary wealth. The monarch, furthermore, appointed national and royal preceptors, who served as religious advisors to the king and maybe more importantly provided the stamp of Buddhist blessings on the monarchy. Perhaps the most eminent monk to be named national receptor, albeit posthumously, was Chinul, a figure of the late twelfth and early thirteenth centuries. Chinul developed a unified system of thought and practice for Korean Buddhism, which had long been divided, sometimes bitterly, into the meditation (*sŏn*) and textual (*kyo*) schools. The largest Buddhist order in South Korea today counts him as its founder.

What proved most distinctive about Koryŏ Buddhism, however, was the incorporation of shamanistic and geomantic elements. As the Ten Injunctions strongly suggested, Korean Buddhism by this time drew from a great mixture of Buddhist orthodoxy, underlying folk beliefs in local gods and spirits, and geomancy, or the systematic combination of nature worship with geography. The great state-sponsored Buddhist celebrations, the Lotus Lantern Festival and the Eight Gates Festival, incorporated these various elements. Through this mixture of religious influences, together with the development of Buddhist scholarship, a distinctively hybrid form of Buddhist practice emerged. Indeed, Korean geomancy was itself systematized by a Buddhist monk in the Unified Silla era,

Tosŏn, who integrated the geographical features of Korea into an organic vision of the peninsula as a living entity fed by the spiritual energy of Buddhist temples and practices. Tosŏn's followers, including Myoch'ŏng, cultivated and popularized this perspective, to the extent that geomancy, including the notion of a geomantic unity for Korea, held an influential standing among the aristocracy and monarchy well into the twentieth century. The location of the capital of the next dynasty, Chosŏn—still the capital of (South) Korea today—was determined according to geomantic principles, for example. Well before then, however, geomancy played a central role in a watershed moment in the history of Koryŏ.

MYOCH'ONG'S REBELLION

Aside from the fact that he was a Buddhist monk from Pyongyang, little is known about Myoch'ŏng's life before his role as protagonist in the tumult that engulfed the country in the early twelfth century. The official historical accounts excoriate him for his deceitfulness and cunning, but he clearly had considerable charisma and skill. Like Rasputin, who held an unshakable grip over the Russian royal family at the turn of the twentieth century through his seemingly magical ability to treat the Romanovs' hemophilia, Myoch'ŏng appears to have cast a spell over the monarch, Injong. Most tellingly, the monk convinced him of a direct geomantic relationship between the ongoing misfortunes of the dynasty—especially the constant attacks and threats of invasion from the Jurchen people to the north—and the location of the dynastic capital in Kaegyŏng (present-day Kaesŏng). Myoch'ŏng's solution, not coincidentally, was to move the capital to his home town of Pyongyang, which held more positive geomantic features, he claimed. He also urged the monarch to declare Koryŏ an empire and launch a campaign against the Jurchen, steps bitterly opposed by the king's ministers.

That King Injong succumbed to this line of reasoning cannot be explained simply by dismissing him as a dupe, for the baseline of belief tying geomantic principles directly to the health of the country, as noted above, had an extensive history. Furthermore,

Pyongyang had long enjoyed a centrality in Korean civilization, reflected in the fact that, since the early Koryŏ period, it was deemed the Western Capital (*Sŏgyŏng*), the second most important city. And, as noted in Chapter 1, Pyongyang had served as the administrative center of the Lelang Chinese commandery and the capital city of the Koguryŏ kingdom. Furthermore, according to the conventional understanding of Korean origins codified in the Koryŏ era, this city represented the place of origin for Korean civilization itself. So said the myths of Tan'gun, the founder of the Korean people who established his court there, and of Kija, the Chinese official who transmitted higher civilization to the peninsula and ruled from Pyongyang. From Myoch'ŏng's perspective, and likely that of many elites from the northwest, the transfer of Koryŏ's capital to Pyongyang represented simply the return of this city to its rightful standing, which would in turn lead to better fortunes for a country besieged by both external and internal threats.

The capital region, in fact, was still recovering from the biggest domestic challenge to the dynasty hitherto, the rebellion in 1126 led by Yi Chagyŏm. The powerful scion of a royal consort family and the monarch's father-in-law, Yi attempted a personal takeover of the throne before his uprising was suppressed with tremendous bloodshed. The capital officials, in short, were extremely wary of brewing trouble. These sensitivities were put on high alert when, soon after the Yi Chagyŏm incident, King Injong began to show signs of having fallen under the sway of the mysterious monk from Pyongyang. Injong made frequent visits to Pyongyang and eventually ordered the construction of a royal palace there. The capital elites, fearing a major shift in power to the northwestern region, responded by imploring the monarch to examine the countervailing evidence: the greater attention shown to Pyongyang, including the construction of the royal palace, not only failed to eliminate the Jurchen menace, but also failed to halt a series of natural calamities that beset this region. The monarch became convinced by these arguments and put a stop to his plans for moving the capital city to Pyongyang. Prompted by an official, Cho Kwang, and other cohorts from Pyongyang, Myongch'ŏng's response to this royal turnabout was simple: rebellion.

In the first month of 1135 Myoch'ŏng, Cho Kwang, and the other leaders orchestrated a swift takeover of most of the administrative centers of P'yŏngan province, incarcerating officials sent from the capital and cutting off the major pass that connected this region to the south. They proclaimed their new realm the Empire of Taewi ("Great Purpose"). King Injong, meanwhile, appointed Kim Pusik, a high official, to lead the government armies as Supreme Commander for the Pacification of P'yŏngan Province. Kim's forces entered the breakaway region and issued ultimatums to local leaders, who for the most part quickly capitulated, and soon surrounded the rebels in Pyongyang. In fear and hope for clemency, Cho Kwang, who by now was acting as the true ringleader of the uprising, beheaded Myoch'ŏng and the other rebel leaders and sent the heads to Kim Pusik as a sign of surrender. But Kim would have none of it, and Cho Kwang in turn decided to fight to the end, which came after many more months of bloodletting—including the killing of government negotiators by Cho. Eventually, Cho's troops, holed up in their fortress, ran out of provisions under the government siege. The defeat of the rebels came in the second month of 1136, more than a year after the eruption. It would take much longer for the region to return to normalcy, and for Pyongyang, the city would never be the same.

AFTERMATH

Myoch'ŏng's antagonist in this ordeal, Kim Pusik, would go on to exert an influence on Korean history far beyond his leadership in suppressing the uprising. As the prime representative of the power elite of the Koryŏ capital region, however, his latter exploits can be considered an extension of his role in the Myoch'ŏng saga. Kim was a descendant of the old Silla royal family, which constituted one of the key components of the emerging capital-based aristocracy that the Koryŏ founder, T'aejo, had collectively incorporated into his ruling order. This was significant because Kim would eventually make another mark on Korean history through his compilation, a decade later, of the court-sanctioned history of the pre-Koryŏ era, the *History of the Three Kingdoms* (*Samguk sagi*). This work serves to this day as the core source of understanding of ancient Korea. Beginning with Sin Ch'aeho, who called the Myoch'ŏng Rebellion the "most important event in a thousand years" of Korean history, many modern historians have condemned Kim Pusik's impact. In particular, they have bemoaned Kim's attempt in the *History of the Three Kingdoms* to strengthen the historical legitimacy of Koryŏ through an emphasis on Koryŏ's status as the successor to Silla. This move, they claim, downplayed the standing of Koguryŏ both in the history of the Three Kingdoms era and as a source of the Koryŏ dynasty's own identity.

Furthermore, the capital-based aristocratic elite that Kim represented, which coalesced around bureaucratic domination and hence maintained itself as the official class, would come to be known as *yangban* ("two orders"), in reference to the two sets of high officials, the civilian and the military. But, as symbolized by Kim, a renowned Confucian scholar-official, a firm hierarchy developed between these two strains of the central officialdom, with civilians like Kim enjoying supremacy. The Myoch'ŏng Rebellion and Kim Pusik's centrality in its outcome may have strengthened this civilian domination to the point of excess, and a backlash to this ordering came relatively soon thereafter. In 1170, military officials rose in revolt and implemented a hundred-year period of military domination of the government (Chapter 6), much like the Shogunal system in premodern Japan. But this represented merely a short hiatus in the millennium of Korean history from the tenth to the twentieth centuries, when on the whole the principle of civilian supremacy and military subordination prevailed. Kim's victory over Myoch'ŏng reinforced this order and likely contributed to the permanent branding of Pyongyang, and the northern regions as a whole, as the preserve of the military, rebellious, even uncivilized underbelly of the country. This perspective constituted a very real prejudice in the ensuing Chosŏn dynasty, when the northern regions, considered a backwater, suffered social and political discrimination, and Pyongyang fell further from civilizational centrality.

Little wonder, then, that in the early nineteenth century, another uprising, the Hong Kyŏngnae Rebellion of 1811–12, erupted with remarkable resemblances to the Myoch'ŏng episode: a charismatic malcontent from Pyongyang, preaching the north's geomantic superiority, fought to break away from the capital-based power structure. This, too, was eventually suppressed, and not until the circumstances of the mid-twentieth century brought to center-stage yet another magnetic military leader from Pyongyang, Kim Il Sung, did finally the northern part of the country succeed in recovering its long-lost glory, but at the cost of a nation divided permanently.

6

....

The Mongol Overlord Period

CHRONOLOGY

THE MARRIAGE OF LADY KI TO THE YUAN EMPEROR, 1340

Kaegyŏng, the capital of the Koryŏ dynasty, was abuzz with news from China in the summer of 1340. Seven decades had passed since the Korean kingdom had succumbed to a long siege by invading Mongol forces, and in the intervening period Korea had become suffused with all things Mongol—its culture, politics, and even its monarch bore the stamp of Mongol dominance. Now Koreans received word of an event that showed that Korea, in turn, could wield influence over the stupendously powerful Mongol empire based in China, the Yuan dynasty. Lady Ki, a Korean and favored concubine of the Yuan emperor, had in the previous year given birth to the likely crown prince, and was now being

51

crowned formally as an imperial consort through her marriage to the Yuan emperor. This turn of events could hardly have been imagined two decades earlier, when she was sent as a captive prize of submission to the Mongol rulers. Indeed she and hundreds of other "tribute women" sent to Mongol-controlled China had embodied the Mongols' comprehensive control over the kingdom of Koryŏ, a period in Korean history normally viewed with utter shame.

The period of Mongol dominion over Korea, however, resists easy judgment. Empress Ki's story, in fact, represents a microcosm of Koryŏ's complex relationship to the Mongol empire—an experience of tragedy and horror, to be sure, but also of reform, opportunity, and valuable exposure to the outside world. This period also highlighted important features of Koryŏ as a civilization and its place in Korean history, especially for practices and customs regarding women. In these and other ways, the Mongol era constituted a seminal turning point in Korean history: on the one hand, it directly led to the fall of the Koryŏ dynasty, but in the larger scope of national history it represented a time when Korea was integrated into the world order to a degree not seen again until the twentieth century.

THE MONGOL CONQUEST

The first Mongol invasion, in 1231, led by the son of the founder of the Mongol empire, Genghis Khan, came six decades after the 1170 institution of military rule in Koryŏ that had turned the Korean monarch into a mere puppet. Notwithstanding the many incursions across the northern border, the administrative reforms over the first century of the Koryŏ dynasty in the tenth century had helped to establish firmly the principle of civilian rule. Hence the military officials gradually experienced a decline in authority over the next 150 years, even to the point of humiliating deference to their civilian counterparts. This, apparently, led to the military coup of 1170, which purged top civilian officials and gave military officers power over not only the government but also the throne. By the turn of the thirteenth century, the Ch'oe family emerged to constitute a mini-dynasty of military strongmen, who ruled a land racked by bouts of unrest, including a large-scale slave rebellion at the beginning of the Ch'oe rule. The devastating Mongol invasions, beginning in 1231, eventually forced the House of Ch'oe to flee to the confines of Kanghwa Island, just to the south of the capital. There the Koryŏ court under Ch'oe control successfully resisted final capitulation, even as the rest of the country suffered. The final Ch'oe generalissimo, however, was assassinated in 1261, and this opened the door for the court to enter negotiations of surrender. Given the continuing decimation of the countryside, including the destruction of countless cultural artifacts, the Koryŏ monarchy had little choice but to accept Mongol overlordship. Despite the lingering resistance to the Mongols on Cheju Island off the southern coast, which was eventually put down, for all intents and purposes Korea was now part of the Mongol empire.

That Koryŏ maintained a semblance of autonomy through the maintenance of its own monarchy and government might be considered a fortunate outcome of its defeat, given that the Mongols could have easily wiped out the entire leadership. But such autonomy was severely curtailed, as the Mongols dictated the general direction of the government. This was soon made apparent when the Korean state was forced to provide manpower and expertise for the next stage of Mongol expansion, into Japan, in 1274. Koreans, long known as master seafarers, built and guided the ships, which were loaded with thousands of soldiers from the joint Mongol-Korean forces. This armada twice attempted, and failed in, an invasion of Japan. The military organ devised to oversee these invasions, the Eastern Expedition Field Headquarters, remained intact even after its original purpose expired, serving as the institutional representative of Mongol domination in Korea. The nominal head of this institution was the Korean king, but in reality this and other powerful organs were controlled mostly by Mongol overseers whose interference in Korea was not limited to foreign relations and military matters, but extended to internal Korean affairs as well. The Mongols, in fact, established commanderies in various parts of Koryŏ to reinforce their suzerainty, and this does not even count the northern quarter of Koryŏ territory that now came under direct Mongol control.

Needless to say, politics in the Koryŏ court often hinged on tendencies and sentiments regarding the Mongols, as the monarch himself politically—and in other ways as well—was severely weakened. The Mongols, in fact, dictated everything from the kings' reign names, which humiliatingly bore the word "loyal" ("ch'ung"), to the clothing and even the consorts of Korean kings. The Mongol court also controlled who would be king, on several occasions returning a Koryŏ monarch to the throne not long after deposing him. But on another level, these signs of subservience might have been moot, for within a few decades the Koryŏ king himself was barely Korean. Under the arrangements of Korea's surrender, the crown prince of the Koryŏ royal house had to spend his childhood in the Yuan dynasty capital, where he would marry a Yuan princess, and then return to Korea when it was his turn on the throne. The first such monarch, King Ch'ungnyŏl, married a daughter of the third Mongol emperor, Kublai Khan (of Marco Polo fame), and hence thereafter all the Koryŏ kings, except the last one, were direct descendants of Genghis Khan himself. One could argue that the Korean court had to submit in order to prevent mass slaughter and hence preserve Korean nationhood, or even in order to escape domination by Korean military officials. But one also has to wonder whether the Koryŏ kings under Mongol rule held a meaningful identity as Koreans. Even the monarch credited with anti-Mongol policies in the mid-fourteenth century, King Kongmin—who, by twist of fate, was mostly Korean and served as the last of the Mongol-era kings—was married to a Mongol princess, whom he adored and famously mourned with obsession upon her passing.

This brings us to the greater implications of these circumstances, and here we must tread with some sensitivity. For not only was the Koryŏ monarchy infused with Mongol ancestry, but intermarriage with the Mongols took place among other Korean groups as well, from the aristocracy down to the lowest status groups who had no choice on the matter. This accompanied the significant spread of Mongol influence in Korean culture in the fourteenth century, from language, food, hairstyles, and clothing to even family and marriage customs—to be expected, given the political and military domination under which the Koreans lived. Together, these two levels of Mongol influence led to what many Koreans today would consider embarrassing at best: a significant strain of

Mongol provenance in the Korean people and culture. DNA analysis, which strongly hints that central Asians share widespread common descent from Genghis Khan, would probably show not an insignificant number of Koreans today with the same ancestry. Such are the results, repeated thousands of times throughout world history, of conquest. We can imagine the often horrific circumstances under which such a mixture of peoples took place, and we can abhor, from the Korean perspective, the shameful consequences. Whether one condemns this particular episode in Korean history or examines it with scholarly detachment, however, it undoubtedly complicates any sacrosanct notion of Korean homogeneity.

If we can take a difficult step back from the horrors of war and forced subjugation to forge a longer-term perspective, we should also consider the salutary impact of Mongol domination on the history of the Koryŏ dynasty and of Korea. Under the Mongol empire, Koreans had many more occasions to make their way to China as tributary officials, diplomats, scholars, traders, and others, and once in the Yuan dynasty capital (present-day Beijing), they encountered a teeming tapestry of peoples and cultures from throughout the vast Mongol empire. The exchange of books, ideas, and other artifacts of both high and low culture from these encounters integrated Koreans, for the first time in their history, into a truly global order. The Chinese civilization that Koreans had emulated always aspired to be universal, but in geographical scope and the willingness to embrace other cultures, it paled in comparison to the Mongol empire. And among the great influences that these cultural currents yielded was the introduction of both the cotton seed and Neo-Confucian philosophy to Korea. But this interaction drove the flow of influence in the opposite direction as well.

KORYŎ WOMEN IN THE MONGOL EMPIRE

Among the most intriguing areas of Mongol influence in Koryŏ lay in marriage and family customs, particularly as they affected women. Scholars have suggested, for example, that the practice of taking multiple wives, not uncommon in the late Koryŏ aristocracy, might have expanded under Mongol rule. If so, such an influence presents an interesting comparison with native Korean customs characterized by a relatively high social and familial position of females. This is not to suggest that the Koryŏ era featured something approaching equality between the sexes. It is now commonly accepted, however, that Korean women enjoyed far greater standing in marriage, inheritance, and social status in the Koryŏ than in the succeeding Chosŏn era, especially in the latter Chosŏn period (Chapter 8).

Whatever benefits that Korean women might have enjoyed, the Mongol period reinforced the submissive standing of females through the demand for "tribute women" exacted upon the vanquished Koryŏ. Government records indicate that, between 1275 and 1355, there were approximately fifty instances of the Koryŏ court sending tribute women to the Mongol court, which took almost two hundred girls. But this is likely a gross underestimation, for the officially recorded instances only counted the mostly aristocratic females sent to become concubines for the Mongol royalty and aristocracy, and did not include the hundreds, perhaps thousands, of lower-status females sent under more wretched circumstances. Like the other major group of Koryŏ people sent to China—those males bound to serve as eunuchs for the Yuan court—the Korean tribute women represented little more than human booty, in effect slaves handed over as a sign of tributary subordination. Out of these terrible conditions, however, a fraction of both the eunuchs and tribute women managed to ascend to the highest levels of court life in the Chinese capital. And among these examples, the most fascinating and powerful figure was Lady Ki.

Lady Ki, daughter of a lower-level official's family, was sent, like many others of her status, as a tribute woman to the Mongol capital some time in the 1320s. Little is known about how she came to catch the emperor's attention, but as noted in her biography in the official history of the Yuan dynasty, it is likely that her beauty and her talents in singing, dancing, and poetry were extraordinary. She was formally named an imperial concubine in 1333. The Mongol emperor, who as a boy had fallen victim to political strife and spent over a year in exile on an island off the west coast of Korea, might have had a favorable disposition to Koreans in the first place. And having developed an intense affection for Lady Ki, he treated her as the preferred companion over his queen, who in fact came from a family of political enemies. When he tried to promote Lady Ki to official status as the secondary consort (second wife), it aroused staunch political opposition because it digressed from the standard practice of taking imperial queens only from a certain Mongol clan. In 1339, after she gave birth to a son, who would later become the Yuan monarch, the emperor's determination stiffened, and over weakening political opposition he had her crowned as the secondary imperial consort in 1340. In 1365, as the Yuan dynasty's grip on China was dissolving, Empress Ki ascended to the position of primary imperial consort.

In that intervening quarter-century, Empress Ki exercised great influence over the Yuan court. In addition to her connection to the emperor himself, she enjoyed a powerful institutional base, a special government organ with wide-ranging tax collecting authority created specifically for her use. Through this organ, she amassed tremendous power and initiated several grand projects. After a while she served in effect as the monarch, as her husband gradually lost interest in affairs of the state. She even led a failed attempt to nudge her husband off the throne in favor of her son. The official history of the Yuan dynasty, written by scholars of the successor Ming dynasty, notes that Empress Ki also developed a reputation for corruption and extravagance. This also suggests that her behavior and that of her court allies contributed to the demise of the Yuan dynasty itself. The Yuan experienced a series of rebellions all across China in the middle of the fourteenth century, many at the hands of the so-called "Red Turban" Chinese bandits, a group of which was led by the man who would become the founder of the succeeding Ming dynasty.

Just as important for our story, Empress Ki also exercised decisive power in her home country of Koryŏ. This was done through both her direct intervention in monarchical succession, and through her family members, whose status and influence, backed by the empress of the Mongol empire, increased considerably. Empress Ki's father was formally invested as a "king" in the Yuan empire, and her mother in her old age enjoyed ritualized visits from the Koryŏ monarch. The Ki family is remembered, however, almost exclusively for its lavish lifestyle and venality, on display both among the common people and within Koryŏ elite circles. Outright theft of others' property, including slaves, reached such severity among her siblings in Korea, in fact, that Empress Ki herself had to send a warning to her family members. One of her older brothers in particular, Ki Ch'ŏl, who once headed the Eastern Expedition Field Headquarters and exercised greater authority than the Koryŏ monarch, is especially singled out in the official histories for his corruption and abuse of power. Indeed, his biographical entry in the official *History of Koryŏ* comes under the section on "Traitors" and recounts the sordid deeds of the entire Ki family. Little wonder, then, that when the last Koryŏ monarch under Yuan domination, King Kongmin, unleashed an anti-Yuan policy in 1356, he purged Ki Ch'ŏl and his family in a surprise attack. For this, Koryŏ suffered a reprisal invasion ordered by Empress Ki, but this was successfully fended off, and indeed King Kongmin and others understood that Yuan control over China was in its last throes. Little remains known of the fate of Empress Ki, who fled with her son, the next Yuan emperor, to the Mongol homelands ahead of the Chinese rebels who would establish the Ming dynasty.

Despite this inglorious end, however, Empress Ki's life and times present an intriguing picture of Koryŏ's successful adaptation to the Yuan overlord period. She was likely the one most responsible, for example, for spreading Korean influence in China. She did this through her political authority, to be sure, but also through her incorporation of Korean females and eunuchs into the Yuan court. These Koreans contributed to the flowering of a "Korean style" in the Chinese capital, as things Korean, from clothing to food to lifestyle, became fashionable. As a Korean observer at the time noted, it became almost a requirement for elite males in China to take Korean concubines, who cultivated an aura of beauty and sophistication. Chinese sources, too—and often not in a flattering way—noted that Koreans, in particular Korean women, exerted strong influence over popular taste in China. The flourishing of the "Korean style" may have represented a peak in the export of Korean culture in premodern times, and not until the early twenty-first century would Korean culture, popular or high, enjoy such widespread emulation and popularity outside the peninsula.

This presents, then, another reminder that the Mongol period, while certainly a time of humiliating subjugation to a foreign power, also left a more favorable imprint on Korean culture and identity. We certainly cannot discount the horrific circumstances of the long Mongol siege of the mid-thirteenth century, or of the way Lady Ki and countless other captives went to China in the first place. But her rise to the heights of the Mongol court—and hence to a status as perhaps the most powerful person in the world at one time—shows her as a fitting representative of how Koreans throughout history adapted to the realities of power among their neighbors. Korea's first experience of integration into a truly global order—a mixture of brutal conquest, humiliating submission, and cultural exchange—shared its core features with the experience of other subject peoples in the Mongol empire who spanned all the way to Europe. The implications for the longer view of Korean history are especially important when comparing this interlude to the periods of foreign domination and intervention in the twentieth century.

In the short term as well, there were significant repercussions. The end of the Mongol period, for example, induced a concerted backlash among Korean elites, who, after two centuries of disruptions caused by both domestic and foreign usurpers, sought to restore a more stable and inward-looking form of rule. And in arousing the Red Turban rebellions, the Mongols were responsible for the rise of Yi Sŏnggye, a Korean military leader who made his name in repelling Red Turban invaders (as well as the so-called "Japanese pirates") during the late Koryŏ era. Together, these two outcomes of Mongol rule contributed directly to the fall of the Koryŏ dynasty itself, and to the birth of a new dynastic order in Korea under Yi's command.

7

. . . .

Koryŏ-Chosŏn Transition

CHRONOLOGY

YI PANGWŎN'S PURGE OF CHŎNG TOJŎN, 1398

Six years after the founding of the new dynasty, for which he played the role of mastermind as well as lieutenant, Chŏng Tojŏn was killed by a militia sent by Yi Pangwŏn, the fifth son of the dynastic founder. The prince, furious over Chŏng's betrayal in publicly backing Pangwŏn's half-brother for designation as the crown prince, now considered the scholar-official a major stumbling block to his own ascent to the throne. Despite having worked in tandem to achieve the common cause of toppling the Koryŏ monarchy, the two had grown increasingly at odds over the issue of royal succession. Pangwŏn, uneasy at the prospect of not getting his just reward, purged his former partner, thereby eliminating from the scene the primary intellectual force in the expression of dynastic legitimacy. From the inception of the Chosŏn era, then, a pattern of struggle was laid between ambitious monarchs and pious officials that would feature prominently in the dynasty's politics as a whole.

Had it not been for this bloody moment, Yi Sŏnggye, the dynastic founder, would have enjoyed unquestioned primacy in the saga of dynastic founding. Like Kim Yusin and Wang Kŏn, the leading figures in the Silla unification and Koryŏ founding, respectively, Yi was a military figure who began from the geographical fringes of the reigning kingdom. And it was Yi's audacity, foresight, and capacity to mobilize a wide range of followers—from military men to scholar-officials and even foreigners— that made possible the monumental change of a dynastic turnover. In contrast to Wang, however, Yi had to deal with potential trouble not from rival warlords but rather from rival sons. When he formally proclaimed the new dynasty in 1392, Yi could scarcely have foreseen that the monarchy he labored to establish would almost immediately begin to fray from the ravages caused by his own progeny. From the historian's vantage point, this particular episode—indeed, the entire process of dynastic turnover from Koryŏ to Chosŏn—brings into relief major issues affecting the historical judgment of the Chosŏn dynasty as a whole, even of premodern or "traditional" Korean civilization itself.

CHŎNG TOJŎN: FROM MASTERMIND TO POLITICAL POWER

In 1383, after nine years of political exile, the up-and-coming Confucian scholar Chŏng Tojŏn visited the northeastern frontier of Koryŏ. There, in General Yi Sŏnggye's home region, Chŏng had his fateful encounter with this future founder of the next Korean dynasty. Whatever took place in their meeting, it was enough to forge a strong alliance, with Chŏng hitching his ideals and destiny to the man who had amassed heroic feats in repelling marauding Japanese pirates and Red Turban raiders (Chapter 6). As it turned out, this bond could be characterized as an alliance of mutual convenience, with Yi using the scholar as much as Chŏng used the general. When, as Koryŏ's second-ranking military officer, Yi Sŏnggye was sent to lead a Korean expedition to invade Ming dynasty China in a show of force during a border dispute in 1388, he recognized this as folly and instead turned his army toward the Koryŏ capital. There he arrested his commander and effectively took control. Waiting for him was Chŏng Tojŏn, who quickly led efforts to implement the political changes that allowed Yi to rule, including the forced abdication of the Koryŏ monarch in favor of Yi's hand-picked one. Chŏng's increasing influence accompanied his accumulation of political offices, and he even went on a diplomatic mission to China to soothe the concerns of the Ming court. Chŏng's rivals managed to send him to a brief exile in 1391, but to his rescue came Yi Pangwŏn, who killed many of these rivals, including the most prominent loyalists to the fading Koryŏ monarchy. In 1392, freed from his imprisonment with the help of Pangwŏn, Chŏng Tojŏn joined dozens of other top scholar-officials in officially pleading for Yi Sŏnggye, the man who had effectively ruled the country since 1388, to take the final step and establish a new dynastic order. For all of these efforts on Yi's behalf, Chŏng Tojŏn was awarded the designation of Dynastic Foundation Merit Subject, First Rank.

Chŏng's role in this story invites comparison with other lieutenants of military leaders who established new political orders in Korea, such as Kim Ch'unch'u, the mastermind behind General Kim Yusin's campaigns to unify the three kingdoms (Chapter 2), and later Kim Jong Pil, the dutiful assistant to General Park Chung Hee in the 1960s (Chapter 23). Unlike these two, however, Chŏng Tojŏn would not survive the turmoil of the takeover process, and so he came to resemble more the many scholar-officials in the Chosŏn era who would become embroiled in royal disputes and pay for this involvement with their lives. Like his successors, Chŏng was driven by a fierce insistence on his own interpretation of Confucian ideology, and by the official's obligation to remonstrate the monarch when the latter strayed from the proper path. As part of the earliest cohort of Confucian scholar-officials in the Chosŏn, however, he helped lay down the original blueprint of the dynastic order, and thereby exerted a far greater influence than his peers would later. Chŏng was by no means the only important figure in this regard, and to some historians his contributions were overshadowed by those of other "founding [Confucian] fathers" of this era. But clearly Chŏng stood as the most versatile and influential in establishing the fundamental contours of early Chosŏn government and society.

In the first few years of the new dynasty, Chŏng authored many of Chosŏn's foundational documents. These included an early version of the dynastic law code that, after decades of gestation, would be promulgated in final form eighty years later. In this and other works, Chŏng displayed a penchant for crafting a working compromise between Confucian ideals, on the one hand, and practical politics on the other. His model for government organization harkened explicitly to the ancient *Rites of Zhou*, one of the core works of the Confucian canon. Chŏng's reverence for China's classical age brought about an affirmation of a universal civilizational order centered on Korea's allegiance to the Ming dynasty. He did not view this arrangement in terms of China and Korea as separate countries as much as partners reviving the original glorious connections of the mythical era when a Chinese sage, Kija, purportedly brought civilization to Korea. Chŏng also helped to institutionalize Confucian meritocratic ideals further through an emphasis on using examinations instead of connections to recruit government officials. This likely reflected his own relatively low birth status (he came from a family of local officials, it appears), a point exploited by his enemies throughout his career. Also arising from his own experience—namely, his near-decade spent in political exile—was his emphasis on the welfare of the peasantry, the meek majority whose struggles he witnessed directly in the remote corners of the country. As if these political and philosophical works were not enough, Chŏng helped to design the layout of the new capital city of Hanyang (Seoul), drafted an official history of the Koryŏ dynasty—an important work in legitimating the Chosŏn—and even composed musical paeans to the new dynasty and its founder.

These accomplishments mattered little, however, in the face of naked ambition from members of the royal house, and Chŏng's death served as one of many episodes of bloodshed that surrounded royal succession in the early Chosŏn dynasty. Chŏng's downfall began with his public support of Yi Sŏnggye's decision to appoint Yi Pangsŏk, the founder's youngest son, as the crown prince. Prince Pangwŏn, who had long supported Chŏng's preeminent standing in the circles of royal advisers, considered this a betrayal and took action, just as he had done several years earlier when he did away with scholar-officials, like Chŏng Mongju, who had opposed the toppling of the Koryŏ monarchy. Now Pangwŏn set his sights on

Chŏng Tojŏn, who was beaten to death by Pangwŏn's agents in 1398, just as other assailants eliminated the crown prince. The dynastic founder, unable to bear any more of this mayhem among his children, abdicated in favor of another son and returned to his home town of Hamhŭng. Pangwŏn killed yet another fraternal rival in 1400, setting the stage for his ascension to the throne later that year as the third Chosŏn monarch, King T'aejong. The violence would not end there, as T'aejong's efforts to make amends to his father by sending royal emissaries to Hamhŭng were poorly received. Indeed the now "Senior King," still infuriated by his son's bloody actions, either incarcerated or outright killed a series of these "Hamhŭng messengers," or *Hamhŭng ch'asa*, a term that still today serves as shorthand for people, sent for errands, from whom nothing is ever heard. The father finally relented and returned to the capital, where, in a final fit of rage, he fired an arrow in T'aejong's direction, narrowly missing him!

A RENAISSANCE, REVOLUTION, OR COUP?

These disturbing, in some ways horrific circumstances during the opening decade of the Chosŏn can elicit a wide range of perspectives on the significance of the dynastic turnover, and even cast doubt on its authenticity as a major historical event. Indeed, different schools of thought regarding the true meaning of this transition have arisen, and they have heightened the historiographical stakes: the judgment on Confucianism's impact on Korean and Chosŏn history; the location of "legitimate" Korean tradition, especially the underlying tendencies in social and family customs; indeed the larger debates regarding the flow of premodern Korean history, such as stability vs. change, external inducement vs. internal propulsion, and so on. In fact, the prominence of both Yi Pangwŏn and Chŏng Tojŏn can illuminate and support each of the main perspectives on the historical significance of the dynastic transition.

Historians who tend to view this moment as a kind of Confucian renaissance emphasize the primacy of ideology in driving the events. Officially, at least, the scholars, officials, and even military men like

Yi Sŏnggye drew explicitly from the teachings of what Western historians commonly call "Neo-Confucianism" in establishing and justifying the new dynastic order. Neo-Confucianism, a scholarly and ideological movement that, in Korea, began to brew in the late Koryŏ era, had begun in Song dynasty China in the eleventh and twelfth centuries. It sought to resuscitate and refashion the classical texts of Confucianism in order to apply them, expansively, to addressing contemporary problems. The particular version of Neo-Confucianism that came to hold sway in the Chosŏn dynasty has often been called the "School of Nature and Principle," which more specifically referred to the firm link established between human nature and metaphysical doctrine. The proper understanding and practice of human connections lay at the heart of Confucian moral teachings, with filial piety—reverence for one's parents, explicitly invoked in the Confucian Five Relationships—serving as the core ethic that, when flexibly applied, guided all human interaction. The "great chain" of Confucian cosmology began with the individual's self-cultivation of filial piety through ritual and learning, which in turn facilitated the application of morality to achieve familial and social harmony, a just political order, and peace under heaven. The founders of Neo-Confucianism in China and their transmitters to Korea preached the need to implement systematically these latent Confucian teachings.

One can see why, then, Chŏng Tojŏn, Yi Pangwŏn, and other Chosŏn founding fathers perceived in Neo-Confucianism not only an update to the millennium-long influence of Confucianism as a group of political doctrines, but a comprehensive approach to ethics, politics, social order, economy, and culture. The impressive range of Neo-Confucian legislation in the first few decades of the Chosŏn era reflected this ideology's systematic reach, and indeed the intricate attention given to even the realm of the family was among the most striking features (Chapter 8). Nevertheless, it bears noting that some Neo-Confucian practices, such as the state examination system and even male primacy in tracing family heritage, had long been in existence in Korea. Conversely, most of the new legislation inspired by Neo-Confucianism, especially in regard to instituting a patrilineal lineage system, took centuries to implement. In short, it can be said that Neo-Confucian ideology, however important, cannot account for all or even most of the thrust behind the dynastic turnover. Chŏng Tojŏn and Yi Pangwŏn, both successful passers of the Confucian civil service examination in the late Koryŏ, subscribed to this ideology, for example, and Yi still found reason to eliminate Chŏng.

An alternative viewpoint claims that the dynastic turnover represented a revolutionary moment, but one driven not by ideas but rather by material changes and socioeconomic imperatives. The agitation of lower-level elites, and specifically the middle- and small-scale landowners, stood as the indispensable source of support for Yi Sŏnggye's efforts to dismantle the late Koryŏ aristocratic order. To this vanguard, the significance of Neo-Confucian doctrine was utilitarian—in the service of class interests of smaller landowners struggling against the stranglehold on power of the capital elites and estate landlords. The rise to prominence of both Chŏng Tojŏn, from a lowly local official background, and Yi Sŏnggye, scion of a military family in the far northern fringe of the Koryŏ realm, would seem to validate this perspective. In spite of the attractiveness of this theory in suggesting a deeper desire for social change and, by extension, a great rupture and hence a compelling story of historical progress, it appears somewhat overdrawn. Notwithstanding the dynastic founder's family history and Chŏng Tojŏn's own humble background, extensive studies of the social background of the new capital elites have shown that, for the most part, they came from the Koryŏ aristocracy.

A third vantage point, in fact, prefers to consider the dynastic turnover as representing neither a social nor an ideological revolution, but rather a historical moment limited in significance, at least initially, to the realm of politics. It required a combination, in other words, of a military strongman's grab for power and a committed group of scholar-officials, like Chŏng Tojŏn, who had long attempted to implement major reforms, both in line with Neo-Confucian doctrine and in order to curb the abuses of the Buddhist establishment. The dynastic transition, then, represented the culmination of institutional reforms that had begun in the late Koryŏ dynasty to address decays in the socioeconomic and political system. It took simply the decisive contribution of military and political power (and ruthlessness) provided by Yi Sŏnggye and his son, Yi Pangwŏn, to bring this promise to fruition. Critics of this stance, which appears to emphasize continuity over historical rupture, have objected to what appears an insufficient consideration of the wider circumstances of political change, especially one as momentous as the toppling of a five-century-old dynasty. One could also level the charge that this interpretation suspiciously resembles the one put forth by Japanese colonialists to justify the takeover of Korea in the early twentieth century: what happened between 1388 and 1392 was merely a drawn-out palace coup. Few historians would seriously dismiss the dynastic turnover as just a coup, but the resistance to this theory reflects a wariness of undervaluing the impact of large historical forces in what appears, on the surface, a monumental transition.

YI PANGWŎN'S IMPACT

Whatever the answer to the question of the historical meaning of the dynastic transition, one must reserve judgment until considering more fully what took place both before 1392 and after this initial decade-long period of turmoil at the hands of Yi Pangwŏn. Upon ascending to the throne to become King T'aejong (r. 1400–18), he placed the floundering new dynasty on firm footing as a Confucian polity. Under his direction, the Chosŏn state established the basic structure of government that would endure until the late nineteenth century, especially in defining the state's deliberative and administrative authority. These duties were headed, respectively, by the High State Council and the Six Boards, a kind of cabinet-like division of managerial responsibility. For the provinces, the early Chosŏn reforms stretched the state's administrative control to the farthest reaches of the realm and institutionalized the eight-province division of the country that still is in effect (at least in South Korea) today. T'aejong also took decisive steps to further the disenfranchisement of the Buddhist establishment, the only viable rival to the new dynasty in its claims to ideological supremacy. He did this by closing down many temple complexes

King Sejong the Great

Only one monarch in the long history of Korean royalty commands the universal appellation of "the Great" following his name: Sejong the Great, the fourth king of the Chosŏn dynasty (r. 1418–50). Sejong enjoys a standing in Korean civilization that is akin to George Washington's in the US, with his name attached to everything from universities and cultural institutions to civic organizations and state projects. That his portrait graces the most familiar South Korean currency, the 10,000 *won* bill, is itself a reflection of his perceived supreme stature in Korean civilization. Most Koreans attribute to him what is widely considered the nation's signature cultural accomplishment, the promulgation of the native Korean alphabet in 1446. They also know that he instituted innovative state policies and sponsored the invention of advanced scientific instruments such as the rain gage, water clock, and sun dial. He is seen, in short, as having come closest to the ideal of the sagacious monarch who promoted the welfare of the common people above all. But one can also summarize his accomplishments and historical significance with the claim that, more than anything else, King Sejong the Great completed the foundation of the Chosŏn state's great task of Confucianizing Korea.

Even the development of the Korean alphabet itself was part of Sejong's wide-ranging efforts to enhance the state's dissemination of Confucian teachings. Overlooked in the ceaseless and ubiquitous mythologizing of this great feat (there is even a national holiday honoring the alphabet) is the fact that Sejong, in addition to standardizing the Korean—that is, "correct"— pronunciation of Chinese characters, found the alphabet a potentially breakthrough instrument for public education. In his famous preamble to the "Proper Sounds to Educate the People" (*Hunmin chŏngŭm*), the document introducing the new alphabet, Sejong stated not only that the Korean language is different from Chinese, but also that the common ("ignorant")

||||➡

people needed a simplified system of written communication. The Chosŏn government in fact soon began to publish numerous didactic works featuring glosses with the new alphabet, all preaching the core values of Neo-Confucianism. And indeed, Neo-Confucian scholarship and education was the basic charge of the Hall of Worthies, a state research institute that Sejong established soon after ascending to the throne. Today there remain questions about the precise balance of contributions from the Hall of Worthies and King Sejong the Great to the alphabet project, but in accordance with the Confucian values that Sejong so eagerly sought to instill, there was no difference: he gets the credit.

and appropriating the Buddhist clergy's human and material resources. And further attesting to the state's ambition for population control, he instituted the obligation to carry an "identity tag" for people traveling outside their home regions. Above all King T'aejong strengthened the position of the monarchy in relation to the bureaucracy, presenting himself as the model of both an authoritative and sagely Confucian monarch.

As noted above, the Confucian transformation of Korea by the Chosŏn dynasty took a very long time to accomplish, but T'aejong's actions helped to set the parameters of Confucianization, characterized by a comprehensiveness of ambition and scope, especially under the direction of the state. The institution of the tributary relationship with China as a means of integrating Korea into the universal civilizational (i.e., Confucian) order represented one of the key steps in this direction that T'aejong, even before he became king, directly ensured. Some modern historians have criticized this and other steps taken by the Chosŏn founding fathers like T'aejong and Chŏng Tojŏn as having led the Koreans to subsume their native ways, indeed their cultural autonomy, to the foreign ideology of Neo-Confucianism. The early Chosŏn's explicit reference to the Confucian canon as the basis for comprehensive changes appears indeed to have set the stage for an obsessive and at times stultifying preoccupation with asserting the country's

Confucian credentials. But Confucianism, like Buddhism, also contained the potential to highlight and heighten native customs and identity. T'aejong's son and successor, King Sejong the Great, considered the greatest of all Korean monarchs, served as convincing testimony to this potential.

8

....

Confucianism and the Family in the Early Chosŏn Dynasty

CHRONOLOGY

THE DRAFTING OF THE YI FAMILY INHERITANCE TESTAMENT, 1541

In 1541, a family inheritance document was drawn up to designate the division of an aristocratic female's possessions, mostly in the form of slaves. Though normally an unremarkable event, this particular occurrence was notable because some of the recipients of this estate, along with its attendant responsibilities, included a mother and son who later became the most celebrated such tandem in Korean history: Lady Sin Saimdang, the venerable poet, painter, and calligrapher who epitomized Confucian ideals regarding females; and her son, Yi I, better known by his pen name of Yulgok, recognized as one of the foremost Confucian scholar-officials and a towering genius. This will is valuable also because it represents one of the few surviving such works from the early Chosŏn era, and because it distributes the estate of a female to her female offspring—something that would be increasingly rare as time passed.

71

Image 8   Lady Sin Saimdang (front) and one of her bamboo paintings (back) featured on the Bank of Korea's 50,000 *won* note, issued June 2009. (Courtesy of Bank of Korea.)

In 2007, South Korean officials chose Sin Saimdang as the historical figure to grace the new 50,000 *won* note, the fourth bill in South Korean money, and the first new one in several decades (see Image 8). Given that the hallowed figures on the other three bills were all men, including Lady Sin's son Yulgok, anticipation over the selection of the new personage drew great attention, with the tacit understanding that the figure would be a female. To the surprise of many, however, when the selection committee announced its choice, a strong reaction arose from women's organizations and feminist groups, who viewed Lady Sin as a representation of the harmful impact of the Chosŏn era and of Korean tradition itself. This opposition provided a reminder of, among other things, the ongoing significance of the early Chosŏn dynasty, in particular of the Confucianization of society and family, in Korea's past and present.

EARLY CHOSŎN CONFUCIANISM

It is commonly accepted that the Chosŏn dynasty, which endured from the late fourteenth to the early twentieth centuries, permanently

Confucianized Korean civilization, in effect rendering Korea's premodern culture inseparable from Confucianism itself. In modern times, this has provided the impetus for an ongoing reconsideration of Korean tradition by distinguishing the Chosŏn era from a "pre-Confucian," and presumably more genuine, Korea. In North Korea, the official historical view dismisses Confucianism as a reflection of backward feudalism and toadyism. In the South, the nationalistic thrust of this critique has fused more recently with the continuing struggle over the proper place of Confucian teachings, especially regarding females and the family, in contemporary identity. While this division of Korean history tends to obscure the millennium of Confucian political thought on the peninsula before the Chosŏn dynasty, the notion that the Chosŏn rulers and social elites instituted Confucianism as a totalizing, dominant thought system appears warranted.

The early Chosŏn state stood at the center of these efforts at Confucianization and, regardless of whether Confucianism drove the dynastic transition or simply acted as a convenient political tool (Chapter 7), the state was infused with this greater purpose. Due to the immediate demands of state strengthening and centralization, Confucian statecraft in the early Chosŏn appears to have had a major impact even in the economy. Officials pursued a grand effort to fortify state finances while attempting to adhere to the Confucian ideals of eliminating unjust tax burdens and of reinforcing the centrality of agriculture over other economic activities, such as commerce. This required, then, a land tax policy of shifting revenues toward the central state's officials and organs at the expense of other social sectors that, in the Koryŏ era, had grown very wealthy, especially the landed aristocracy and the Buddhist establishment. These measures did not go so far as to completely monetize the economy, however; land taxes were paid in kind through grains and cloth. A complex system of personal tribute taxes also constituted a large proportion of the state's revenues. The population was responsible for service duty, such as military service or labor for state projects, as well as for providing material goods, ranging from luxury items to household goods, for government organs, the royal family, and even foreign dignitaries. The precise balance between land taxes, personal service, and tribute items is difficult to gage, but all of these duties had the effect of reinforcing the centrality of agriculture in the country's economy. Commercial activity and foreign trade appear to have been relatively unchanged or even curtailed through the central state's increasing control over the circulation of material resources. Confucianism, and hence Confucian statecraft, expressed little interest in encouraging private accumulation.

Confucianism did, however, encourage the pursuit of intellectual wealth, and the first two centuries of the Chosŏn dynasty witnessed the peak of Confucian philosophy—indeed, the peak of philosophy, period, in Korean history. Through a richly productive exchange of letters, memorials, and publications, Confucian philosophers partici-pated in a thriving republic of letters in sixteenth century Korea that tackled fundamental problems in connecting the cosmos to human experience and morality. The preeminent figures in these develop-ments were Yulgok and Yi Hwang, better known as T'oegye (who also is canonized by his appearance on one of the South Korean currencies). Although they were not of the same generation and likely met only a couple of times, T'oegye and Yulgok stood as the dueling representatives of a great debate that consumed Korean philosophy in the sixteenth century and went on to exert a profound impact on politics and society the rest of the dynasty (Chapter 10). The foremost issue, now commonly called the "Four-Seven Debate," revolved around how to reconcile basic psychological drives behind moral behavior (the "four basic feelings" and "seven emotions") with the Neo-Confucian metaphysics of reality and being. T'oegye appears to have further refined and clarified the orthodoxy, with great effectiveness, and gained acclaim for unveiling a convincing schematic for self-cultivation. Yulgok, meanwhile, won renown for tackling these questions through a novel, synthetic approach that reflected well the creative forces of the sixteenth century, and indeed the great cultural achievements of the early Chosŏn as a whole.

CONFUCIAN FAMILY LAW AND WOMEN'S STANDING

One must be mindful, however, that the Chosŏn dynasty lasted over five centuries, and the historical perspective on Confucianism's impact on Korean civilization is closely tied to this durability. Had the Chosŏn system ended with the lifespan of a typical Chinese dynasty—for example, if the Japanese invasions of the 1590s (Chapter 9) had led to a new sociopolitical order after only two centuries of the Chosŏn—then Confucianization might have been judged as incomplete. In fact, in terms of the political or socioeconomic hierarchies, the dynastic changeover appears to have fallen far short of a major shift. Rather, the most pronounced impact of Confucianization came from the comprehensive approach to remodel Korean customs, religious practices, and human interaction, down to the level of the family itself. The signal transformation, in fact, came in the realm of family law, with the most dramatic effects felt in the familial and social standing of women. The intimate setting of the family, though, is also where entrenched customs naturally take the longest to change—as witnessed in modern Korea, for example, with the century-long, grinding progress to *overturn* Confucian family law.

The Chosŏn dynasty eventually did manage to install a new family system as a central feature of the Confucian transformation of Korean civilization. The legislative blueprint appeared in the opening decades of the Chosŏn dynasty at the turn of the fifteenth century, based largely on "Master Zhu's Family Rituals," written by the great twelfth-century systematizer of the Neo-Confucian renaissance in Song dynasty China, Zhu Xi. *Master Zhu's Family Rituals* designated four such ceremonies and contained detailed instructions on how to carry them out: capping (a coming-of-age ritual), wedding, funeral, and ancestor worship. With the exception of capping, these rituals had long been practiced by Koreans, but the Neo-Confucian instructions integrated them systematically into a cosmology that extended to dictums on politics, society, religion, and other realms. Because of their divergence from previous practices and their centrality to the overall Confucian program, the propagation of Confucian family teachings received a lot of attention from the state. Korean scholar-officials and even female royal family members glossed Zhu Xi's work, with a consideration of native circumstances, in order to disseminate publications on core Confucian principles. This effort was enhanced by the Korean alphabet beginning in the mid-fifteenth century.

The Confucian family laws also demanded a strictly patrimonial system, one that not only traced lineage identity and legitimacy through the males, but also required that all rituals conform to this orientation. While the intricacies of the new wedding rites seem to have faced the most difficulty in gaining complete acceptance, the Confucian ancestor worship requirements had the most far-reaching impact. The lifelong responsibility of descendants to observe regular sacrificial rituals carried an acute economic burden, for example, and this demanded that inheritance practices, too, be gradually modified.

Historical events and documentary evidence from the early Chosŏn dynasty bear witness to the fits and starts of this wide-ranging effort to implement Confucian family law throughout the realm. Work on producing a final version of the dynastic code, or *Kyŏngguk taejŏn*, which would serve as a kind of constitution for the remainder of the Chosŏn, in fact took seven decades following the establishment of the dynasty, with promulgation coming finally in the 1460s. But the dynastic code represented just the first step, and the greater challenge of Confucianization lay in getting the people, beginning with the aristocratic elite, to follow the code's instructions in their own family practices. This is why documents such as the Yi family inheritance testament of 1541 are so illuminating, for they reflect the ongoing, though not always smooth, transition to a Confucian family system that would eventually transfer privileges—as well as responsibilities—exclusively and permanently to males.

The Yi family inheritance document in fact suggests the resilience of older practices mixed with the demands of the new, even as late as the mid-sixteenth century. Strikingly, it shows a female, albeit a female aristocrat, holding considerable economic resources in her name and, apparently, at her disposal. This female, Lady Yi, would go down in history as the maternal grandmother of the great philosopher Yulgok, whose deeply affectionate biography of his grandmother provide all we know about her, aside from the information presented in the will. As to be expected for a local aristocrat, Lady Yi had impeccable family credentials, with both of her parents coming from prestigious lineages. She had grown up in Kangnŭng, on the east-central coast, and had wed a young man from Seoul with the surname of Sin (pronounced "sheen"). Following long-established native practices, after her wedding the couple lived initially in the wife's natal home before, in accordance with Confucian teachings, moving to Seoul to be with the husband's family. But she quickly returned to her natal home, with blessings from her husband and in-laws, to care for her aging parents. She and her husband lived apart like this, interspersed with frequent visits, for over a dozen years. In Kangnŭng she raised their five children, all daughters, including the second daughter, Sin Saimdang, who would become the mother of Yulgok.

The 1541 inheritance testament, however—drafted nearly thirty years, as it turned out, before Lady Yi's death—provided no special consideration for Sin Saimdang. In accordance with a long-held custom, Lady Yi's substantial estate of 173 slaves was divided more or less equally among her five daughters, with the inheritances ranging from twenty nine to thirty five slaves each. The document meticulously notes the name, age, gender, family relationship, and current residence of each of the slaves, who were scattered throughout the country except for the northwest and southeast regions. While this shows a continuation of native inheritance practices that divided estates equally among children regardless of gender or order, the Confucian demands made their presence felt in the special designation of the "ritual heir," the descendant responsible for leading the ancestral rites. The extant inheritance documents from the early Chosŏn show a gradually increasing appearance of this provision until it became standard practice by the late sixteenth century. Here the Yi family will is especially instructive, for, in the absence of any sons, the person designated to lead the ancestral ceremonies was none other than a five-year-old grandson, Yulgok, who was given land and five slaves to provide the financial wherewithal to sustain this task indefinitely. One presumes that, had Lady Yi died soon after this document was drafted, either this boy's father or an uncle would have temporarily taken responsibility, but this provision is still notable on two levels: first, that it was the third son of the second daughter who was chosen, suggesting that this boy, Yulgok—who later, as a thirteen-year-old, would pass the introductory level state civil service examination, in first place (!)—was already demonstrating his precociousness; and second, that no daughter, despite receiving a substantial inheritance, could be deemed fit to lead the sacrificial rites, suggesting strongly that some legal and, by now, customary restrictions on females were taking hold.

In the late Chosŏn dynasty, this trend would become even more restrictive, with far greater social consequences. By the eighteenth century, the increasing centrality of the ancestor rites in the Confucian lineage system standardized the practice of primogeniture, or preference for the oldest son, not only in selecting a ritual heir, but, due to the cost of such a responsibility, in inheritance practices as well. Daughters and even younger sons received far less, if anything, and when it came to the children of concubines, the exclusion was complete. Indeed, when families in the late Chosŏn era encountered a similar situation as that of Lady Yi in 1541—that is, lacking a (non-concubine's) son—the prevailing practice was to adopt a nephew, however distant, from the same lineage, to act as both the ritual and family heir. Customs like primogeniture that later developed out of the Confucian family system hence eventually weakened the standing of women in many ways. They left women mostly with few possessions and hence little economic independence, in stark contrast to Lady Yi. They diminished women's ritual and lineage roles. And they stigmatized the descendants of secondary wives, whose status as concubines reinforced the centrality of sexual exploitation in the social hierarchy.

It is no wonder, then, that contemporary women in South Korea look back on the early Chosŏn with deep regret about what might have been—that is, without the incorporation of Confucian family practices. In modern terms, as noted above, the Yi family inheritance document and other evidence suggest strongly that pre-Chosŏn Korea was relatively "advanced" in the social and familial standing of females. Without Confucianization, so the thinking goes, the country might have taken a more enlightened historical path. The sixteenth century, more specifically, is fascinating in this regard, for it could have represented the last gasp of relatively high female standing before the momentum of state instructions would overwhelm it. At the court, for example, for two decades in the early sixteenth century, practical power was wielded substantially by two women: the first was the mother of a young king who acted as his regent, and the second was her niece, who had begun her life as a slave and ascended to a position in the court that allowed her to push for greater social opportunity for the lower classes. And in literary circles, two other women, Hŏ Nansŏrhŏn and Hwang Chini, appeared far more accomplished than even Sin Saimdang.

Given this, one could suggest that Lady Sin might not have been the Bank of Korea's best choice even from her own historical period. In any case, one can understand the disappointment expressed by women's organizations over the selection of Lady Sin, long celebrated for her supposed dedication to Confucian family values in her role as a daughter, wife, and mother. Critics of this choice suggested that Lady Sin's claim to fame was based not on her artistic talents, however admirable they might have been, but rather on the fact that she raised a celebrated scholar and statesman who, along with his admirers, placed Lady Sin on an undeserved pedestal. Lady Sin, in other words, was seen as a paragon of traditional (male) Confucian—not modern—virtue, and hence her selection was considered somewhat patronizing. Tellingly, before the selection South Korean women's organizations and feminist groups had put forward another female, Yu Kwansun, as their preferred candidate for the new currency. As a cultivated teenage girl armed with modern schooling, Yu had been martyred while rallying her home town's residents to participate in the independence movement of 1919 against Japanese colonial rule. Within the overarching, persistent framework of nationalism and modernity, then, Sin Saimdang serves as another symbolic object of contestation over the place of tradition, especially the Confucian heritage, in contemporary Korean identity. But all four historical figures, including Sin Saimdang, who are now celebrated on the South Korean bills hail from the first two centuries of the Chosŏn dynasty. This suggests strongly, then, that the early Chosŏn era continues to hold a commanding significance in Korean history.

9

....

The Great Invasions,
1592–1636

CHRONOLOGY

THE RETURN TO DUTY OF ADMIRAL YI SUNSIN, 1597

Though little known outside of Asia, the East Asian war of 1592–8 stands as one of the major events in world history. For the first time since the aborted Mongol invasions of Japan in the thirteenth century, the major civilizations of East Asia became embroiled in a single conflict, with consequences that would far exceed any other in this region's history until the late nineteenth century, perhaps indeed until the Pacific War of 1937–45. Begun through the Japanese invasion of Korea in 1592 in a bid to conquer Ming dynasty China itself, this war, fought exclusively in Korea, brought together all three countries in a fierce seven-year period of conflict. The destruction was enormous—to the Chinese who sent huge armies in Korea's defense, and even to the Japanese. In Korea, the scale of the devastation can scarcely be imagined: hundreds of thousands killed, millions injured or uprooted, and a poisoning of relations with Japan that would never disappear.

That Korea survived this onslaught is itself a miracle. The most common Korean perspective relates that the country was rescued by its greatest military hero, Admiral Yi Sunsin, who helped staunch the destruction in 1592 by leading the Korean naval forces to key victories over their Japanese counterparts. Not long after his heroics, however, Admiral Yi found himself in a Seoul jail, awaiting judgment on charges of treason and incompetence. When, after four years of stalemate, peace talks collapsed and the Japanese sent another invasion force in 1597, Admiral Yi was freed and ordered back to the Korean coast to coordinate his command with the Chinese allies. This helped bring the conflict to an end in 1598. But the significance of this conflagration, albeit different in each country, would extend both geographically and temporally thereafter. It may have even paved the way a few years later for the rise of the Manchus, who also launched destructive invasions of Korea. For the Koreans, these wars exposed grave problems in the Chosŏn polity, but they eventually provided also an opportunity for sharpening their national identity and reassessing their civilizational standing in the northeast Asian region.

PROBLEMS IN THE KOREAN RESPONSE

Although some Korean officials had suspected trouble brewing in Japan and even anticipated a conflict, the utter scale and catastrophic force of the Japanese assault in the spring of 1592 came as a shock: a landing force of hundreds of ships and tens of thousands of soldiers. The county officials of Tongnae, now part of the city of Pusan in the southeastern corner of the peninsula, managed to send messengers immediately on horseback to Seoul before the siege overwhelmed the Tongnae fortress. But the samurai soldiers, taking two invasion routes northward, tore through the country so quickly that within two weeks they were at the gates of the capital. After much hand-wringing with every report of the collapse of the country's defenses, the Korean monarch, King Sŏnjo, took the advice of his ministers urging him to abandon Seoul and flee northward. Along his path of evacuation, common Koreans, who enjoyed no such option, pleaded with him not to forsake his duties of protecting the capital, but clearly any attempt to withstand the barrage would have proved suicidal.

With the failure of its land defenses, the Korean court had to turn to its formidable navy, sending two naval commanders for the southernmost provinces, Wŏn Kyun and Yi Sunsin, to engage the Japanese within a few days of the invasion. Admiral Yi Sunsin, in particular, enjoyed tremendous successes in these battles, destroying much of the Japanese fleet and thereby managing successfully to cut off Japanese supply lines along the coast. He is credited in particular with skillful deployment of smaller, highly maneuverable attack ships, including the famed "turtle boats" that were protected by a spiked armored shell. These breakthroughs proved sufficient to hold off the invaders until the Ming dynasty forces, sent by the Chinese emperor at the request of the Korean monarch, arrived to halt the Japanese advance in the decisive Battle of Pyongyang. The combined Korean–Chinese army pushed the invaders gradually southward, and as the Japanese retreated to fortresses along the southern end of the peninsula, negotiations began for a peace settlement.

Meanwhile, in spite of the recognition of his heroics accorded him by the court, Admiral Yi found himself embroiled in the factional struggles among high officials over responsibility for the stunning failure to prepare for, then counter, the invasion. Factionalism, a form of party politics, had evolved from the early-Chosŏn ideological conflicts among the throne and high officials (Chapter 7) to a system, ironically institutionalized in King Sŏnjo's reign, of hereditary political affiliation. Perspectives on Chosŏn dynasty factionalism have varied widely among historians, while the Japanese who colonized Korea in the early twentieth century cited factionalism as another example of the debilitating Korean political system.

Regardless of its ultimate significance in explaining Chosŏn dynasty politics as a whole, factionalism did play a central role in this period of major invasions from 1592 to 1637, as partisan disputes became entangled in formulating the court's responses. One key example of this phenomenon came in the two years preceding the Japanese attack, when the Korean monarch sent a diplomatic mission to Japan to gauge the intent of Toyotomi Hideyoshi, the Japanese leader who would later launch the invasions. The embassy's report to King Sŏnjo showed a division among its top two officials, members of rival factions. In implementing a response, one official's warnings of an imminent Japanese invasion lost out to the reassurances of peace by the second official, whose faction enjoyed the upper hand in court. The court's fateful decision not to mobilize the country in preparation for war proved disastrous. And, once again, partisan politics inserted itself into the government's handling of crisis amidst the Japanese war, as Admiral Wŏn Kyun, who, in contrast to Yi Sunsin, had largely failed in his efforts to defeat the enemy at sea, blamed Yi for not carrying out orders to support him. As a stalemate in the war ensued, Wŏn's factional ties to those in power in Seoul produced the amazing scene of Admiral Yi's becoming incarcerated for insubordination and incompetence, and indeed of even being sentenced to death. The scramble to save his life by a few top officials was enough to prolong the stay of execution until the second Japanese invasion of 1597, which highlighted the folly of locking up Admiral Yi. Freed from prison and reinstated to his command, he immediately turned his attention to the southern coast. Alas, his leadership appears to have been critical to the conclusion of the war in 1598, as the joint Ming-Chosŏn forces, buoyed by news that Hideyoshi had died, chased the remaining Japanese soldiers off the peninsula—though not before a stray bullet killed Admiral Yi.

NARRATIVES OF HEROISM

Admiral Yi's death in a blaze of glory has served as the integral conclusion to the great narrative of heroism centered on this figure, whose feats of bravery and skill in the face of impossible odds are commonly recounted by Korean schoolchildren. By all viable historical accounts, Yi Sunsin was indeed an accomplished soldier, gifted strategist, and charismatic commander. From a prominent aristocratic family that had produced mostly civilian officials, he chose another path in his youth and, after passing the military examination with honors, soon ascended the ranks of the military officialdom. As naval commander of Chŏlla province, he stood as one of the few officials who foresaw the danger from Japan, and his preparations appear to have served him well once he engaged in battle, as chronicled in his diary-like official reports to the court. These sources, as well as other eyewitness accounts and government records, all point to Yi's great deeds. But perhaps the source that contributed most to the mythologizing of Yi Sunsin as Korea's greatest war hero was the *Book of Corrections* (*Chingbirok*), written by Yi's staunchest supporter in the upper echelons of government officialdom, Yu Sŏngnyong. Yu had acted as one of Yi's early patrons before the outbreak of war, and the *Book of Corrections*, in reference to the lessons that must be learned from the country's failures in the Japanese invasion, likened Yi to a great spiritual force who almost single-handedly saved Korea. And Yi's stoic righteousness in the face of factional injustice only heightened the impression of his purity.

In the modern era, another source of heroism has gained prominence in the conventional perspective on the Japanese war: the "Righteous Army" guerilla bands mobilized throughout the country to attack the invaders and obstruct the Japanese lines of communication and supplies. In the North Korean account of this war, for example, it is the Righteous Armies, representing the mass of the common, downtrodden people, who came to the rescue when the upper classes, including the monarchy, utterly failed to protect the nation. Such a populist perspective has become more accepted in South Korea as well, but, as scholars have pointed out, these bands, for all their effectiveness, appear to have been led by local aristocrats and thus replicated the hierarchies of society at large. To what extent these militias played a decisive role in the war's outcome remains a point of contention. But regardless of the precise impact of these guerilla units, it seems fitting—given who suffered the brunt of the Japanese invasions—that they would be featured prominently in the national memory of the war. Indeed, their deeds lingered in the popular imagination thereafter, as seen in the reprisal of the "Righteous Army" moniker for ragtag militias that formed in the early twentieth century to resist, once again, the Japanese. In this sense, the prominence of the Righteous Armies in the narratives of national struggle reflects the intensification of Korean identity in opposition to Japan.

There remains, however, one final major factor in the war's outcome that, in Korea at least, has not been readily highlighted: the Chinese. North Korean accounts understandably do not even mention the Ming dynasty's assistance, for this would run counter to their hyper-nationalist narrative of Korean history. Even in South Korea, conventional perspectives on the war give little credit to the Chinese assistance. As for Yu's *Book of Corrections* from the early seventeenth century, it paints the Chinese in mostly a negative light, focusing on their abusive behavior, their commanders' neglect of Korean concerns in the negotiations with the Japanese, and their battlefield failures. Other recent scholarship, however, has questioned this longstanding impression and suggests that the Chinese forces played not only a key role in the allied victory over Japan, but indeed an indispensable one.

THE REGIONAL ORDER REMADE

The significance of the Chinese contribution highlights the fact that, notwithstanding Korea's suffering, this war's impact spread far beyond the peninsula and may have been the most widely encompassing East Asian regional event until the modern era. Indeed the consequences extended even to an area originally untouched by the invasion, Manchuria. While there remains historical debate over the precise connections between the Japanese invasions and the conquest of Korea and China by the Manchus three decades later, the destructive force throughout East Asia could only have had a staggering, profound effect on the region.

Often overlooked when considering the fallout from the Japanese invasions of Korea is the pronounced impact on Japan itself, much of which, ultimately, was in fact beneficial. The lessons learned from the failure of Hideyoshi's grand scheme, not to mention the expenditures of resources and lives, cast a long shadow over Japan's subsequent history. Aside from megalomaniacal delusion, Hideyoshi's primary reason for launching the invasion was to provide an outlet for the energies of his warrior retainers, who had proved instrumental in his completing the project of politically reunifying Japan after centuries of fragmentation. After his death, Japanese leaders would not again venture beyond their borders for over 200 years. In fact, the leader who emerged as Hideyoshi's successor, Tokugawa Ieyasu, instituted a peaceful, stable, and in many ways a thriving dynastic rule based partly on the policy of "closure" to the outside world until the middle of the nineteenth century. The salutary effects of the Hideyoshi misadventure would extend to unforeseen realms as well: the many Korean artisans—artists, potters, smiths, ship builders, and others—taken as war captives back to Japan appear to have made a lasting contribution to the development of Japanese culture and technology.

As for China, the dedication of massive resources to the war against Japan—an act, admittedly, that was not devoid of self-interest, since Korea served as a buffer against the Japanese—could not have helped the Ming dynasty's increasingly fragile grip on rule. After more than two centuries, the Ming government, having concentrated its energies on internal stability through limited foreign adventures, found itself having to beat back not only the Japanese, but also Chinese rebels and ultimately yet another "barbarian" group to its immediate northeast. The Manchus, descendants of tribesmen who had periodically organized them-selves into a formidable military force throughout East Asian history, had suddenly done so again while the rest of the region was preoccupied with recovery from the Japanese invasion. By the 1620s, the Manchus, following the familiar pattern of the Northmen of East Asia in previous eras, appeared on the verge of striking Korea on their way to the big prize of China itself. The brooding specter of this invasion instigated a major factional struggle in Korea over how to respond, and eventually the king, who favored a policy of accommodation with this new power, was overthrown by Chosŏn's high officials in favor of a more explicitly pro-Ming monarch. This soon brought forth the first of two devastating Manchu invasions of Korea in 1627, to be followed by the finish-ing blow in 1636, when the Korean monarch surrendered in ritual-ized humiliation to the Manchu emperor just outside of Seoul. This paved the way for the Manchus' march into Beijing in 1644 and their takeover of China.

Despite succumbing themselves to the irrepressible Manchu force just a few years earlier, the Koreans were completely shocked by the Ming dynasty's fall, which constituted, from the Korean perspective, an event on the level of a cosmic shift. For all the diplomatic subordination that the Koreans endured thereafter, the legitimacy of the ensuing Qing dynasty of the Manchus was never accepted by most Korean elites, who harbored a deeply ethnicized scorn for these "barbarians." Indeed for well over a century Koreans openly retained fantasies of engaging in a "northern campaign" to overthrow the Qing. Koreans, now deprived of their long held assumptions about civilizational order, were forced to reconsider their larger standing Under Heaven. A belief hardened among Korean elites that, with the fall of the Ming, only Chosŏn remained as a bastion of (Confucian) civilization. This accompanied the equally fascinating emergence of a more widespread sense of national consciousness among lower groups of people, as seen in the expressions of popular culture from the seventeenth century onwards (Chapter 12). Indeed, the rallying cry of Yi Sunsin, Righteous Army leaders, and others around the common cause of national survival during the Japanese and, later, Manchu invasions laid the foundation for fortifying the idea of Koreanness itself.

10
. . . .
Ideology, Family, and Nationhood in the Mid-Chosŏn Era

CHRONOLOGY

THE BIRTH OF A SON TO LADY CHANG, 1688

In late 1688, news quickly spread that Lady Chang, the favored concubine of King Sukchong, had given birth to a son. Though certainly not an unusual event in the annals of the Korean monarchy, in the tense atmosphere of court politics at this time, it carried strong repercussions. For Lady Chang, known commonly as Chang Hŭibin, was not just a royal concubine. Through her actions and her unwitting status as a political symbol, she also embodied the tensions and conflicts that had roiled the capital for years involving fundamental issues of Korean identity and civilization. Lady Chang had so smitten the monarch that he promptly designated the newborn as the crown prince, divorced his own queen, who had yet to bear a son, and promoted Lady Chang as her replacement.

The vehement objections to this move from many top advisors, including the most notable Confucian scholar of the era, unleashed a storm of political strife. Within fifteen years, this conflict would ultimately victimize dozens of high officials on all sides and end with Lady Chang's own execution ordered by the monarch himself.

A riveting story that has been replayed countless times on Korean television dramas and movies, this episode's historical significance extends far beyond the realm of the inner palace quarters. It underscores, for one, the conflicts surrounding ideological and factional struggles, family practices, social organization, and even civilizational identity that had been stirring for decades as the country recovered from the Japanese and Manchu invasions (Chapter 9). From the historian's perspective, these wider implications in turn highlight the significance of this middle period of the Chosŏn dynasty, when some of the most familiar features of Korea's Confucian society came into form.

KING SUKCHONG'S TRIANGLES

The mid-Chosŏn, in turn, can be further divided: the half-century of devastating invasions from 1592 to 1637, and the seven or eight decades thereafter of recovery and reconstruction. The political figure dominating the latter period was King Sukchong, who ascended the throne in 1674 and survived to reign for forty five years. His longevity alone suggests a strong monarch ruling at a time of welcome stability, which indeed was the case for the country as a whole. King Sukchong bolstered Korea's defenses and stabilized its northern frontier, implemented major tax reforms that contributed to the growth of agricultural production, and chipped away at the social discrimination against lower status groups in the government and military. All these deeds for the public good, however, are overshadowed in the prevailing historical perspective by his private failings—his quick-tempered, inconstant, and often scandalous behavior—which in turn had a great bearing on the history of this period.

The consequences of these personal weaknesses might not have extended beyond his private quarters had he not ruled amidst the peak of factional wrangling among high officials, a phenomenon that he actually furthered. The bitter partisan court battles of the late sixteenth century, which affected Korea's preparations for and response to the Japanese invasions, had again undermined Korea's preparations for and response to the Manchu incursions beginning in the 1620s (Chapter 9). But it did not stop there; following the Manchu conquest of Ming China in 1644, factional wrangling in Korea became intricately tied to sophisticated debates concerning the country's place in the larger realm of civilization. Indeed, since the early Chosŏn era, philosophical differences had often spawned factional divisions. This relationship became crystallized in the arcane metaphysical rivalry of the sixteenth century between the forerunners of the Southern School, who followed the great philosopher T'oegye, and the Westerners, forming around the teachings of Yulgok (Chapter 8). Such a close intertwining of ideological and political affiliations had overwhelmed the political system and debilitated the monarch. Sukchong, though, used factional hostilities as a political tool even while claiming to abhor it. Partisan strife, a phenomenon commonly associated with the institutionalized weakness of the Chosŏn crown, stood in this case as a manifestation of a powerful king attempting to increase his leverage through his triangulation between two bitterly opposing sides.

Sukchong was also immersed in another, better-known triangle, however—the love triangle involving his wife and his concubine. The troubles arising from this particular dynamic were commonplace in Korean elite families throughout the Chosŏn era (and beyond), but, when these private travails racked the royal family, they had a pronounced effect on politics. The two-decade drama involving these three figures resulted in major political upheavals leading to the deaths of dozens of people. It also highlighted the tensions of the mid-Chosŏn era between the ongoing efforts at Confucianization and the great native impulses—socially, culturally, and in the realm of the family—continuing to resist a complete makeover.

Sukchong's second wife, Queen Inhyŏn (his first had died at an early age), had impeccable family credentials and, according to both official and unofficial historical sources, was widely revered for her grace and character. But as time passed these qualities were overshadowed by the lack of a male heir. In the meantime, the king grew strongly fond of one of the palace ladies, Lady Chang, who had already developed a reputation for her spellbinding beauty and cunning. She even suffered expulsion from the palace for her potentially dangerous effect on the harmony of the royal family. Queen Inhyŏn herself, credited with selflessly putting her husband's desires above those of her own, urged that Lady Chang be allowed to return. In early 1688, when news of Lady Chang's pregnancy spread, it seemed to validate Queen Inhyŏn's noble move even as it threatened to unleash yet another struggle for royal succession. When, in answering the monarch's fervent wishes, Lady Chang bore a son, King Sukchong's affection for her grew immeasurably. In the midst of this euphoria, the monarch named the newborn the crown prince. An explosion of political strife quickly followed.

The high officials belonging to the Westerners faction immediately protested *en masse* to this move, arguing that Queen Inhyŏn was young and thus could still bear a "legitimate" crown prince. Not only did King Sukchong react angrily to this protest by purging some of these officials, he immediately ratcheted up the confrontation to another level by divorcing Queen Inhyŏn, stripping her of her title as queen. He accused her of insufficiently embracing, both figuratively and literally, the baby boy, and further rationalized this move as necessary for the crown prince when he eventually became king. The uproar that followed induced another purge of the Westerners, this time killing the faction's intellectual leader, Song Siyŏl, who was forced to drink a bowl of poison. In 1694, however, King Sukchong, fickle as ever, changed his mind again and returned Queen Inhyŏn to the palace, demoting Queen Chang back to her original status as a palace lady. This would not be the end of the drama, however, for Queen Inhyŏn, still without having borne a son, died suddenly in 1701. When it was discovered that Lady Chang, in her attempt to regain the monarch's affections, had constructed a shamanistic altar where she put curses on Queen Inhyŏn through the use of figurines, King Sukchong blamed her for his queen's death and had Lady Chang executed. But Lady Chang, as if remaining true to her reputation, would not go quietly and fiercely resisted any dignified death. The executioners had to force feed her the poison.

If we take a step back from the titillating combination of sex and politics that enveloped this long-running drama, we can rightfully place it in the larger currents of Korean history and even draw comparisons to similar situations in other parts of the world. To many readers, this episode will evoke thoughts of the notorious behavior of King Henry VIII of England from a century-and-a-half earlier. Like King Sukchong, Henry was willing to go to extremes in order to divorce his queen for a favored concubine, and, like Lady Chang, Anne Boleyn in the end paid the ultimate price for the monarch's inconstancy. In the meantime, the political order was upended and led to the execution of the widely revered great man of letters, whether Song Siyŏl or Thomas More, who led the righteous opposition. And in the wider consequences as well, there are important similarities. While a new religious order like the Church of England did not materialize from this episode in Korea, in both countries the larger stakes concerned the country's place in the realm of the dominant religio-ethical civilization.

In this sense, Song Siyŏl and Lady Chang stood as the dueling parties in King Sukchong's most important triangle. In determining the future direction of Korea's Confucian civilization, the monarch had to balance his personal desires against the two extreme priorities represented by Chang and Song. Song Siyŏl, in fact, had served as the resilient ideological fount of classical East Asian and Neo-Confucian orthodoxy for much of the seventeenth century. Since the 1640s, he had engaged in prominent battles against scholar-officials arguing for Korean exceptionalism in the Confucian world order. The latter view, given the fall of Ming China to the Manchu "barbarians" in 1644, emphasized Korea's position as the lone standing source of civilization and called for an adjustment to orthodoxy that would accommodate historical change and national interests. Song, on the other hand, in condemning such "heterodoxy," always maintained that Korea, precisely because of the fall of Ming China, must firmly adhere to the traditional understanding. Little wonder, then, that Song is sometimes cited as "Korea's Zhu Xi," in reference to the great Chinese scholar credited with formulating the foundation of Neo-Confucian doctrine in the twelfth century. In stark contrast,

Lady Chang can be seen representing the nativist impulses of folk religion, the primacy of the crown, and the complications of hereditary social hierarchy. She also represented the heritage of strong-willed Korean women whose public prominence reached a high point in the mid-Chosŏn era.

FAMOUS FEMALES

Neither Lady Chang nor Queen Inhyŏn, who have always been joined at the hip in historical lore, wished to be swept up and exploited by the political combatants of the day. Likewise, neither likely could do anything to prevent their fates from being determined, in the end, by a mercurial monarch. But in other ways, these two opposing females served as models of strength in Chosŏn Korea, although in very different ways. Queen Inhyŏn has always stood as the paragon of Confucian female virtue. Unable to gain the affection of her husband due to the lack of a son, she subsumed her personal feelings and interests by inviting Lady Chang back into the palace. And when Lady Chang gave birth to a boy, Queen Inhyŏn again selflessly supported the monarch's designation of the baby as the crown prince. Lady Chang, on the other hand, has traditionally been portrayed as the evil opposite—the stubborn, licentious, and decadent *femme fatale*. But she could also be considered a model of the boisterous, passionate, clever Korean female who more recently has been celebrated, especially in popular culture, as a forerunner to the confident modern woman who takes her fate into her own hands.

Unlike Lady Chang, most palace girls, who were servants attending to mostly female members of the royal family, had little chance of becoming a royal concubine, much less of exerting great influence on political affairs. But, as with other privileged females, they could express themselves through a discreet but historically significant medium of empowerment at the time, vernacular writing. The Korean alphabet had been devised and promulgated in the mid-fifteenth century, but well into the nineteenth century literary Chinese remained the dominant form of writing in the circles of learned elites and government affairs. Females, who could not expect to become literate in the high culture, took advantage of the alphabet's great functionality to leave behind a treasure trove of valuable writings, ranging from letters and diaries to poetry, novels, and chronicles. Among the most illuminating examples of the latter came from a palace lady who apparently had witnessed the events surrounding the Queen Inhyŏn–Lady Chang affair. This author penned the "Biography of Queen Inhyŏn," a sympathetic portrayal of the queen that still stands as a precious unofficial source of information about these events.

The vernacular culture exerted perhaps the greatest influence in regard to females by shining a spotlight on the social class of "kisaeng," or courtesans. Like the Japanese *geisha*, the *kisaeng* courtesans carried out both sexual and artistic functions. And, like the palace ladies, many courtesans were attached to government service, usually provincial or county government offices. This reflected also their "base" social status, which put them in the same category as slaves. Their sometimes scandalous love affairs and renowned talents in music, dance, and letters gave these women prominent standing in the folk culture as a whole, while the lives and accomplishments of certain *kisaeng* became legendary. In fact, a disproportionate number of famous females from the Chosŏn era were *kisaeng*. In addition to Hwang Chini, the early-sixteenth century figure renowned for both her great beauty and extraordinary literary skills, many other *kisaeng* gained fame for their talents and romances. The sorrowful tales of their forced parting from their lovers became the basis for some of the great literary and musical expressions of premodern Korea (Chapter 12), and they constitute a rich source of information about Korean culture and society at the time.

The prominence of such low-status females in the historical memory of the Chosŏn dynasty, especially of the mid-Chosŏn era, also testifies to the solidification of the decrease in standing of females as a whole, especially of the aristocracy. It became rare, for example, for daughters to gain equal inheritance with their brothers, especially the oldest son, and movement and visibility for women were significantly curtailed. These developments also went hand-in-hand with the hardening of the hereditary social hierarchy beginning in the seventeenth century. The social and political discrimination against the offspring of concubines and remarried widows, a semi-Confucian legal measure from the early Chosŏn, now took firm root throughout society. One consequence was the increasing practice, among elite families, to adopt nephews—often distant nephews—into a household instead of allowing a concubine's son to become the legal heir. These concubines' descendants, including those of *kisaeng* courtesans, became a distinctive hereditary status group that, by the nineteenth century, swelled in numbers to constitute a major social force.

LATENCY OF THE MID-CHOSŎN ORDER

As suggested by the formation of these conventionally "traditional" Korean social patterns, the mid-Chosŏn era stood as a time of reconstruction and systematization in the wake of the foreign invasions. The Japanese invasions might have been more devastating in terms of human and material loss, but the Manchu invasions, particularly the Manchu conquest of China shortly thereafter, dealt a greater blow to Koreans' sense of self and propriety. At the heart of the political conflicts and social strife lay the task of implementing a sense of Confucian order, and of reformulating a national identity as that of the sole remaining true civilization. The bloody contests that embroiled Song Siyŏl and others also demonstrated that a significant strain in Korea's sociopolitical leadership sought to reassess Korea's place Under Heaven by asserting native practices that transcended Confucian orthodoxy. And as the Lady Chang episode demonstrated, the self-styled rationality of Confucianism, now after nearly three centuries as the official social ideology, still had to contend with longstanding native beliefs and practices.

One possible consequence of the persistence of native tendencies was the rise of money as a social force, particularly amidst the economic expansion and advances in agricultural techniques and production of this era. Lady Chang, who is conventionally known as someone from low social origin befitting her position as palace lady, actually entered the royal compounds through the maneu-vering of her wealthy family. Her social status, in fact, was that of a "chungin"—hereditary lineages of technical officials such as interpreters, physicians, and accountants. Her father was a promi-nent interpreter who likely used his great wealth, gained through his trading activities while accompanying government embassies to China, to wield political influence. There is strong evidence that many of the rich but sub-aristocratic members of society who could not hope to enter high office or marriage relations with the ruling aristocracy—i.e., those belonging to the secondary status groups—turned to monetary influence-peddling to gain the pres-tige that otherwise was denied them. If so, the Lady Chang story unveils a significant undercurrent of social fluidity in her time.

The secondary status groups

One of the enduringly fascinating features of Korean civiliza-tion since the beginning has been the commanding influence of social status in determining both social interaction and structure. And perhaps the most compelling manifestation of the Korean social hierarchy was the emergence, in the mid-Chosŏn, of the secondary status groups. To a far greater extent than the hereditary aristocracy or commoner peasantry, which were not significantly different from their counterparts else-where in the premodern world, the secondary status groups embodied Chosŏn Korea's systematic integration of political power with the delineation of ascriptive social privilege.

Five secondary status groups, who collectively constituted a hallmark of late Chosŏn society, came into distinctive form beginning in the post-invasions recovery period of the seven-teenth century: the lineages of technical officials, such as the family of Lady Chang; the hereditary clerks of local govern-ment who descended from local elites of the Koryŏ era; the many concubine descendants, who constituted one of the largest social categories in the late Chosŏn period; the local elites of the northern provinces, victimized by a regional bias with origins deep in Korean history; and the military officials who, in an earlier era (however briefly), stood as equals to their civilian counterparts. Though originating under different circumstances, these secondary status groups all suffered discrimination both socially and politically, and hence embodied the core principle linking hereditary social status to political power, or, to be more precise, to bureaucratic eligibility. Their existence as sub-aristocratic groups, in other words, both determined and was determined by their lower possibilities for gaining government office.

The secondary status groups acted as a kind of buffer between the ruling aristocracy and the majority mass of commoners. Hence they embodied the complicated mixture of the rock-solid principle of hereditary status and the sporadic possibilities for some social mobility in the mid- to late-Chosŏn. They had a foot in the realms of both the ruling class, with whom most of them had an ancestral connection before being sloughed off into secondary status, and the ruled, with whom they could commiserate about the injustices of the system. They represented, then, the Chosŏn social structure in its full range of characteristics, from the dominant Confucian ethos and socioeconomic system to popular culture and sentiment (Chapter 12). And therein lay the latency of their historical significance: while they absorbed social conventions and internalized the Confucian orthodoxy, as time passed they demonstrated an increasing desire for social recognition and privilege, which remained largely thwarted until the modern era.

That Lady Chang's ascent to the royal palace created such an uproar, however, testified also to the reverse: the firm limits to social mobility irrespective even of material wealth. The chaos of the invasions led to a determination on the part of the aristocracy, armed with its command of political institutions and Confucian orthodoxy, to maintain its dominant social standing through a creative combination of factors. While allowing room for sub-aristocratic groups, such as the technical official class, to gain a small measure of social mobility through material accumulation, the preeminence of birth and marriage in determining privileges and sociopolitical power remained intact.

11

· · · · · · · ·

Intellectual Opening in the Late Eighteenth Century

CHRONOLOGY

THE RETURN OF PAK CHEGA TO KOREA, 1778

In 1778, Pak Chega, a little-known intellectual, gained the privilege of accompanying a close friend on a tribute mission to China. So inspired was he by this trip that, upon his return later in the year, Pak wrote the *Discourse on Northern Learning*, at once a travelogue as well as a wide-ranging social commentary on the ills of his native country. Through this work, Pak Chega voiced the views of a scholarly movement that drew together some of the country's brightest minds, who together pushed for a thorough renovation of Chosŏn dynasty society, and particularly its economy, by looking to the example of contemporary China. While

99

Koreans had a long history of adopting Chinese models, for over a century before Pak's appointment most Korean elites had dismissed Qing dynasty China, established by the Manchus in 1644, as a country ruled by barbarians.

From the vantage point of Pak Chega and those in his intellectual circle of "northern learning" advocates, the urgency of reform directly correlated to the challenge of overcoming this long-held, ethnicized bias against the Manchu-run Qing dynasty—the "north". Nearly all of these scholars had visited Qing China and come back with an eye-opening impression of its socioeconomic advancement. These advocates of northern learning declared not only that Koreans must overcome their prejudices regarding the Manchus, but that this must in turn spur a comprehensive reconsideration of long-held Korean tenets and practices, including those of the Confucian orthodoxy. In this way the northern learning movement constituted, however briefly, an apt capstone to the Chosŏn dynasty's "golden era" of the late eighteenth century, marked by peace, relative political stability, and cultural flowering. Little wonder, then, that this period is also preferred by Koreans as a truer representation of the latter Chosŏn era, before the ravages of the nineteenth century led to the tragedies of the twentieth.

"UTILITY FOR THE GREATER GOOD"

The unofficial motto for the northern learning school, appearing repeatedly in the writings, was "iyong husaeng," a term that can be translated in many ways, including "utility for the greater good," and reflects an approach to solving problems practically and logically. Historians tend to identify the northern learning cohort as part of a wider scholarly movement in the late Chosŏn era called "practical learning" (*sirhak*), but this was a coherence constructed mostly by modern historians. Furthermore, one could argue that all Confucian reform proposals that targeted policies affecting the lives of people, by their very nature, were a reflection of "practical learning." The northern learning movement, however, was real— nearly all of the movement's figures had a singularly influential experience of visiting China, befriended each other and, in their writings and advocacy activities, supported common core principles. These principles in pursuit of "utility for the greater good" included an embrace of foreign models, especially the scientific teachings of the West; an encouragement of manufacturing, trade, commerce, and even consumption, as well as the concomitant removal of the social stigma attached to profiteering and commercial activities; and the leveling of the social hierarchy. Together, these positions, in fact, went about as far as one could in questioning Neo-Confucianism itself—or at least the domination of its long-held tenets in Korea—without explicitly rejecting it.

The apex figure of this movement was Hong Taeyong, who visited China as part of a tribute mission to Beijing in 1765. There he became well acquainted with Chinese scholars, Catholic clergymen, and a plethora of writings about the world beyond the peninsula. Hong's experience left him in stunned awe, and he meticulously recorded his observations in a travelogue he wrote following his return. In this and other works, Hong noted the extraordinary energies in the daily lives and economic activities of the Chinese, even beyond the showcase capital of Beijing itself. He took this as an impetus to launch a general critique of Korean customs and Confucian orthodoxy, most clearly in evidence in his "Ŭisan Mountain Dialogue," which features a conversation about the world and nature between the imaginary characters "Empty" and "Substantive." Needless to say, Empty reveals himself as a thinly veiled caricature of the Korean scholar mired in the abstractions of Neo-Confucian philosophy. As seen in this work and others, however, the interaction with Chinese and Western scholars seems to have most affected Hong's received view of the larger cosmos, and indeed it is Hong's scientific writings for which he is best known. In them he propounded and legitimated, mostly through deduction, the ideas of a round, rotating earth that encircled a stationary sun, and of humanity's commonalities with the rest of the natural world. Some historians consider Hong Taeyong the greatest scientific thinker of the Chosŏn era.

Hong's circle of like-minded colleagues included his protégé Pak Chiwŏn, who finally took his own trip to China in 1780 and returned to write the best-known travelogue of this period, the "Diary of the [Journey to the Chinese Emperor's] Summer Palace." Like Hong, Pak admiringly described the flourishing lives of the Chinese, whose use of advanced practical technologies was directly connected to their economic productivity and governmental efficiency. This work was far more than a travelogue, however; his observations of China induced critical reflections on a wide range of topics concerning his home country, to which he applied the extraordinary literary skill that placed him among the most innovative writers of the Chosŏn era. Indeed, aside from the "Diary of the Summer Palace," Pak's best-known works are short stories, written in literary Chinese. Many have in common a satirical portrayal of the late Chosŏn society and mindset, in tandem with allusions to the very different examples found in China. In his "Tale of the Yangban" or "Tale of Hŏ Saeng," for example, Pak takes aim at Korea's hereditary social hierarchy, in which one's social status corresponded little, if at all, to one's contributions to the greater good. These stories depict a parasitic aristocracy that relied upon empty learning and the privileges accorded by birth, while people of lower standing were engaging in socially productive, practical work and even growing rich.

Such themes were perhaps most systematically integrated into a prescriptive for national renovation by the work and writings of Pak Chiwŏn's close friend Pak Chega, whose renown extended to poetry, painting, and calligraphy. Pak Chega's appointment in 1779 to a high position in the Royal Library by King Chŏngjo, newly enthroned three years earlier, allowed him to further elaborate on the points made in the *Discourse on Northern Learning* and to influence the formulation of government policy. By the time the final revised version of the *Discourse* appeared in print more than two decades after its unveiling, it contained the most systematic expression of the northern learning program, garnished with the wisdom gained from Pak Chega's experience in government service.

Among the most striking ideas appearing in this work and in Pak Chega's policy proposals was the explicit endorsement of the pursuit of private wealth. According to Pak, the core problem facing late Chosŏn Korea was widespread poverty, both in relation to China as well as in absolute terms. This condition stemmed in part from the ruling ethos of austerity that discouraged the consumption of high-quality goods, which in turn destroyed any incentive to produce, improve, and circulate material items. One solution, then, was to encourage the aristocratic *yangban* to engage freely in commerce, trade, and manufacturing—all areas of activity that, in the Chosŏn era, had been scorned as unbecoming of the nobility. This would, Pak stated, discourage idleness and serve as a model for "pursuing profit," which in turn would enrich everyone.

Korea also was beset by decay in the infrastructures of commerce and manufacturing, according to Pak. Along these lines, he seemed almost obsessed with the simple wagon, which was the first of dozens of novelties—ranging from sericulture and paper currency to buildings and boats—that he describes having seen and studied while in China. He noted that ancient Koreans effectively used wagons, and even in contemporary times one could find a few of them in scattered areas. So why were wagons not in greater use as a central mode of transportation and transport? Nothing so encapsulated his homeland's backwardness, Pak appears to have been saying: widespread use of wagons internally, in conjunction with open trade externally, would boost the circulation of goods, promote the diversification and improvement of locally produced specialty items, and benefit the economic conditions of the country as a whole.

Indeed the northern learning school's "utility for the greater good" motive constituted very much a materialist proposition: only after the basic economic conditions are met can other concerns be addressed. In laying out the interconnectedness of the material with other realms of existence, scholars like Pak Chiwŏn in fact aped the great Confucian chain of being, as expressed famously by Confucius in *The Great Learning*, a core book of the Confucian canon. But instead of locating self-cultivation at the most fundamental level, the northern learning advocates designated material well-being. This in effect overturned the long-held spiritual and ritualistic basis of Chosŏn Neo-Confucianism, and it was even done with the rhetorical tool of appealing to the classics. In his introduction to the *Discourse on Northern Learning*, for example, Pak Chega quotes the ancient sages, including Confucius himself, to emphasize the economic foundation of ritual and morality— that the people's welfare must be secured before focusing on enlightening them in spiritual propriety. In this sense the northern learning school presented one of the most compelling intellectual challenges to the orthodoxy of Neo-Confucianism in the Chosŏn.

THE SPROUTS OF MODERNITY?

Historians have suggested that the northern learning school, as part of the "practical learning" trend, demonstrated the stirrings of Korea's own drive toward modern ideas and institutions. The calls for a centrality of the people's welfare in statecraft and the leveling of the hereditary social hierarchy ostensibly represent modern ideals. And the prioritization of material welfare as well as the promotion of industry and trade to increase national strength suggest not only a vibrant mercantilism but indeed the shift toward capitalism. Economic historians, furthermore, have dug up evidence that the late Chosŏn witnessed increases in productivity stemming from greater commercial activity and, in the agricultural sector, the adoption of new techniques and technologies. Northern learning scholars, as noted above, certainly did embrace technological advances and the development of industries and infrastructures, as well as the encouragement of consumption, commerce, foreign trade, and manufacturing. But the expression of such ideals and, as it turned out, the lack of sustained implementation of them, reflected more the fact that Chosŏn Korea, despite some advances in productivity, was nowhere close to achieving the critical mass necessary to overturn the basic production modes. In fact, that Pak and others so lamented the *absence* of changes long having been adopted in China testifies to the starker reality of late eighteenth-century Korea. The vociferous opposition to the northern learning school, some of which stemmed from a distaste for its literary conventions, did not counter that Korea's economic conditions were inaccurately portrayed, but rather that they were acceptable given the risk of exposure to corrupting influences.

This takes us to the issue of the historical significance of the northern learning school, given its seeming lack of any major, immediate impact. Was it simply an interesting but ultimately inconsequential intellectual movement? As suggested above, the "what if" questions surrounding these promising developments of the eighteenth century are particularly bitter-sweet due to the solipsistic decay, leading ultimately to calamity, that followed in the nineteenth century (or so it seems—see Chapter 13). The underlying historiographical issue, though somewhat crudely put, is, did the internal development of Chosŏn society have enough within itself to trigger the shift toward the modern? There appears to be a search for a reassurance, almost cathartic in tone, of the validity of Korean tradition and civilization before the nineteenth century as a way to accept the sacrifices and ultimate accomplishments of the modern experience. Over the past few decades in South Korea, as seen in historical scholarship as well as in historical fiction, television dramas, or movies, this search has been narrowed to several benchmarks for measuring the advances of the late eighteenth century, such as capitalism, Catholicism, and royal absolutism. And in this regard, even more than the northern learning advocates, the historical figures who have been featured most prominently are two with direct personal connections to Pak Chega: the great philosopher Chŏng Yagyong, better known as Tasan, and King Chŏngjo.

King Chŏngjo in fact brought Pak and Chŏng together to work in the Royal Library. The king was an accomplished scholar in his own right. And his charge to his officials in the new Royal Library was to compile and organize a grand repository of works in order to advance scholarship and government policy, just as the Hall of Worthies had done for King Sejong the Great. Like Sejong, Chŏngjo has enjoyed great acclaim for personifying the ideals of the sagely Confucian monarch. He was the third in a triumvirate of long-reigning, powerful, reform-oriented kings under whose rule Chosŏn culture and civilization reached a peak: Sukchong (r. 1674–1720), Yŏngjo (1724–76), and Chŏngjo (1776–1800). King Yŏngjo, the longest reigning monarch in Korean history, not only brought stability but introduced a series of state reforms, including a major update to the dynastic code, that spurred cultural and social advances. Many restrictions on hereditarily discriminated groups were eliminated under his leadership, and he is lauded for having striven, somewhat successfully, to control the factional strife among his officials. Despite these accomplishments, however, Yŏngjo also is remembered for a tragedy in his family: in 1762 he ordered that his murderous, mentally disturbed crown prince wither away while locked in a rice chest. King Chŏngjo, Yŏngjo's grandson and the doomed prince's son, had witnessed this horror as a child, and it is a wonder that the psychological scarring did not overwhelm him once he ascended to the throne in 1776. Indeed, on the sixtieth birthday of both of his parents in 1795, Chŏngjo formally rehabilitated his father through a lavish royal outing to his father's new grave site south of Seoul.

Chŏngjo's own accomplishments as monarch might have matched those of his predecessor in half the time, although it is widely lamented that he did not reign longer. While maintaining Yŏngjo's intolerance for factional strife, Chŏngjo was keen to promote cultural advances through the circulation of new ideas. The combination of his interest in new models and publications from China and his desire to cultivate talented young officials appears to have brought Pak Chega to his attention. A year following the publication of Pak's *Discourse on Northern Learning*, King Chŏngjo appointed him in 1779 to his compiler's position in the Royal Library. Pak in fact was one of four new pathbreaking officials in this post—all of them were concubine's children or descendants. The monarch had earlier proclaimed a policy of opening the path toward higher government office for these long-discriminated men. Indeed, Pak appears to have enjoyed the favoritism of King Chŏngjo, who in 1790 sent him as a special ambassador to China.

By then Pak had served for over a decade in the Royal Library, where he befriended and mentored other young officials, none more accomplished than Chŏng Yagyong. Beginning with his entrance into government service in the 1780s, Chŏng went on to establish himself as one of his era's foremost intellectuals and is today commonly cited as the greatest thinker of the late Chosŏn. He was certainly one of the most prolific authors and versatile minds. He produced hundreds of masterful writings on topics ranging from the core Confucian pursuits of statecraft, philosophy, and social criticism to history, economy, science and engineering, architecture, and religion. In the realm of religion, in fact, Chŏng may have been the first major scholar-official of his time to embrace not only the scientific but the religious and philosophical teachings of Catholicism. He may even have converted.

Korean visitors to China had begun to notice the Catholic presence in the form of Jesuit priests in Beijing in the sixteenth century, but it was not until the closing years of the eighteenth century that the potential challenges from this religion became a serious issue in Korea. The first Korean Catholic was baptized in China in 1784, and soon Korean and foreign missionaries clandestinely pursued their work in Korea itself, converting thousands by the turn of century, including many from the aristocracy and secondary status groups. Over protests urging a harsh crackdown on a set of teachings that appeared to promote an abandonment of one's social and ritual responsibilities, King Chŏngjo cautioned patience and treated this religion as a superstitious curiosity that needed to be monitored. Following Chŏngjo's death in 1800, however, the Chosŏn court soon pursued a mass persecution of Catholics, and amidst this tumult Chŏng Yagyong was stripped of his position and sent into exile.

Chŏng would never recover his political or intellectual influence, even after his exile of over fifteen years ended while in his late fifties (he would live into his seventies). But the second half of his life that he spent in exile and recovery proved extremely fruitful for him intellectually: it allowed him to reorganize his thoughts, synthesize the various strains of reformist policies that had circulated in the late eighteenth century, and witness directly the plight of the people in the countryside. As a result, he could provide an exhaustive diagnosis for Korea's systemic ills. His proposed solutions in many ways reflected the influence of the northern learning school, especially given his embrace of new technologies—and particularly in agriculture—though with a more reserved enthusiasm for copying the Qing model. In contrast to his friend Pak Chega, Chŏng directed more of his attention to fixing statecraft, with an emphasis of fundamental points inherent to Neo-Confucian doctrine but left neglected over the years amidst the wrangling over abstractions. Chŏng's premise, then, was that a good society began with good governance more than with material or technological advances. This perspective was reflected in his most famous work, *Core Teachings for Shepherding the People*, which harkened back to the focus in the Confucian classics on proper education, guidance, and care for the people as the basis of proper government and society. On one level, this work was a handbook on how to be an effective county magistrate, based on Chŏng's own experiences as both a magistrate and exiled observer. On another level, the reform measures advocated in this work extended to lessons on administration that applied on a far wider scale. Chŏng argued, for example, that real-life administrative problems were handled poorly due to the government's reliance on a stilted examination system to recruit officials, which rewarded rote learning and empty philosophy.

That Chŏng Yagyong, like Pak Chega and Pak Chiwŏn, faded into the political and intellectual wilderness in the early nineteenth century heightens the contrast with their prominence in the late eighteenth century, and in turn the sense of what might have been. Their fates, then, constituted a regrettable end to the intellectual and cultural flowering of the Chosŏn golden age: a whimper instead of a bang. The bang would have to await the tumult of the ensuing era.

12

....

Popular Culture in the Late Chosŏn Era

CHRONOLOGY

early 17th c.	Publication of the *Tale of Hong Kiltong*
1844	Publication of the *Hosan Unofficial History* by Cho Hŭiryong
1850s	Standardization of *p'ansori* librettos by Sin Chaehyo
1858	Publication of the *History of Sunflowers*
1862	Publication of *Observations from the Countryside* by Yu Chaegŏn

PUBLICATION OF *OBSERVATIONS FROM THE COUNTRYSIDE*, 1862

"Many upstanding people have lived in our country, which stretches for hundreds of miles in all directions. How can it be, then, that we know about only a few of these people whose stories deserve to be passed down through our words and literature?" So asks the scholar and renowned painter Cho Hŭiryong in the preface to the book, *Observations from the Countryside*, on behalf of the book's author, Yu Chaegŏn. Yu's work meant to address Cho's rhetorical question by presenting the biographical portraits of almost 300 notable people whose lower social status had prevented their upstanding actions and lives from having become more widely known. Their backgrounds ranged from the well-educated but subordinated groups of people holding technical positions in the government—or *chungin*, like Yu himself—to local military officers, clerks, doctors, artists, peasants, and merchants, as well as slaves, monks, and other "mean" people. People of all such backgrounds lived as models of filiality, morality, self-cultivation, and sacrifice, Yu wanted to show.

Observations from the Countryside typified a flurry of such publications in the mid-nineteenth century. Biographical compilations of lower status groups, including a work that had appeared a decade earlier authored by Cho Hŭiryong himself, were published in tandem with a growing poetry movement headed by non-aristocratic literary figures like Yu and Cho. In turn, this literary movement partook in a trend that figured prominently in the latter half of the Chosŏn dynasty: a greater awareness of the plight of the common people through the increasing expression of their voices in popular cultural forms, from novels to music, dance, and painting. The most well-known folk stories today in Korea, in fact, originated in this era, crafted and transmitted through both written and oral means. The flourishing of these cultural expressions in the late Chosŏn also presents a treasure trove of clues about the everyday lives of the people, as well as subtle digs at the injustices and sorrows of the hereditary social hierarchy. Literature and art thus expressed discontent in a way that circumvented the political and social structures of authority, until it became a palpable groundswell of challenges to the status quo.

TALES OF THE PEOPLE

Little wonder, then, that the adventures of Robin Hood-like righteous bandits held a prominent place in this body of literature. Such tales provided a scenario that, on the one hand, espoused the orthodox values of righteousness and benevolence, and, on the other, addressed the social yearnings of lower status groups through escapist fantasy involving heroic exploits. One such story was *The Tale of Hong Kiltong*, centered on the story of Hong, a concubine's son abused by both his family and society at large due to his birth status. Unable to endure the rampant prejudice against him, he runs away and leads a group of bandits that attack corrupt officials and distribute the booty to those exploited by them. This story ends with Hong and his followers settling into a kind of socialist utopia without hierarchies and discrimination. In written form, *The Tale of Hong Kiltong*, which appeared in the early seventeenth century, might have represented the first Korean novel in the vernacular. Clearly, however, the story did not originate with its putative author, Hŏ Kyun, but rather had circulated since the times of a real historical figure named Hong Kiltong in the fifteenth century.

The legendary elaboration on his life probably drew also from a similar story involving another, better-documented bandit, Im Kkŏkchŏng, of the early sixteenth century. Im's adventures were similar, but his background was even lower than that of Hong Kiltong: Im came from the social outcast group of butchers, tanners, and other "unclean" people.

Another marginalized group, namely women—or, more often, girls—also appeared prominently in the popular tales circulating in the late Chosŏn. Like those of the righteous bandits, these stories of virtuous women also appealed to the Confucian ethos propagated by the elite. That these stories' protagonists were females from lower backgrounds showed that such values had penetrated the masses while also promoting these common people's humanity and goodness. The most famous such story is *The Tale of Ch'unhyang*. Ch'unhyang, the teenage daughter of a courtesan concubine, falls in love with and betroths the son of the local county magistrate. While her beloved returns to Seoul and becomes a successful young official, she endures a series of hardships stemming from the next magistrate's evil cravings for her in expectation that she, like her mother, would serve her "duties." Ch'unhyang, though, resists with her insistence that she remain faithful to her husband despite her social background, and in the end her lover returns as a secret government inspector and rescues her just before she is to be executed. The *Tale of Simch'ŏng* was another popular narrative of a virtuous woman who demonstrated the core Confucian values of filial piety, loyalty, and sacrifice. Simch'ŏng, having acted on her belief that she could cure her father's blindness by sacrificing her own life, is instead rescued from the underworld and delivered intact to the king, who falls in love with her and marries her. The story ends with a joyous reunion with her father, whose sight is restored. Like Ch'unhyang, the reward of reunion comes from Simch'ŏng's faithfulness to her Confucian duties. The larger message of cosmic justice arriving through good acts also drew from Buddhist under-currents as well as from the centrality of a common woman over-coming her tribulations despite the odds arrayed against her. Indeed, these latter narrative elements are the most compelling and likely contributed most to the popularity of these stories.

It appears, in fact, that both the tales of Ch'unhyang and Simch'ŏng began not in written form but rather as orally transmitted stories used as songs in shamanistic ceremonies, a genre that ultimately developed into what we now call *p'ansori* (see below). The elaboration and transmission of these tales through a more definitive, written form were made possible by the gradual spread of the vernacular as a means of communication among those unable to acquire the high culture of literary Chinese. Despite the great effort that went into the creation of the native alphabet back in the mid-fifteenth century, for the most part the social elites shunned the use of what they called this "vulgar script." Until the end of the nineteenth century, then, the alphabet's usage and development remained consigned to the lower social orders and, significantly, females. But these groups discovered what is today commonly touted as the great strength of this alphabet—namely, its efficient simplicity and versatility—and likewise, beginning in the seventeenth century, there appeared a surge in mostly informal works employing the vernacular. Not surprisingly, the popularization of the tales of common people accompanied the increasing use of the Korean alphabet among the lower social orders. That these tales also featured compelling plots and characters (including historical figures), especially for the benefit of illuminating social injustices, likely also contributed to their popularity.

OTHER CULTURAL FORMS

P'ansori, a distinctive "opera" genre that emerged in the eighteenth and nineteenth centuries, stands today as perhaps the best-known traditional Korean musical form. The singer or singers, accompanied by a drummer who keeps the beat and occasionally shouts responses and encouragement, recount a sprawling tale full of characterization, plot twists, and long monologues. The great challenge to the singers comes from the demand to voice several different characters as well as the narrator, and from the enormous stamina necessary to pull off a complete performance. The most popular works of the *p'ansori* repertoire, such as the "Song of Ch'unhyang" and "Song of Simch'ŏng," invariably date from the late Chosŏn era, and the successful transmission of these works through the ages owes much to the efforts of systematizers, in particular Sin Chaehyo of the early nineteenth century, who standardized the librettos and performance styles.

Mask dances (*t'alch'um*), a theatrical performance genre comprised of one to several characters dancing to accompanying instrumental music, also became standardized in the late Chosŏn into the form that we know today. As the name suggests, the performers wore masks of exaggerated expressions representing the status and emotion of the characters involved. Their "dances" combined choreographed displays and spontaneous movements that, when supplemented by spoken dialogue, furthered the story along its trajectory. The different elements of artistic expression that went into this Korean version of the *Gesamtkunstwerk*—theater, music, song, dance, colorful costumes—usually served the purpose of satire. The aristocratic and other characters with pretenses to authority, including even Buddhist monks, were usually depicted with ridicule, as if this comedic context presented the most effective means of expressing the grievances of lower-status people. Not coincidentally, like Sin Chaehyo, the great systematizer of *p'ansori*, the creative figures behind the promotion and development of mask dances came from the ranks of the hereditary local clerks in the late Chosŏn, the *hyangni*. Due to their administrative duties, these clerks were literate, organized, and able to measure the pulse of the local mood.

Examples of the final major art form of the late Chosŏn, genre painting, have come down as among the most cherished and representative expressions of traditional Korea. Unlike dramatic singing and satirical mask dances, which boasted a history of development before their respective standardized forms of the late Chosŏn, genre painting—the depiction of daily life—could not draw upon a definitive heritage before the eighteenth century. The extant Korean paintings preceding that period are mostly portraits, Buddhist works, landscapes, or drawings of plants and animals. In fact one has to turn all the way back in time to the Koguryŏ tomb paintings to find a similarly lively attention to people in everyday settings. But unlike these Koguryŏ wall paintings' preoccupation

Image 12 "Wrestling", by Kim Hongdo, eighteenth century. (Courtesy of the National Museum of Korea.)

with the social elite, the eighteenth-century genre paintings are concerned also with showing commoners and even low-born peoples. In style as well, due likely to the influence of Western painting techniques by way of China, one sees a turn in perspective and spacing that corresponded to the shift in subject matter to the commonplace and ordinary. So representative of "traditional" Korean life and culture have these paintings become that the two most prominent masters of genre painting are also the two best-known painters of Korean civilization—perhaps even the two best-known artists: Kim Hongdo, whose expertise extended to all other painting forms but is most beloved for his uncanny, sympathetic depictions of commoners and slaves (and the occasional aristocrat) going about their daily lives (Image 12); and Sin Yunbok, whose beautiful pictures of glamorous courtesans and aristocratic lovers evoke scenes in the *Tale of Ch'unhyang*.

POPULAR CULTURE AND SOCIAL CONSCIOUSNESS

One of the most remarkable aspects of these developments in late Chosŏn popular culture is that the subject matter of these works seems to have mirrored the lower social status of those responsible for their production, standardization, and dissemination. When we dig a little deeper, however, we find that actually the creative forces—whether court painters like Kim Hongdo and Sin Yunbok, clerks promoting the mask dances, or the *p'ansori* "composer-authors" like Sin Chaehyo—came not from common or low-born backgrounds, but rather from secondary status backgrounds: families of technical officials in Seoul, hereditary clerks in the countryside, or the descendants of concubines. While the secondary status groups played an integral role in maintaining the Chosŏn structures of state and social authority, they also suffered from the restrictions of the aristocratically driven hereditary status system (Chapter 10). They were caught, in other words, between a fervent desire to emulate the rituals, behaviors, and education of the aristocracy and thereby be considered social elites themselves, and the frustrations at the fruitlessness of most such efforts to attain true recognition for their talents. This explains, perhaps, why their artistic works rarely featured themselves, but rather focused on mostly downtrodden commoners and the low-born. Even in the genre paintings there are subtle hints of the social critiques that were more openly expressed in the tales, songs, and mask dances. Neither revolutionaries nor even effective agitators, the artists and intellectuals of secondary status background had to achieve a delicate balance between social recognition and social reality.

The former tendency of emulating the aristocracy can be seen in their emphasis on the Confucian values of filial piety, loyalty, reverence for political authority, and chastity (for female characters) in these works. Even Sin Chaehyo's *p'ansori* librettos, full of allusions to the Confucian canon, point to his absorption of the dominant value system. The capital-based poetry societies of the late eighteenth and nineteenth centuries also reflected this sentiment. While a separate literary movement was necessary for talented figures of non-aristocratic background who wanted to organize themselves, these authors did not produce vernacular verse on themes of social injustice, but rather poetry in literary Chinese on traditional themes. Meanwhile, the subject matter of their contributions to the vernacular poetry form, *sijo*, remained mostly the yearning for love, nature, and contemplation.

The reflective tendency of subtler protest against social discrimination, however, also spawned an undisguised effort among the secondary status groups to proclaim a higher place in the social order. And here the genre of choice was not poetry but rather the more mundane prose of biography. Works of literary biography had long taken their position as central elements of what can be considered this era's contributions to a "national literature"—in the true sense of the term given these works' use of the vernacular. They included the "court diaries" written by palace ladies as well as fictionalized or partially fictionalized biographical novels of historical figures. While the biographical compilations that the secondary status groups produced were mostly in literary Chinese, they were equally important because of their subject matter: a focus on people beyond the examples of heroic and court figures. The secondary status groups had begun these efforts with profiles of those from their own ranks. A history of hereditary clerks, for example, emerged in the late eighteenth century, featuring the lives of exemplary figures mixed among appeals for greater social recognition. Genealogies for secondary status groups also appeared, mimicking the form of traditional aristocratic genealogies.

The real breakthrough, however, in not only the social history but also the literary history of the late Chosŏn, came via the biographical compilations, such as *Observations from the Countryside*, of people from all non-aristocratic backgrounds. These works truly reflected an ideology of social rectification in the guise of popular culture. The profiles of "Interpreter Hong" or "Filial Lady Yi," for example—among close to 300 separate biographical portraits in *Observations*—provide examples of lives worth remembering as well as a clear sense of these people's adherence to common values. As the author of *Observations* notes in his preface, "Since long ago there have been wise and good people throughout the countryside who have gone unnoticed [because of social status]. How could the disappearance of their memories not be lamentable?" It was precisely such a sentiment that pervaded the growth of popular culture in the late Chosŏn.

13

Nineteenth-Century Unrest

CHRONOLOGY

THE DESTRUCTION OF THE AMERICAN MERCHANT SHIP, THE GENERAL SHERMAN, 1866

In the summer of 1866, residents of Pyongyang saw something very strange in the middle of the Taedong River: a black, iron-clad merchant steamship, with cannons, carrying mostly Chinese and Malay sailors but headed by a few pale-faced men. This American ship, called the "General Sherman" in honor of a union commander in the recent American civil war, had become stuck on a sandbar in the middle of the river. Impatient with the progress of negotiations regarding their demands for trade, the officers of the ship began firing on the shore and even abducted a Korean negotiating official. Soon, the order from the authorities came down to attack the vessel, and after a few days of fighting, Korean soldiers managed to set the ship afire. The crew members who swam to shore were all killed. The Pyongyang governor who directed the attack was none other than senior high official Pak Kyusu, grandson of the famed scholar-official of the Northern Learning School, Pak Chiwŏn. As it turned out, the *General Sherman* was not simply a wandering intruder, but rather the harbinger of an ominous phenomenon. It marked the onset of imperialism, a force that had already engulfed China and induced great internal disruption in Japan, and would soon push Korea onto the currents of a new world order. Within a month, in fact, Korea would be attacked again, this time from French forces.

The arrival of imperialism, and all that it implied for Korea's existence as a nation and state, dominates historical consideration of the latter half of the nineteenth century. It marked the beginning of Korea's unwitting entrance into the cutthroat system of competing nation states that would eventually strip the country of its autonomy. While imperialism ushered in the transition to the modern era, however, significant internally driven upheavals also proved essential to this process. Both sets of developments also stimulated, however, the rise of a concerted reform movement that questioned almost every aspect of Korean society and eventually led to the formal "opening" of the country through the Treaty of Kanghwa in 1876. Pak Kyusu, the Pyongyang governor at the time of the *General Sherman* incident, found himself in the middle of several seminal moments of this period. His role in guiding the government through the winds of change, like the events of the era as a whole, complicates any easy judgment on the nineteenth century, which has long been dominated in historical memory by perceptions of decay and decline.

THE NINETEENTH CENTURY ISSUE AND INTERNAL PROBLEMS

The nineteenth century, marked by both internal uprisings and external threats, continues to stand as a troubling historical fulcrum in Korea's transition to the modern era. In this regard, the period is taken simply as the prelude to "the end," that is, the loss of national sovereignty and other calamities of the early twentieth century. The shadow cast by the nineteenth century on Korea's modern experience is so long and dark that attempts have arisen recently to suggest that, given the flourishing of culture and statecraft in the eighteenth century (Chapter 11), the nineteenth century was more of an anomaly. Both of these perspectives situate the nineteenth century in longer, and presumably more significant, historical developments—that of the late Chosŏn era that preceded it, and of the modern era that succeeded it. While such a long-term historical approach is always edifying, it is equally important to take the nineteenth century on its own terms and show how it represented a distinctive period in Korean history.

Many factors contributed to the major events that racked the nineteenth century, but we must look first to politics. Here, an event took place—conveniently, for arranging historical eras, at least—at the very beginning: the death of King Chŏngjo in 1800. As discussed in Chapter 11, King Chŏngjo has come to embody in the historical annals all that was hopeful and healthy in the Chosŏn dynasty, and his sudden death while still in his forties represented the end of the comprehensive reform movement that he had been leading. He was followed on the throne, coincidentally, by a succession of four kings too young to exert authority on their own when they began their reigns. Not so coincidentally, throughout the nineteenth century the court came under the corrupting influence of royal family members, especially those of the queen. The network of corruption extended all the way to local administration, and this constituted a fundamental cause behind the eruptions of rebellious violence—the largest in the Chosŏn dynasty until that time—in northern Korea in 1811 and southern Korea in 1862.

The Hong Kyŏngnae Rebellion of 1811–12 is striking for its many similarities to the Myoch'ŏng Rebellion of 1135–6 (Chapter 5): a charismatic malcontent, convinced by divination of Pyongyang's rightful place as the center of Korean civilization and, seething at the discrimination against the northwestern region of the country, leads a devastating uprising to overthrow the reigning dynasty. On both occasions, the central government's forces eventually crushed the rebels after a long siege, but the negative reverberations in P'yŏngan province, and indeed throughout the country, would last for decades. The lingering bitterness following the Hong Kyŏngnae Rebellion, however, would prove especially consequential because, unlike the Myoch'ŏng Rebellion, the uprising was instigated by rampant corruption by local government authorities. Indeed, the venality came at a particularly acute time—amidst near-famine conditions. And this largely explains how, under the banner of regional solidarity, the rebel leaders could mobilize so many people from different socioeconomic and status backgrounds to join the cause.

While the court undertook a thorough investigation of the rebellion, it could do little to overturn the most entrenched cause, which was not the famine nor even regional discrimination, but rather local corruption. For misconduct by local officials was rooted in the chain of graft emanating from the central court itself, chronically headed by a weak king and beset by strife. Hence, smaller-scale uprisings continued, and it was almost inevitable that another major peasants' revolt would erupt. Half a century later it did, striking this time the southern provinces. In early 1862 residents around the southern coastal city of Chinju, fed up with the extortionate local military commander, rose up to kill local officials and take command of government offices around the area. The central government hurriedly dispatched Pak Kyusu to investigate the uprising and mollify the local populace. This did little to stop the spread of the revolts throughout the southern provinces—and indeed all the way to some counties in the north as well. Eventually Pak came to recommend several systemic reforms in the taxation system as a way to address the grievances of the populace. His recommendations, however, were swallowed up by the festering dysfunction of the central government.

Indeed, the most consequential result of the 1862 rebellions might have been to alter the growth of a nascent religious movement. In the tense atmosphere of southern Korea following the uprisings, the authorities arrested a wandering preacher, Ch'oe Cheu, for spreading heterodoxy and subversion. He was quickly tried and executed in 1864, and hence began Ch'oe's status as that of a martyr. By then, his teachings, which he labeled "Tonghak," or "Eastern Learning," boasted several thousand followers organized into geographical units in over a dozen localities. Ch'oe's story, and that of his movement in the early years, diverged little from the familiar path followed by the founders of other religions: an early life of doubt and restlessness leading to a path of self-discovery, followed by a moment of extraordinary revelation of universal truths so powerful that they compelled the receiver of this vision to initiate a religious and social movement. The Tonghak theology, however, was particular to the conditions out of which Ch'oe arose. It blended elements of native Korean spirituality, Confucian ethics and cosmology, Catholic teachings of a single divinity, and a timely message of universal brotherhood and equality. What was most striking were the distinctively Korean prayers and incantations, methods of divination, and healing practices. Even the name of "Tonghak" referred to Korea—traditionally, the "eastern country"—and contrasted consciously with "Western Learning," or Catholicism. The Tonghak theology's incorporation of a strong native, even nationalist, identity compels a comparison to other nation-centered religious movements that arose in the nineteenth century: the Taiping in China and the Mormon Church in the US, both of which were founded by extraordinary men who blended nativist elements with established religious practices. Not surprisingly, Ch'oe's execution in 1864 only served to harden the resolve of his followers, who flourished underground for the next three decades before erupting through an explicitly nationalistic revolt in 1894 (Chapter 14).

To the governing authorities, Ch'oe—despite his movement's profession of a faith that deliberately contrasted with Catholicism—looked very much like someone trying to spread a subversive tenet like Catholicism. Like Tonghak, Catholicism, with its call for an ontological equality under a personal deity, was considered gravely threatening to the carefully crafted social order. While King Chŏngjo had found this religion a curious but potentially disruptive superstition that demanded surveillance, after his death in 1800, the overwhelmingly hostile sentiment from the central elites was unleashed on the small but growing Catholic community in the country. The first state-led persecution of Catholics in 1801 killed several thousand converts, and when this failed to exterminate the movement, further roundups and mass executions took place periodically over the next several decades. The final anti-Catholic campaign took place in 1866, and by then, thousands of Korean Catholics had been martyred. Even today parts of the countryside are dotted by memorials to individual followers who were captured in a particular spot and executed for their faith. To Korean Catholics, this experience of mass persecution represented the searing trial that ultimately strengthened their faith and church. To the historian, the Catholic persecutions represented yet another sign of domestic turmoil in the nineteenth century.

THE ARRIVAL OF IMPERIALISM

The persecution of 1866 was significant also because it helped trigger the arrival of imperialism to Korea, a force that had already struck its East Asian neighbors. Qing dynasty China had suffered the woes of actual military confrontation against these "barbarians from the oceans" (the British) beginning in the 1830s, and this set the tone for China's tragic difficulties with both internal and external challenges through the rest of the century. While not lacking in institutional reforms, the Chinese response to the impending crisis, for complicated reasons, did not amount to a fundamental reorientation of the country's sociopolitical system. Japan, on the other hand, managed to escape foreign depredation. This was due mostly to its relatively mild initial confrontation with the West, in the form of the US, which nonetheless sparked fiery domestic struggles that led to the overthrow of the Tokugawa shogunate and to an intensive drive for institutional reform. By the 1870s Japanese leaders sensed that influence over (and even conquest of!) Korea would constitute the logical extension of this self-strengthening effort, and hence they applied the same kind of gunboat diplomacy practiced by the West to "open" Korea to unequal terms of trade and diplomacy. The resulting Treaty of Kanghwa in 1876, for good reason, is commonly seen as the beginning of Korea's modern era.

The opening shots of imperialism, however, were fired a decade earlier along the banks of the Taedong River in Pyongyang. The American officers and owner of the *General Sherman* had set sail from China in the summer of 1866. They had loaded the ship with trade goods and were determined to force open trade relations with the recalcitrant "hermit kingdom." When the ship first stopped near the mouth of the river, the local magistrate sent word that the Korean government forbade such relations with foreigners and demanded that the visitors leave. The Americans ignored this request by sailing further up the river and, buoyed by some heavy rains, made it past the shallows to Pyongyang itself. After the rains subsided, however, the ship found itself stuck on a sandbar. Negotiations between Pak Kyusu, the city's governor, and the *General Sherman's* officers reached an impasse, and when the Americans abducted a government representative and held him hostage, hostilities broke out. After a few days of cannon, rocket, and archery fire going back and forth, the end of the standoff came when the ship was set ablaze, forcing the crew members to swim to shore, where they were beaten to death.

Within a month, however, it became clear that these incursions were not going away, as a French armada raided villages and fortresses on Kanghwa Island on the west coast, establishing a temporary base. Soon, it made its way up the Han River leading to Seoul, proclaiming itself a punitive expedition and demanding reparations for the nine French priests who had been killed in the Catholic persecution earlier in the year. The Korean defenses

Image 13 "The Martyrdom of Reverend Thomas," depicting the attack on the General Sherman in 1866. Painting by Kim Haksu. (Courtesy of the Council for the 100th Anniversary of the Korean Church.)

successfully beat back the ships after several days of fighting, but not without heavy casualties and the loss of something equally valuable: hundreds of books and cultural artifacts taken by the French forces from Kanghwa Island. The fear of the Korean leaders, especially the xenophobic Prince Regent, the *Taewŏn'gun* (father of the boy king), that had led to the mass persecution in the first place had been their belief that Catholicism was simply an instrument of Western imperialism. The French invasion seemed to validate these fears.

Kanghwa Island and the lower reaches of the Han River again served as center stage for imperialism five years later in 1871, this time for a punitive expedition carried out by American marines in response to the destruction of the *General Sherman*. As the French had done, the American invasion force left behind a path of destruction on the island and along the banks of the river, suffering only a handful of casualties while killing hundreds of Korean soldiers. But once again, the invaders ultimately beat a retreat without accomplishing their aims of battering the capital. And once again, this episode intensified the anti-foreign sentiment among Confucian scholars, high government officials, and a court still dominated by the Prince Regent's policies of anti-foreign resistance. His response was to erect stone tablets in front of government offices throughout the country inscribed with a stern warning: "Western barbarians are invading. Failure to fight amounts to appeasement. Appeasement is treason."

A countering sentiment, however, was also forming among some influential scholar officials, led by none other than Pak Kyusu himself. Soon after the 1871 episode, Pak went on a diplomatic mission to Qing dynasty China. He returned with a resolve to convince the Korean court to break away from its policy of disengagement. Despite his central role in repulsing the *General Sherman*, Pak was actually intrigued by the possibilities of learning from the outside world. He belonged to a small circle of such advocates for greater opening, which included also two gentlemen who, unlike the aristocratic Pak, came from the secondary status group of technical officials: O Kyŏngsŏk and Yu Honggi. O, an interpreter, had brought back books and stories

The "Uphold Orthodoxy and Reject Heterodoxy" movement

The teleological tug of the nineteenth century tends to direct the observer's gaze toward the forces calling for "opening" among the Korean reactions to imperialism, but the more substantial and influential responses came from the opposing view that adamantly condemned the West. Advocates of this perspective formed a concerted movement beginning in the 1860s called *wijŏng ch'ŏksa*, or "uphold orthodoxy and reject heterodoxy." This term starkly delineated the moral differences, and reiterated the urgency of acting on those differences, between the Confucian and Western civilizations. The practice of labeling opposing ideas as heterodoxy had a long history in the wrangling over Confucian propriety in the Chosŏn dynasty, but this time, as with the Manchus in the seventeenth century, the notion of heterodoxy carried an ethnicized contempt. In contrast to the Manchus who conquered Korea and China but sought to maintain Confucian civilization, however, the "barbarians from the oceans" challenged Confucianism's supremacy. Though later eclipsed by the forces of imperialism and internal reform, this fervent rejection of any contact with the West exerted a tremendous influence on the subsequent trajectory of conservative responses to the outside world and of nationalism itself. Indeed this nineteenth-century movement's successors included not only the Righteous Armies that fought the Japanese takeover in the opening years of the next century, but ultimately also the isolationist "self-reliance" ideology of *Juche* that came to define North Korea.

Though most readily associated in historical lore with the Prince Regent, or *Taewŏn'gun*, who carried out the Catholic persecution and feverishly beat back the American and French incursions in 1866, the intellectual leader of the "reject heterodoxy" movement was Yi Hangno. Yi was actually one of the most accomplished Confucian philosophers of his time, but it was through his explication of the rationale for rejecting all intercourse with the West that his influence became paramount. Based on the premise of Confucian civilization's unalterability, Yi found the news of China's own fall at the hands of the British deeply disturbing, and he claimed that these developments portended grave dangers for Korea as well. Even the slightest accommodation to these corrupting external overtures, he noted, would place the Chosŏn state, populace, and civilization on a slippery slope toward disaster. Before Yi died in 1868, he served as mentor to the next generation of "uphold orthodoxy and reject heterodoxy" advocates, including those, such as Ch'oe Ikhyŏn, who led the Righteous Army campaigns half a century later. For Yi, the events of 1866 only reinforced his original warnings, and although he eventually fell out of favor with the court, his advice of absolute resistance resonated with the Prince Regent, who made this stance the state policy.

The official North Korean historical view claims that Kim Il Sung's own great grandfather led the people's charge against the *General Sherman* that year. In an odd way, this might as well have been true, for the "self-reliance" isolationism of North Korea brought to full circle the historical trajectory that began with these events. The makeup of the dangerous outside changed from Westerners to Westerners pushing capitalism, but the claims that contact with the external world endangered the survival of Korean civilization itself remained in force.

from his trips to China that aroused the interest of both Pak and Yu. Together, these three men stood as the founders of the Korean enlightenment movement, tutoring the first group of young activists who would gain prominence in the 1880s and 1890s, and helping to drive a shift in government policy. Such a change in the court's diplomatic stance finally materialized in 1875, when King Kojong, now with full royal authority, was persuaded to open formal trade relations with Japan instead of continuing to resist these forceful overtures. As officials, both Pak and O played key roles in the negotiations that led to the Treaty of Kanghwa the next year.

What followed quickly was a series of study missions sent by the Korean government to Meiji Japan and Qing China to imbibe the basics of modern statecraft and technology. Participants in these trips, from high officials to young students, returned and helped implement major changes in government organization and direction in the early 1880s. The full-fledged "enlightenment" movement behind these developments challenges, in turn, the conventional view of the nineteenth century as one of decay and decline, a historical anomaly that led directly to the tragedies of the early twentieth century. Rather, the enlightenment movement, which drew partly upon the late Chosŏn reform movements—and, indeed, even on the rise of the *Tonghak* religion—showed that the nineteenth century represented the logical outgrowth of the late Chosŏn era. The developments in the nineteenth century also paved the way for the emergence of a fiercely indigenous voice in the opening stages of modern transition.

14

....

1894, A Fateful Year

CHRONOLOGY

THE OCCUPATION OF THE ROYAL PALACE BY JAPANESE SOLDIERS, JULY 1894

In July of 1894, Otori Keisuke, Japanese minister in Korea, presented to the Korean government a set of demands for domestic reforms that would protect Japan's security interests. Otori could act with such impudence because his soldiers were encamped in and around Seoul. They had been sent to the peninsula in the wake of China's own entrance into the country, which had come, officially at the behest of the Korean court, to help pacify the Tonghak rebellion. This uprising had exploded in the southwest earlier in the spring and threatened to bring down the five-century-old Chosŏn dynasty itself. When the Korean government refused to respond directly to Otori's demands, Japanese troops stormed the royal palace and sent most of the government leaders scurrying. The *Taewŏn'gun*, father of the Korean king and former Prince Regent, now re-established his power with the support of the Japanese and formed a Deliberative Assembly, with sweeping governmental powers, to take charge of reform efforts. The Deliberative Assembly consisted of conservative opponents of the Korean government (like the *Taewŏn'gun*), as well as moderates and progressives who had long been chafing at the bit to take control over a court dominated by the royal consort family, the Min.

This hodgepodge of elements in the Deliberative Assembly, however, soon developed into one of the most significant forces in Korean history. Thus what began as an uprising against local corruption soon engulfed the country in a region-wide confrontation and helped to usher in a new age in Korea, a process driven by the elite admirers of foreign ways as much as by the peasant followers of the native Tonghak religion. Over the long term, therefore, one could argue indeed that the Tonghak rebellion led to the downfall of the Chosŏn dynasty, or at least of Korea's long-established sociopolitical system.

THE TONGHAK SPARK

In the summer of 1894, the ill will from the Tonghak uprising was still festering in the countryside, for the end of the rebellion's fiercest battles earlier in the spring had not brought an end to the underlying troubles that had touched off the uprising in the first place. Venality by local officials had been a constant problem in the nineteenth century, but the exploitation practiced by the magistrate of Kobu county in Chŏlla province, in the form of debilitating local taxes, appears to have come at a particularly sensitive moment. The local followers of the Tonghak religion had been unhappy with deteriorating economic conditions, local corruption, and foreign, especially Japanese, commercial influence. They were also upset at the difficulties of rehabilitating the reputation of their martyred founder, Ch'oe Cheu (Chapter 13). When their grievances about excessive local taxes went unheard, these Tonghak villagers, led by their local religious leader Chŏn Pongjun, swiftly ransacked the Kobu county office and redistributed the ill-gotten grain taxes to the people. The rebellion thereafter spread like wildfire through the southwest, and within a few weeks, many county governments in this region had been seized. The battles against government troops, now supplemented by Chinese reinforcements, abated in the early summer of 1894 through a settlement, only to revive in the fall in protest against the Japanese occupation of Seoul. The bloody confrontations that ensued between the Tonghak followers and the joint Japanese–Korean force ended the rebellion in the winter, but not before costing the lives of tens of thousands of peasants.

Interpretations of the Tonghak rebellion and its historical significance have tended to focus either on the systemic ills of the late Chosŏn state, or on the suffering of the common people besieged by a stifling social hierarchy, government exploitation, and poor economic conditions. The former perspective tends to view the Tonghak rebellion as the culmination of a gradual decay in the central government over the course of the nineteenth century. By contrast, the latter historical perspective, which accentuates the plight of the people, establishes the Tonghak rebellion as the basis and inspiration for the modern struggles against domestic oppression and foreign domination. The manifestos, declarations, and demands that the Tonghak leaders issued in 1894 do indeed appear somewhat forward-looking: calls for an end to hereditary social discrimination, for an expulsion of seedy foreign influences, and even for the redistribution of property seem, upon first glance, not merely progressive but revolutionary. While both historical viewpoints concerning the Tonghak movement are somewhat problematic when examining the sources, especially regarding the claims for economic redistribution (likely an embellishment added later), on the whole there are also strong merits to both perspectives. The implications for Korean history, furthermore, were not limited to internal developments. The Tonghak rebellion's most widespread impact, in fact, might have come from serving as a trigger to events that overturned the millennia-long regional order in East Asia.

A SHRIMP CAUGHT IN A WHALE FIGHT

The Japanese incursion into Korea following the Treaty of Kanghwa in 1876 would not go unmet by the Chinese, who understandably were not keen on allowing any challenge to their special supremacy in Korea. (This was, after all, a relationship that had endured, for the most part, since a unified state came into existence on the peninsula in the seventh century.) Thus in the 1880s Korea became entangled in the growing feud between China and Japan over dominance in northeast Asia, a situation that Koreans referred to proverbially as "the breaking of a shrimp's back when caught between fighting whales." This rivalry took many forms—in the availability of intellectual and institutional models, in diplomatic influence, and in competition among merchants—and twice grew into military skirmishes in Seoul. In 1882, a group of common Korean soldiers, unhappy with their treatment compared to that of the new crack unit trained by Japanese advisors, rose up in revolt against the Korean government's growing ties to foreign influence. Taking the *Taewŏn'gun* as their inspiration and leader, the soldiers instigated attacks on Japanese compounds and threatened members of the royal family. Although the initial target was the Japanese presence, the Chinese military was dispatched to put down this rebellion, which it quickly did. With the staunchest anti-foreign activist, the *Taewŏn'gun*, seized by the Chinese and taken to China, the pro-reform elements in the Korean elite circles, favorably disposed to following the Japanese model, were emboldened. In 1884 a particularly brazen group of young radicals, impatient with the slow pace of change despite the signing of treaties with Western powers (beginning with the US in 1882), killed conservative high ministers and took over key government buildings. Despite the tacit support of the Japanese officials, as in 1882, this putsch, known as the Kapsin Coup ("Coup of 1884"), met its end at the hands of the Chinese military. The coup plotters able to escape the backlash fled all the way to Japan.

Gaining the firm upper hand through this event, the Chinese established preeminent influence over the Korean government for the next decade through a "residency" headed by the powerful Chinese official Yuan Shikai. While scholars have termed this a "dark period," characterized by stifling Chinese intervention and commercial exploitation, a languid pace of Korean institutional reforms, and the house arrest of enlightenment activists such as Yu Kilchun, the Chinese impact was not so clear-cut. Qing China in fact played a central role in the establishment of the first Korean telegraph lines, the Korean Customs Service, and even formal diplomatic relations with Western governments. Furthermore, Korea's government restructuring efforts continued, the enlightenment movement grew further through publication and educational activities, and moderate reformers in government remained in power, supported by a sympathetic monarch often hemmed in by his queen's ties to the Chinese. These tendencies might have produced an interesting result had the Tonghak uprising not triggered a clause in a treaty, signed in 1885 by the Chinese and Japanese, acknowledging each other's interests in Korea.

This treaty had called for the notification of the other side if ever there was a cause for dispatching troops to Korea. And this is exactly what happened in June of 1894, when the Korean government turned to China, almost reflexively, to help put down the Tonghak rebellion. The influx of Chinese troops was met by a quick Japanese response likewise, and before long this powder keg was lit. Under the pretext of protecting the Japanese consulate and other possessions, Japanese soldiers filled the Seoul streets. They provided support for the diplomatic pressure exerted by envoy Otori, who demanded fundamental government reforms at self-strengthening that would ensure a Korean buffer against Chinese threats to Japan. When these troops chased away the conservative pro-Chinese government leaders, the Japanese orchestrated the creation of the Deliberative Assembly (*Kun'guk kimuch'ŏ*), which would henceforth act as the highest governing body.

While the Deliberative Assembly went about its work, the Japanese forces prosecuted their confrontation with China, declaring war on August 1 and swiftly gaining the upper hand. In a series of clashes, from Pyongyang, where the largest land battle of the war left much of the city in ruins, to the Manchurian areas of Dalian and the Shandong peninsula, to naval exchanges in the Yellow Sea, the Japanese won decisively. Just as they had attempted, but failed, to do in the 1590s, the Japanese sought supremacy in East Asia by provoking a direct confrontation with China in Korea, and this time the result was a shift in the East Asian regional balance of power that would endure for a century.

THE SPIRIT OF KABO

This momentous reversal of the East Asian order would present a psychological and cultural shock to the Koreans, akin to the effect of the fall of the Ming dynasty two centuries earlier (Chapter 10). But for many Koreans, China's downfall represented good riddance, a crucial external ingredient for furthering the internal processes of enlightenment, reform, and self-strengthening. The Deliberative Assembly in fact could not have been clearer in its approval of this newfound independence from the centuries-long subordination to the Chinese: the first article of its reform program declared that Korea's official dating system would no longer be based on the Chinese imperial calendar but rather on the founding, in 1392, of the Chosŏn dynasty—1894, for example, was now "Year 503 After Foundation." The second article called for a new kind of diplomatic relationship between Korea and China. But the articles that followed definitively set the stage for the staggering changes in state and society that the Deliberative Assembly would promulgate. In the rest of the first ten articles, in fact, the Deliberative Assembly declared an end to hereditary social status and slavery, a cessation of contract marriages of adolescents along with a lifting of the prohibition on widow remarriage, and the opening of the path to government service by commoners. By the time the Deliberative Assembly gave way to a cabinet-based government at the end of 1894, it had passed over 200 such bills, systematically overhauling patterns of Korean government, society, and economy that had been in place for centuries. With the exception of those concerning governing structure, most of these resolutions were not immediately implemented into practice, but they provided a blueprint and impetus for reform that would continue for decades.

The end of slavery in Korea

"Laws allowing public and private public slavery are completely abolished, and the sale of human beings is forbidden." One is tempted to take this resolution of July 1894, the ninth passed by the Deliberative Assembly, as the Korean equivalent to the American Emancipation Proclamation of three decades earlier. Indeed this comparison inspires thinking about the striking parallels as well as differences between the Korean and American forms of slavery. Korea's system was more ancient and endured in a population with no physical differences, while that of the US was based on, and had a lot to do with furthering, the notion of race. But the two slave systems shared fundamental features: hereditary slave status, the treatment of slaves as chattel property, and the dependence of the social structure and economy on their exploitation. In both cases as well, the perpetuation of slavery and discrimination relied upon the insistence of the "one drop of blood" rule in the face of widespread "miscegenation" through sexual exploitation. The similarities extended, in fact, to the gradual and pained process of true emancipation following legal eradication.

The fading of slavery in Korea had actually begun long before the Kabo Reforms, both legally and customarily. After reaching a peak, according to estimates from household registration records, of approximately 30 percent of the population in the late seventeenth century, economic trends toward the use of more wage labor made slavery gradually less efficient. And growing calls from scholar-officials condemning the practice as a violation of Confucian morality contributed to the government's decision to eliminate the holding of "public," or government, slaves (*kong nobi*) in the early nineteenth century. By the time of the Kabo Reform declaration that extended this ban to the private slaves, slavery had already been significantly diminished. The official emancipation of 1894, then, was largely a symbolic gesture; indeed, some forms of servitude did not end,

||||➡

and even the first major revision of the household registration system in 1896 still made room for bound servants. It was not until 1909 that the registration form eliminated any possibility of accounting for them. Even these steps, however, did not totally destroy the reality of bondage, especially in the countryside, where servile laborers (*mŏsŭm*) continued to tend to their masters until the Korean War (1950–53) period.

These legal steps of the late nineteenth and early twentieth centuries, however, were still significant, for once slavery, bound servitude, and the legal distinction of "mean" or "low-born" people were eliminated from Korean society, their descendants truly enjoyed social liberation. This perhaps stems from the fact that Korean hereditary slavery, though meticulously maintained through record-keeping and other factors, had not been based on physical differences like "race." In other words, in the modern era, with increasing urbanization and mobility, no one could really know who was a slave descendant. The contrast with America could not be starker. The flip side to this, however, is the contemporary Korean tendency, bordering on national amnesia, regarding this troubling component of the past: the casual claim that Korea's form of slavery was somehow less inhumane finds easy support in the quirky belief among almost all (South) Koreans that they are descendants of the Chosŏn aristocracy.

The Deliberative Assembly, in short, kick-started the Kabo ("1894") Reforms of 1894–6, the significance of which would reverberate over the course of Korea's modern transformation.

The makeup of the Deliberative Assembly and of the Kabo Reform governments was equally revolutionary. Of the twenty or so members of the Deliberative Assembly, half came from the non-aristocratic secondary status groups. And while the Kabo government cabinets were formally led by men with traditional aristocratic ancestry, the ranks immediately below, from vice minister to administrators and their assistants, were filled with those from non-aristocratic backgrounds. This bespoke the prominence of people from secondary status groups, especially northerners and the *chungin* technical specialists, in the Korean enlightenment movement from the 1860s onward. Their ascendance to the higher ranks of the new officialdom, in breaking through the centuries-old barriers of hereditary status, had much to do with the particularities of their longstanding roles, but also with their readiness to discard traditional ideas and ways. This tendency, shared by the enlightenment activists as a whole—both aristocratic and not—also drew them to Japan as a model of reform and self-strengthening. Such ties were reinforced in the fall of 1895 by the assassination, at the hands of Japanese soldiers and Korean accomplices, of Queen Min, who from the beginning had been a thorn on the side of Japanese interests.

The uproar over this craven act eventually engulfed the political scene and, by the opening weeks of 1896, anti-Japanese elements close to the monarch spirited away the Korean king to the safe haven of the Russian consulate, beyond the reach of the Japanese soldiers and Korean government officials. This provided the impetus for the widespread distaste for the Kabo government to erupt into a mob that helped to kill several top officials while chasing the rest to Japan. Thus ended the Kabo Reforms, the same way as they had begun back in the summer of 1894, with Korean progressives under the protection of the Japanese.

The forces unleashed by the events of 1894, however, would pave multiple paths of historical development determining the country's modern fate: China would weaken further and not regain its dominant standing in northeast Asia for another century; the Tonghak uprising would inspire countless other eruptions of armed anti-foreign resistance movements well into the period of Japanese colonialism (1910–45); and the Kabo Reforms would stand as a microcosm of Korea's uneasy transitions at the turn of the twentieth century—at once embracing the models of the outside world, but ultimately becoming swamped by forces beyond Koreans' control.

15

· · · · · · · ·

The Great Korean Empire

CHRONOLOGY

THE OPENING OF THE SEOUL–INCH'ŎN RAIL LINE, 1899

"The noise from the rolling fire-wheeled chariot was like that of thunder, as the earth and heavens shook and the smoke from the chimney of the engine erupted into the air," wrote a newspaper reporter who rode the inaugural rail trip in Korea in September of 1899. "As I sat in the car and looked out the window, the whole world seemed to be racing past us, and even flying birds could not catch up." Such awestruck accounts accompanied the introduction of railroads throughout the world in the nineteenth century, as the enormous bellowing machines heralded the onset of a new era. In Korea, the opening of the first rail line between Seoul and Inch'ŏn, a distance of approximately twenty miles, took on a similarly epochal significance. This event furthermore came to reflect the mixture of confidence, potentiality, and wariness that came to mark the "Great Korean Empire," the brief period, from 1897 to 1910, when the Chosŏn kingdom became an "empire" in line with the foreign powers that surrounded the country. As with the railroad, the Great Korean Empire period witnessed the birth of many fundamental features of the modern era, not only in communications and transportation infrastructure, but in the wider realms of technology and commerce, and as well as in culture and institutions.

However profound its altering of life and perception, the railroad in Korea also cannot escape the discomfiting connections to the history of national misfortune, for these early rail lines eventually served the purposes of the Japanese takeover of Korea. The initiation into the modern era, like the railroad, constituted a double-edged sword, as the promises of "enlightenment" and progress were tempered by threatening forces beyond the Korean people's control. It is this duality that renders judgment on the Great Korean Empire contentious. Once largely derided for its failures, this period is now mined for signs of an autonomous Korean modernity.

KOREA AND THE NEW EMPIRES

At the turn of the twentieth century, Korea was immersed in the age of high imperialism. The social Darwinian ethos of the "strong eating the weak" played itself out in the global arena, and northeast Asia became one of the fiercest zones of competition. Once again, Korea, at the center and crossroads of this region, unwittingly stood as a target for territorial gain or commercial exploitation. The imperialist rivalry penetrated and, in turn, was appropriated by competing political groups at court. During the closing years of the nineteenth century a new imperial power, Russia, eyed the peninsula as a key component in its geopolitical strategy, and likewise the pro-Russian sentiment among higher officials, who looked upon Russia as a protector, gained the upper hand. But the Russian empire's ambitions of establishing a strong presence in northeast Asia clashed with those of another rising power with support from Korean high officials: Japan. The Japanese empire had defeated Qing dynasty China in the 1894–95 war on Korean soil and gained Taiwan and parts of Manchuria as its war booty. At the turn of the twentieth century, however, it found itself chafing against the constraints on its regional ambitions imposed by the European powers, especially Russia. And finally, China, too, lurched toward refashioning itself as a modern imperial power even while trying to fend off the Western forces.

Korea, traditionally China's most reliable tributary state, now sought to escape this subordinate relationship altogether. "Independence" from China had been a central motive behind the Kabo Reforms of 1894–96 (Chapter 14). And even after the fall of the Kabo government in early 1896, the Korean monarch and government advisors pursued this diplomatic path in order to establish autonomy not only from China but from all the ravenous imperial powers that surrounded the country. After months of entreaties, from both within and beyond the court, to take a bold step in this direction, in 1897 the Chosŏn monarchy officially joined the ranks of empires. On the surface, this seemed delusional, for Korea, with no command over different ethnic or civilizational groups, did not look anything like an empire. But in traditional East Asian statecraft, the distinction between empire and kingdom was one of diplomatic recognition and self-declaration. When the Chinese "Son of Heaven" no longer appeared as the pinnacle Under Heaven, Korean officials felt compelled to take such a step, believing this would bestow equal standing in the global order. Hence the birth of the "Great Korean Empire," or "Taehan cheguk"—shortened to "Han'guk" then as now (at least in South Korea, or *Taehan min'guk*)—and, with it, the coronation of the Korean monarch in 1897 as emperor. One of the best known images from this period shows Emperor Kojong, appropriating the circulating symbols of imperial splendor and might, posing resplendently while dressed in a faux Kaiser uniform. Little wonder, then, that henceforth his reign would be called officially that of the "Glorious Military" (*Kwangmu*).

The construction of the Korean monarchy's new status and legitimacy went far beyond the emperor himself, however. It encompassed a range of changes, both symbolic and organizational. The ceremonial declaration of the "Great Korean Empire" borrowed from a mixture of old and recent traditions, surrounding the monarch in ancient customs and symbols while emphasizing that his ascent represented "the foundation of independence" in the new era. The standardization of other symbols accepted globally as emblems of state sovereignty soon followed, including a flag and national anthem, and even national holidays. The strengthening of the monarchical state progressed on the level of institutional changes as well. The formal description and proclamation of the "Imperial System," which appeared two years later in 1899, employed concepts and terminology establishing legitimacy in the vocabulary of late nineteenth-century international law. But most of the content in this proclamation reinforced the ties to the Chosŏn dynasty and declared monarchical absolutism, with each article explicitly covering a different realm of governance over which the emperor had total control.

Even the economic activities directed by the royal house contributed to this emperor-centered state legitimacy, for they bathed the monarchy in the aura of modern advances. The Office of Crown Properties and a host of other organs subordinated under the Royal Household Ministry took the lead in sponsoring major economic projects in electricity, streetcars, waterworks, telegraph and telephone, printing, and minting. Furthermore the monarchy rescinded the concessions already granted to foreign railroad and mining operations and took control over the further development of these industries. This pattern of connecting the imperial state's legitimacy to economic development would serve as the basis upon which the intensified developmentalist efforts of Korean states would emerge later in the modern era. The Korean government that coexisted uneasily with the Royal Household Ministry did its part, too, in strengthening the state, particularly by revamping the household registration system and undertaking a nationwide land survey. Both efforts sought to increase the central government's capacities for mobilization and extraction, and to a certain extent they achieved these goals. But ultimately they paled in comparison to the accomplishments of the Royal Household Ministry in solidifying legitimacy through the promotion of material advances.

TRADE AND INDUSTRY

The Royal Household Ministry was, in fact, responsible for a substantial portion of the many developments in commerce, industry, and infrastructure during the Korean Empire, which laid the foundation for the material transformation of modern Korea. In some areas, such as electricity generation, Korea benefited from a "late developer" status, gaining immediate access to recent technological breakthroughs through borrowing. The first and most advanced electrical generation system in East Asia had been installed in the royal palace in Seoul in the mid-1880s and built by the Edison Electrical Company. Within a decade, Korea's capital city could boast of hundreds of electric streetlights. By May of 1899, four months before the opening of the Seoul–Inch'ŏn railway, the Seoul Electrical Company unveiled, to great fanfare, the first electric streetcar line, connecting the city's East Gate to a neighborhood on the outskirts of the city. The Seoul streetcars, appearing frequently in photographs that implied a range of accompanying social and economic changes, would remain the most visible symbol of rapidly changing Seoul in this era.

As an emblem of modern technology and material change, however, the railroad came to dominate the popular and historical consciousness in Korea during the opening decades of the twentieth century—serving, as it did around the world, as a metaphor for progress and transformation. The fanfare that greeted the opening of the Seoul–Inch'ŏn line on September 18, 1899, reflected the momentousness of the event, as dignitaries from the political, diplomatic, and business worlds gathered in a station on the south bank of the Han River, just outside Seoul, for the inaugural ride. News reports and official pronouncements heralded this event as a momentous step toward a new era. One newspaper account noted with awe that, "On the inside, the rail cars were divided into three classes—high, medium, and low—while the outside of the cars was decorated in such a [lavish] way as to be indescribable." The train departed with the first group of passengers at 9am, and "within a short time" found its way to Inch'ŏn, where a magisterial welcoming ceremony awaited them at the station. At the festivities, according to another newspaper report, the head of the Japanese company that operated the rail line concluded his congratulatory address with three cheers of "Long Live the Korean Emperor" and "Long Live the Japanese Emperor." He was followed by Korea's Foreign Minister, who also ended his remarks by leading three shouts of "Long Live the Korean Emperor." The reporter noted that the throng of people at the Inch'ŏn station looked "like a cloud," and pondered, along with a bystander, that this might have signaled Koreans' overdue achievement of "enlightenment." They also noted regrettably, however, that this wondrous technology had been built by foreigners.

An American company had won the concession from the Korean government to construct the Seoul–Inch'ŏn rail line, which broke ground in 1896, but a few months before completion had sold these rights to a partially government-owned Japanese company. In hindsight it was clear that the Japanese had eyed this short stretch as the prelude to the larger prize of building two "trunk lines" that would extend from the capital to the port city of Pusan in the southeast and to Ŭiju in the northwest. These two lines, with the former completed in time to aid the Japanese effort against Russia in the 1904–5 war, would greatly aid Japan's expansionist aims. But the Korean imperial government had sold many concessions to representatives of various countries for transportation and communication networks, mines, and industries. These concessions all had in common favorable terms for the foreign enterprise and a potential, often met, to retrieve great returns on the investment. From the Korean government's (or monarchy's) vantage point, selling these rights did not constitute a giveaway, but rather an opportunity to import commercial and industrial technologies while expanding the coffers of the state. The Korean rulers could hardly have envisioned that some of these ventures, especially the railroad, would also serve literally as a vehicle for imperialist aggression.

Furthermore, as Korean governments later in the twentieth century discovered, it was difficult to separate the general well-being of the country from the influx of foreign capital, technologies, and industries. The economic gains in the Korean Empire period would not have materialized without foreign commercial intercourse.

The rise of Korean port cities

An unlikely symbol of the ambiguous position of the Great Korean Empire period in modern Korean history is the city, or more precisely, the rapid growth of urban centers from the late nineteenth to early twentieth centuries. As with so much else associated with the modern era in Korea, the emergence of modern cities is entangled with the unsettling impact of external forces, in particular the transformation of the country into first a target of imperialism, then a Japanese colony. Imperialist and colonialist interests, especially regarding trade and transportation, launched the rise of many of the familiar cities today. These places include Sinŭiju, Kaesŏng, and Hŭngnam in the North, and in the South, Kunsan, Mokp'o, and especially Taejŏn, now South Korea's fifth largest metropolis, which went from small town to provincial capital during the colonial period. Outside the traditional centers of Pyongyang and Seoul, however, the two largest cities by the end of the colonial era were Pusan and Inch'ŏn, which grew through the regional trading system beginning in the late nineteenth century.

Pusan and Inch'ŏn had long served as ports in the Chosŏn era, but their significance increased dramatically after the 1876 Treaty of Kanghwa with Japan. Afterwards they served as two out of the three official "treaty ports," along with Wŏnsan (now in North Korea), where officially sanctioned foreign trade could occur. Through the accelerated influx of foreign merchants, interests, and conflicts at the turn of the twentieth century, the stage was set for these two ports to grow rapidly as Korea's meeting points with the larger world. Inch'ŏn, the gateway to the capital, grew into a hotspot teeming with Korean, Chinese, Japanese, and other foreign merchants, who set up their own communities and worked with the native population to gain favorable terms for extending their commercial ventures into the interior. Though the port became a battleground for the imperialist rivalry between China and Japan, by the end of the Russo-Japanese War in 1905

⫸

Japanese interests had gained the firm upper hand and soon began to construct not only railroads but also electricity, gas, and telegraph lines. Presently South Korea's fourth largest city and home to the country's gleaming flagship airport as well as other enormous development projects, Inch'ŏn (Incheon) now touts its long ties to China and its status as Korea's most visible global hub.

Pusan, by contrast, was always a creature of Korea's relations with Japan. A port that had long facilitated the minimal official trade between the two kingdoms during the Chosŏn era, in the late nineteenth century Pusan quickly developed into an almost extra-territorial base for Japanese commercial, agricultural, then military ambitions. By the turn of the twentieth century the harbor area had a large Japanese settlement and served as the primary entrance point for Japanese merchants wanting access to Korea's internal trading networks, and for Japanese companies supplying the amenities of the modern commercial world. Railways and electricity lines that began as short networks within Pusan during the pre-annexation period, for example, soon extended to neighboring areas in the southeastern region of the peninsula. And, not surprisingly, this Japanese largesse continued into the colonial period, when Pusan's expansion swallowed up its adjacent towns and eventually turned the city into an official provincial capital. The rapid development of Pusan served it well when, during the opening months of the Korean War in 1950, it functioned as the interim capital of South Korea that held at bay the North Korean siege until American reinforcements, through an invasion of Inch'ŏn, provided relief. Today Pusan (Busan), as South Korea's "second city," ranks as one of the largest ports and most dynamic metropolises in the world.

What is also lost in the narrative of imperialistic encroachment in Korea at the time is the blossoming of native enterprise and the training of thousands of Koreans in the labor and expertise needed for an increasingly diversifying economy. From the workers who laid the tracks, mined the mines, and toiled in the nascent textile sector, to the operators of the streetcars and telegraph lines,

Koreans began to forge a modern commercial realm. They were joined by those who established the first Korean banks, with some even succeeding sufficiently in this difficult venture to survive for decades to come. And many Koreans, like these early bankers, formed the first group of modern entrepreneurs by learning how to integrate their ventures into the regional and global trading system. These businessmen had an indelible impact, whether as transporters or handicraft manufacturers peddling their goods in the ports, or as traders taking advantage of their connections to the heartland, or even as officials using their political connections to gain access to capital and materials. Dozens of companies, including joint-stock companies, were founded during the Korean Empire.

One of the best known representatives of this early Korean business class was Yi Sŭnghun. Yi hailed from the county of Chŏngju, north of Pyongyang and famed for its late-Chosŏn commercial prowess as well as for producing many prominent cultural figures in the early twentieth century. Yi traversed a variegated life course, but he was first and foremost a manufacturer-merchant. He got his start as an apprentice in a local enterprise that produced brass wares, and by the late 1880s he had borrowed enough money to establish his own brass factory. During the Korean Empire period Yi expanded his business activities through his trading company based in Pyongyang. This company eventually gained a prominent position in the rapidly developing commercial sector, especially along the trading networks on the west coast between Pyongyang, Inch'ŏn, and Seoul. In addition to brass and other handicraft goods, his company traded in petroleum, medicinal products, and paper items. He also accumulated a small fortune as a renowned investor in new enterprises. He was a founder in 1908, for example, of one of the earliest joint stock companies in Korea, the Pyongyang Porcelain Company. He was, in some ways, the first modern Korean tycoon.

THE SPIRIT OF ENLIGHTENMENT

For all of his success as a leading figure in the first wave of modern Korean entrepreneurs, Yi Sŭnghun is better known for his activities, made possible by his wealth, in the realms of education and publishing. He stood at the forefront of the cresting enlightenment movement through his sponsorship of educational ventures in his home region. The schools that he and other activists founded around the country would educate the first generation of Korean school children in the "new learning," the popular term for Western knowledge and enlightenment in general. Yi established and ran, most notably, the Osan School in Chŏngju, founded in 1907, which would go on to produce some of the best-known literary and intellectual figures of modern Korea. Yi's passion for spreading new knowledge and raising national consciousness also resulted in his sponsoring the activities of acclaimed nationalists, including An Ch'angho. Yi's most celebrated accomplishment, in fact, came in 1919, when he served as one of thirty three signers of the March First Declaration of Independence from Japanese colonial rule.

Yi Sŭnghun also became active in newspaper publishing, a realm that began to wield social influence during the Korean Empire through the activities of the Independence Club, a civic group founded in 1896 by Sŏ Chaep'il. Sŏ (anglicized to "Philip Jaisohn") was a plotter of the Kapsin Coup of 1884 who had fled to the US and lived there for a decade before returning, with an American education and an American wife, to his homeland in 1895. The Club's ideas and ideals, which centered on "independence" from old ways as well as from China, appeared in *The Independent* newspaper, the first modern newspaper in Korea. In its inaugural issue in April 1896, *The Independent* served immediate notice of its radical program by its choice of the written language: the Korean vernacular, with even a page in English. When Sŏ opted to head back to the US in early 1898, another enlightenment activist schooled in America, Yun Ch'iho, stepped in as the next leader of the Independence Club. Under Yun's guidance the Club and *The Independent* maintained the spirit of the Kabo Reforms, constantly prodding the Korean government and monarch toward autonomy, reform, and self-strengthening. The Club sponsored the erection of the Independence Gate, still extant, at the site of the old gate where the Korean monarch used to greet ritually the Chinese envoy, and it organized a series of mass, open-air debates that promoted the participation of people regardless of social status.

In late 1898 the Independence Club was shut down by the government, which suspected the Club of republican leanings. *The Independent* newspaper had to follow suit a year later, but not before spawning a revolution in mass culture. People associated with the Club started other newspapers, which all sustained the general spirit of using these organs to disseminate information and knowledge, and thereby to build a strong, independent nation and state. Of particular note was the establishment of the *Cheguk sinmun* ("Imperial Post") and *Hwangsŏng sinmun* ("Capital Gazette") in 1898, the former written in native script and targeted at the masses, the latter written in mixed Sino-Korean script and aimed at a more educated population. Both newspapers survived largely intact until 1910, serving as the twin pillars of the growing world of publishing during the Great Korean Empire. This sphere of public discourse received its next major boost after 1905, as the forced implementation of the Japanese protectorate in Korea provoked an urgent outpouring of publishing, from newspapers and intellectual journals to books.

As with the railroad and other technological changes, the enlightenment movement's embrace of the "new learning" to further the aims of Korean self-strengthening and reform constituted a double-edged sword that marked the Korean Empire as a whole. As noted above, the railroad, for all its benefits, ultimately served in 1904–5 to facilitate Japan's prosecution of its war with Russia over supremacy in northeast Asia. Likewise, the discourse of "civilization and enlightenment" that dominated the public debate during the Korean Empire period proved just as useful to the imperialist forces wanting to conquer Korea as to those who touted this creed in defense of autonomy. To the Japanese (and many Koreans), Korea fell far short in its degree of civilizational advancement, and this served to justify another power's ambitions to take control of the country. For centuries dating back to the Spanish conquest of the Americas, after all, Europeans had deployed the same rationale to colonize much of the known world. Not surprisingly, Japanese and even many Korean elites argued that Japan had not only an interest but a duty in shaping

Korea's destiny—out of security concerns, if nothing else, for Korea was too weak to withstand the pressures of Western imperialism. The promotion of railroads, streetcars, electricity, mines, and other hallmarks of modern technology and infrastructure ultimately would prove incapable of overcoming these geopolitical tides.

Thus we return to the problematic place of the Great Korean Empire in the story of Korea's modern transition. Long stained historically by a perception of failure on the part of the state, elites, and even the masses to withstand imperialist pressures, which led directly to the Japanese takeover, the Korean Empire has recently enjoyed a historiographical resuscitation and an increase in popular and scholarly interest. At one level, the responsibility for the loss of autonomy has shifted more to imperialism as a whole—and not just that of Japan—which exacerbated the complex political rivalries among Korean elites, including the monarch himself. Korea, then, could not have possibly escaped unscathed in this era. At another level, contemporary historians and shapers of popular opinion have accentuated the need to appreciate all the major advances that marked this period, whether in culture, economy, or politics. But such a position has served only to sharpen the condemnation of Japanese actions, for the Korean Empire developments demonstrated that Korea was heading toward an autonomous modernity had Japanese imperialism not intervened. The subsequent colonial period from 1910 to 1945 represented, then, a dreadful "distortion" of national history that robbed the Koreans of the capacity to forge their own modernity. This goes too far—one cannot write off thirty five years of history, after all—but one can understand how the Korean Empire can be considered a major moment in the annals of Korean civilization, and at the very least a key component in Korea's modern transformation.

16

. . . .

The Japanese Takeover, 1904–18

CHRONOLOGY

1904 February	Outbreak of the Russo-Japanese War; signing of the Korea–Japan agreement
1904 August	Signing of treaty allowing Japanese intervention in Korean government affairs
1905 September	Treaty of Portsmouth ending the Russo-Japanese War, recognizing Japanese supremacy in Korea
1905 November	Protectorate treaty establishing Japanese Residency General in Korea
1907 June	Arrival of secret Korean emissaries in The Hague for the World Peace Conference
1907 July	Forced abdication of Emperor Kojong; signing of a treaty giving Japan appointment power in the Korean government
1907 August	Disbandment of Korean army, swelling of ranks of Righteous Armies
1909 October	Assassination of first Resident General Ito Hirobumi
1910 August	Signing of the annexation treaty, commencement of Government General of Korea
1910–1918	Comprehensive land survey by colonial government

THE SECRET MISSION TO THE HAGUE, 1907

On June 25, 1907, three curious-looking Asian men carrying the Korean flag and a fierce determination appeared on the grounds of the Second World Peace Conference in The Hague, Netherlands. They had been sent clandestinely by the Korean monarch, Emperor Kojong, and after a long journey had arrived in Europe to plead the case for Korea's independence from the encroaching Japanese empire. The three "secret envoys," however, were turned away by the Conference's officials and denied a platform to make their case before the gathered diplomats. These representatives from dozens of sovereign states were seeking to codify and institutionalize a global peace regime for a world increasingly marred by conflict. From their perspective, they could not grant the Koreans formal recognition because Korea itself simply had no diplomatic presence on the world stage, having been stripped of its autonomy in foreign relations by the onset of the Japanese Protectorate in late 1905. But the Koreans were ready to demonstrate that the "treaty" that the Japanese claimed authorized its Protectorate had been garnered fraudulently.

Declaring the 1905 treaty invalid and illegal was not a simple matter, however, and neither was the Japanese takeover of Korea that began in 1904. This process in turn reflected the complexities of Korea's modern history itself. The way one views the Japanese takeover and the nearly four decades of Japanese rule invariably dictates one's perspective on Korea's modern experience as a whole, particularly on the immense influence exerted by the outside world. Seen from this angle, the Hague incident showed Koreans taking matters into their own hands despite becoming swamped by overwhelming historical forces, including those that would rob them of their political independence.

AUTONOMY AND MODERN HISTORY

The Japanese conquest of Korea, which led to a period of colonial rule that lasted until 1945, constituted the first time since the era of Mongol suzerainty in the fourteenth century that Korea was directly controlled by a foreign power. Understandably, most historical perspectives have tended to focus on the political rupture and to treat the loss of Korean autonomy primarily as a matter of domination, collaboration, resistance, and victimization. They also extend this inquiry to raise questions about the nature and even historical validity of the period under foreign rule, so large was the imprint of the Japanese takeover on the rest of Korea's twentieth century: how did this happen, and why? In addition to imperialism, historians have cited numerous internal factors, some going as far back as the early nineteenth century (Chapter 13), and including a series of "missed opportunities" by the state and elites to avert the oncoming disaster: the reactionary responses to Western contact in the 1860s; the tepid changes of the 1870s and 1880s; the Chinese domination of the 1880s and 1890s; the incomplete reform movements of the 1890s; and the unsuccessful efforts, hampered by corruption and carelessness, to improve Korea's diplomatic, military, and economic conditions in the opening years of the twentieth century. Social and cultural factors cited include the stifling effect of a recalcitrant social hierarchy, the weakness of Koreans' sense of sacrifice and national collectivity, even the Korean customs in marriage, hygiene, and work ethic. Undeniably, many if not all of these factors did indeed ultimately contribute to the end result, but it is difficult to determine their relative significance, especially regarding those events that took place long before the first decade of the twentieth century.

On the other hand, one must also not overestimate the significance of the immediate circumstances, namely the 1905–10 Japanese protectorate period leading to outright annexation in 1910. First, such an approach would inflate the impact of two treaties—the 1905 treaty installing the Protectorate and the 1910 Treaty of Annexation—as the boundaries for the takeover process. In fact, one could even argue that these did not even constitute the most important *treaties*, as those in 1904 and 1907 can be considered more consequential (see below). Second, one must be careful not to exaggerate the historical rupture of 1910, as if the annexation acts as a conceptual black hole that sucks in all historical perspective. Such a fixation also leads to a preoccupation with the issue of the "legality" of the Japanese conquest, which, while not unimportant, is mostly moot given the larger historical forces at work. The takeover did not rely on a treaty, and it could not have been legal in any sense but the most absurdly legalistic. And certainly one cannot believe that in 1910 everything changed; indeed, it took another decade for the colonial regime to implant foreign rule securely. The colonial period itself subsequently developed in different ways at different times, and we must situate the colonial experience, as well as the takeover process itself, within the longer processes of modern change.

In the end, the most decisive factor was Japanese imperialism, and the series of events that led to Korea's loss of political autonomy began in 1904 with the onset of the Russo-Japanese War. The rivalry between these two powers for dominance in northeast Asia had been brewing for some time, and the eruption of hostilities in early 1904 off the west coast of Korea provided the Japanese the justification for taking control of the peninsula. Without the Japanese ambition to first coerce Korea and then to control it directly, Koreans would not have lost their sovereignty—at least not to the Japanese and not at that time, and possibly not at all.

Having said this, it is imperative to maintain the centrality of Koreans in Korean history, an obvious point that often gets lost when revealing the multiple means by which a foreign power imposed its rule over the country. Koreans not only challenged and resisted this effort, but in many ways also aided it, both willingly and not. The path leading to the loss of Korean autonomy, then, was paved by the interaction of imperialism and Korean consent. And one can further divide these factors into the "soft" and the "hard," with the latter in reference to the mechanisms of suppression engendering various means of resistance.

FORCE AND PUSHBACK

Until recently a historical narrative of domination and resistance prevailed in the common understanding of this period. Even with the emergence of a refreshingly more complex historical picture over the past two decades, it still bears reiterating that the loss of Korean sovereignty depended ultimately on force. The thousands of Japanese soldiers and policemen who entered the peninsula beginning with the Russo-Japanese War established the coercive framework for foreign domination, including the intimidation of Korean officials into signing, without royal consent, cooperative treaties. The first such pact in February 1904, immediately after the outbreak of the war, allowed Japanese soldiers to be stationed on Korean soil. Later, in August, another treaty stipulated a strong role for Japanese advisors in the financial, military, and diplomatic sectors of the Korean government. This served as prelude to the Protectorate Treaty of November 1905, which followed a peace agreement between the warring sides, brokered by the US, that recognized Japan's pre-eminent interests on the peninsula (in return, apparently, for Japanese recognition of American imperial interests in the Philippines). This notorious "1905 Treaty," signed by Korean ministers under coercion, established the Japanese protectorate government, the Residency General. The Residency General controlled the Korean government's foreign and financial affairs and put in place regional consulates around the country overseeing the Japanese migrant population and military presence. Ito Hirobumi, the venerable "senior official" at the center of Meiji Japan's modern transformation since the 1860s, arrived in Korea in early 1906 to serve as the first Resident General.

At first, Ito appears not to have envisioned a complete takeover of Korea, but rather a civilizing mission that would curb Korea's potentially dangerous decay. This outlook took a dramatic turn in the summer of 1907, however, with news of the secret mission to The Hague. Emperor Kojong, who had been a thorn in the Japanese side throughout this period, was forced to abdicate the throne in place of his meek son, who became crowned as Korea's new emperor. A treaty to accompany this move put in place the framework for total Japanese control over the Korean government by allowing the foreigners to determine appointments to the highest government posts. The disbandment of the Korean army quickly followed, along with the swelling of the combined Japanese–Korean military police force under Japanese control. The assassination of Ito in October of 1909, just a few months after he stepped down as the Resident General, appears to have accelerated the move toward outright annexation, which took place within a year thereafter. But, for all intents and purposes, the 1910 annexation treaty merely formalized the Japanese political control over Korea that had been completed in 1907.

An Chunggŭn, Ito's assassin, has long stood as the heroic representative in Korea of the combative resistance to the Japanese takeover. An gunned down Ito in plain sight at a train station in Harbin, Manchuria, and, following a legendary interrogation in which he laid out the principles behind his actions, he was executed. Prior to this An had led some bands of "Righteous Army" guerillas who were operating throughout Korea and beyond, targeting Japanese soldiers as well as Korean collaborators—from officials and policemen down to villagers. Active sporadically after 1894, the Righteous Army guerillas had risen up spontaneously in force following the 1905 Protectorate Treaty. Some of these groups were led by prominent elites, including the Confucian scholar Ch'oe Ikhyŏn, whose anti-foreign activism dated back to the 1860s (Chapter 13). It was the disbandment of the Korean army in the summer of 1907, however, that truly triggered an explosion in Righteous Army activities, as thousands of disaffected former soldiers entered the ranks of anti-Japanese guerillas. Battles raged throughout the peninsula, with one dramatic showdown taking place on the outskirts of Seoul in late 1907 involving upwards of 10,000 Korean resistors. Though they would never again be so well organized, they quickly formed the most serious obstacle to the Japanese takeover, and the full thrust of Japan's imperial might was directed at suppressing them. Pacification would not come until well after the 1910 annexation, and the bitter memories of the brutality deployed to hunt down the guerillas would continue to fuel anti-Japanese activities indefinitely.

Notwithstanding his military deeds, An Chunggŭn also belonged to the wave of resistance leaders who, after 1904, had pursued their activities through education and publishing. The onset of the Russo-Japanese War and the growing awareness of Japanese designs instilled a sense of crisis that the nation's autonomy and even its future as a civilization were at stake. Sin Ch'aeho, who like An Chunggŭn would later engage in militant activities, was representative of those sounding the alarm. As a writer for a stubbornly critical newspaper during the protectorate period, the *Korea Daily News*, he, like many others, connected the country's imminent danger to the people's lack of nationalistic consciousness. His solution was to raise awareness of the nation's plight through the publication of works on the glories of ancient history, on the often tragic trajectory of national historical development thereafter, and on the pressing need to apply these historical lessons to asserting independence. Other historian-activists included Pak Ŭnsik and Hyŏn Ch'ae, who wrote long treatises on both recent and distant Korean history that sought to instill a sense of urgency. Still other educators, scholars, and journalists appealed for direct action. The most notable example of this was Chang Chiyŏn, who penned a resounding "Lament of Wailing" in a leading newspaper immediately following the signing of the 1905 Protectorate Treaty. The newspapers and journals of the protectorate period stood often as the desperately final means, short of violence, to arouse Koreans and to appeal for international attention.

Little wonder, then, that one of the first steps taken by the colonial government in 1910 was to shut down all private newspapers and publication activities. The first decade of the colonial period, in fact, was marked by a general suppression of unauthorized activity, including in business, and became known as the era of "military rule" in reference to the heavy hand of colonial suppression. The primary aims of the colonial administration were to ferret out and pacify the remaining sources of armed resistance, and to stifle any plots seeking restoration of Korean autonomy. For the latter concern, the colonial authorities directed much of their attention and resources to mollifying the Yi royal house, for, as the secret mission to The Hague had proven in 1907, the long-standing monarch, Kojong, would not go quietly.

In the spring of that year, Kojong, unable to break out of the confines in which the Protectorate had placed him, dispatched three advisors to the Second World Peace Conference in The Hague. They met first in St Petersburg, where they joined up with a former Korean ambassador to the Russian Empire to plead their case for assistance to the Tsar himself. The Russian government, now more interested in allying with Japan, rebuffed them, and they proceeded to the Netherlands on their own. While they were denied a formal audience there, the three emissaries did manage to create a scene of protest, which caught the attention of the press. Indeed, according to the official proceedings of the Conference, one of the Korean delegates, Yi Wijong, pleaded simply for "a judgement on the legitimacy of the 1905 treaty." Later, at a speech he gave, in French, at the foreign press club in The Hague, he was more explicit: the

Japanese have unjustly forced their way onto Korea against the wishes of the Korean people and their monarch; the 1905 treaty was signed at the point of a gun and sword, and hence is illegal according to the standards of international law; and the Korean people are determined to resist this injustice. Much of the press coverage of the Koreans came to sympathize with them, and this only furthered the resolve of the Japanese officials to take more decisive action.

THE DEFT HAND OF CONQUEST

The summer of 1907, which included the forced abdication of Emperor Kojong, represented the culmination of gradual changes in the Korean government that the Japanese had promoted since 1904, the year the Japanese military made its way into the capital to stay for good. Thereafter, the military and police, though not deployed specifically for struggles over control of government, stood as the undeniably powerful presence looming over the developments leading to and securing the Japanese takeover. Under the cause of "reform" the Japanese Residency General, which formally held responsibility only for Korea's diplomatic and financial affairs, pushed many of the most consequential changes. This process witnessed sweeping amendments to the organization and manner by which the Korean government operated, all geared toward a more efficient means of mobilizing human and material resources as well as greater state control and surveillance. Notable targets of this project included the household registration and legal systems, both of which included an explicitly expanded role for, and the implicit threat of, the police. The reorganization of the cabinet and, more importantly, the shift in appointment power to the Residency General took place immediately after Kojong's abdication in 1907. Thereafter the highest posts in the central government, the provincial governorships, and most of the county magistracies were filled by Koreans with reliable ties to Japan.

The formal annexation of the summer of 1910, then, required few major changes to the structure or personnel of the government. The first Governor General, or head of the colonial Government General of Korea, had been in fact the last Resident

General of the Protectorate. He presided over an ambitious colonial state that more or less combined the pre-annexation Korean government and Residency General. One major change in state organization did materialize, however, to oversee the execution of the comprehensive colonial land survey. By the time of its conclusion in 1918, this enormous project would record and standardize the ownership of all parcels of land, consolidate large holdings of both public and private owners, and employ thousands of new officials, mostly Korean, in the process.

The cultivation of Korean officials became perhaps the most overlooked major ingredient in the Japanese takeover. Upon annexation, the royal family and prominent elites were eased into submission through lavish monetary sums, nobility titles, and sinecures. The more reliably friendly Koreans were appointed to high positions in the colonial government, continuing a pattern that had begun in 1907, as noted above. The top Korean appointees after 1907, especially those to the provincial governor positions, had in fact spent most of the previous decade in Japan, having fled Korea following the collapse of the Kabo Reform government in early 1896. Their time in exile had only served to harden their belief that the only hope for their country lay in accepting Japanese direction, and upon their return to their homeland they facilitated this effort. One did not need this formative experience in Japan to concur, however, as demonstrated repeatedly by the top Korean cabinet officials in the 1904–10 period—those who had signed the 1904 and 1905 treaties, colluded to transfer appointment power to the Residency General in 1907, and formally handed over the government in 1910. The central Korean figure in the latter two steps was Prime Minister Yi Wanyong, still reviled today as Korea's Benedict Arnold.

Yi Wanyong, however, represented only the tip of the collaborationist iceberg, for thousands of Koreans in all spheres of life acceded to the takeover process. Yi was actually related to Korea's royal family; he could count Emperor Kojong as a brother-in-law. While a tragic irony at one level, this was emblematic of the messy ties and blurry line between the two sides of resistance and acceptance, and of the less-than-clear-cut choices that many Koreans faced. While many prominent public figures, such as the historians and educators noted above, dedicated themselves to enlightening people in the ways of the modern world for the cause of preserving autonomy, others believed that saving the nation required the relinquishment of political independence. In addition to the maneuverings of Yi and other elites, there were also popular movements promoting the idea of joining the Japanese empire during this period. The most conspicuous of these groups was the *Ilchinhoe*, or "Advance in Unity Society," which counted tens of thousands of members from a wide range of backgrounds, with many formerly belonging to the Tonghak religion and social movement. Originally stirred into organizational activity in the midst of the Japanese entrance into Korea for the 1904–5 war, the Advance in Unity Society's primary goal was to agitate for a greater popular voice in government affairs, especially regarding taxation. To accomplish this, the leadership, led by an interesting figure named Song Pyŏngjun, embraced the annexationist cause in very public campaigns. It hence benefited from and contributed to the ongoing flowering of publishing for educational and political purposes. Although Song himself gained high office, however, the Advance in Unity Society ultimately failed to exert any lasting influence, even after annexation, for the very state power that it tried to curtail became the necessary instrument for implementing foreign rule.

The growth of the state both drove and reflected the dynamics of the Japanese takeover, not only in enforcing a militarily supported conquest, but in penetrating Korean society so deeply that overwhelming force proved mostly unnecessary. The "soft" features of the takeover, in fact, might have had a greater and more lasting impact in naturalizing foreign rule: changes to the financial and banking sectors; the government investments in communications and transportation infrastructure; the construction of schools and technical training centers; and the establishment of hospitals and other mechanisms to improve healthcare and hygiene—including, stunningly, a protectorate-period effort to enforce medical exams for prostitutes! To be sure, all of these measures were aimed first and foremost at facilitating a transition to foreign rule, catering to the Japanese migrants flooding the peninsula, and eventually enhancing colonial exploitation, but these steps also improved the welfare of many Koreans as well. The majority of Koreans—those in the countryside—of course felt little to no change in their daily lives, and they likely sensed few compelling consequences from the political changeover. Many Koreans simply had little incentive to resist the takeover.

Did Koreans, then, "sell out" their country? For two large groups, this might have been the case: the thousands of officials, like Yi Wanyong and Song Pyŏngjun, and other direct beneficiaries who provided legal and institutional assistance; and many, mostly lesser-known Koreans whose actions hinged not on payments but rather on implicit promises and hopes for material improvements and "enlightenment." But one could argue that many societies had to make such a Faustian bargain, often absent of considerations of national political autonomy, in coming to grips with the economic and political dislocations of the modern era. At least the Koreans, whether in accommodation, resistance, or someplace in between, claimed a role in determining their own fate amidst the maelstrom of external forces pushing upon them. They would undergo another such trial of autonomy and modernity following their liberation from Japanese rule in 1945.

17

....

The Long 1920s

CHRONOLOGY

OPENING OF A SPECIAL EXHIBITION OF NA HYESŎK'S PAINTINGS, 1921

On March 18, 1921, a special exhibition of Western-style paintings opened in downtown Kyŏngsŏng (Keijo), the official name of the Korean capital of Seoul in the colonial era. It represented the first such show dedicated to the works of a single painter, but notably, the artist was a young woman in her mid-twenties, Na Hyesŏk. Perhaps more remarkably, just two years earlier Na had been imprisoned for five months for having participated in the March First Independence Movement, a mass uprising against colonial rule that sparked bloody reprisals. Na's quick social rehabilitation and ascent to artistic distinction owed much to the rapid changes that enveloped the lives of Koreans at this time. Her new husband, for one, was a rising young Korean lawyer with connections to the upper echelons of colonial politics, business, and publishing. Indeed the sponsors of her exhibit were the two official government newspapers of the time, one published in Japanese and the other in Korean. The success of this exhibition also demonstrated how dramatically the socioeconomic transformation of colonial Korea facilitated the rise of groups and individuals who relied upon new opportunities and different forms of social identity and collectivity.

Na Hyesŏk, in fact, proved a pioneering figure in another way as well— she was a forceful voice in the flourishing public discourse of her times, in which she argued for greater recognition of both of her primary identities, as artist and as a woman. Her life and work constituted a microcosm of Korea's "roaring twenties," the maturation period of colonial rule that established significant societal patterns enduring well past this decade. One could argue that the 1920s actually began in the opening months of 1919, when the independence uprisings led to the closure of the somber 1910s and the commencement of what officially was proclaimed "Cultural Rule." Henceforth appeared a blossoming of cultural expression, associational activity, and articulations of nationhood in the re-invigorated realm of publishing. As the rise and equally dramatic fall of Na Hyesŏk's public profile demonstrated, the transformation of Korea in the long 1920s was centered on social and economic developments that affected nearly everyone, but especially Korean females.

THE MARCH FIRST MOVEMENT AND CULTURAL RULE

It is difficult to say whether the loosening of social and political restrictions that marked the 1920s would have eventually emerged regardless of the March First Movement of 1919, but certainly the uprisings spurred the colonial authorities to deploy substantial corrective measures. The first decade of the colonial period, the so-called "military rule" era characterized by stifling limitations on social activity, had suppressed the outward expression of people's discontent, but this served only to intensify the ensuing explosion. The trigger came from a confluence of three major events, one in Korea, another in Japan, and a third in Europe. In the West, 1918 was the year of reckoning of the Great War (First World War), and among the resolutions that the victorious powers advanced was to encourage self-determination among fledgling nations.

The Euro-American leaders had in mind the peoples of Europe and did not envision the independence of overseas colonies, but this was exactly how these utterances from Versailles were taken by liberation movements around the world. Indeed, the Korean students who had flocked to the metropole, especially to Tokyo, in the 1910s found there not only greater educational opportunities but, ironically, also a much freer atmosphere for political thought and agitation. They organized themselves into publishing a manifesto of Korean independence in February 1919, and soon they joined forces with like-minded students in their homeland to recruit social and cultural leaders for a mass demonstration for independence. The timing, however, would be dictated by news in late February of the death of Kojong, the last autonomous monarch of pre-annexation Korea, and by the likelihood that people from throughout the country would gather in the capital for his funeral.

The drafting of the Declaration of Independence by a renowned author, the gathering of eminent religious and social figures to serve as official representatives, and other secret planning for the demonstrations targeted March 1, two days before the funeral, as the date. On that morning, the thirty-three signers of the Declaration gathered in Seoul to read aloud the document in Pagoda Park, and soon throngs of people marched down the streets shouting "Long Live Korean Independence!" This scene was soon repeated throughout the country, and everywhere the scale and ferocity of the demonstrations, with upwards of one million participants nationwide, stunned and befuddled the authorities. This undoubtedly accounted for the senselessly ruthless measures taken to crack down on the demonstrators, with the cycle of suppression and resistance escalating into atrocities that included random shootings, massacres, and burnings of churches and entire villages. Perhaps the best-known victim of these reprisals, and hence also the most renowned female of this era in the nationalist annals, was Yu Kwansun. Yu was a schoolgirl in Seoul when March First broke out, but quickly went down to her home town in Ch'ungch'ŏng province to rally the locals for the cause. She was captured, brutalized, and eventually killed in prison, one of countless activists who became martyred. Even the colonial government's tallies totaled more than 500 deaths and thousands of injuries over the course of the spring, with unofficial counts claiming exponentially larger numbers. Pacification would eventually come in the summer, but almost everything had changed.

The one thing that did not change was Korea's colonial status. The March First Independence Movement ultimately failed to achieve its primary goal of gaining Korea's liberation from Japanese rule. But the significance of March First, judged by its effects both internally and externally, was still enormous. Outside the country, representatives of disparate efforts to achieve independence, militarily and otherwise, were inspired to gather in Shanghai in April that year to organize a government in exile. This effort soon faltered due to ideological and other divisions among the activists, but the independence movements continued throughout the colonial period, if along divergent tracks. Within the peninsula, meanwhile, the March First Movement elicited a sweeping reevaluation of colonial rule on the part of the Japanese government. Japanese leaders were not ready to grant independence, of course, but they realized that harsh enforcement was counterproductive. Hence, the new Governor General instituted a comprehensive program that combined a discreet strengthening of bureaucratic and police forces with an outwardly more benign governing approach that encouraged Koreans to pursue social, economic, and cultural activities more freely. This so-called Cultural Rule, then, constituted a strategy of co-opting Koreans into the colonial system by allowing them a greater stake in its development.

The scale and scope of the changes that followed, particularly beyond the political realm, were extensive. Publication restrictions were lifted, and the two oldest Korean newspapers still circulating today, the *Tonga ilbo* and *Chosŏn ilbo*, began publishing in 1920. In the economy, the pursuit of a core benefit of turning Korea into a colony—that is, the exploitation of its natural resources—remained preeminent, but in the 1920s this effort gained improved efficiencies and structural reforms. While these developments consigned more Koreans to life as struggling tenant farmers, they also provided opportunities for other Koreans to gain commercially from the agricultural sector. Furthermore, the

Government General's easing of restrictions on native enterprise stimulated the emergence of many Korean companies, including those businesses that would later turn into the giant conglomerates dominating the South Korean economy, such as Samsung and LG. The most formidable and conspicuous of such family-owned companies, the Kyŏngsŏng Textile Company, eventually branched out into various industries and even different regions, as it built factories and branches in Manchuria and elsewhere. The colonial government's accelerated extension of communication and transportation networks, meanwhile, spurred further urbanization and the concentration of wealth, construction, and influence in these growing population centers. The precipitous migration out of the rural areas and the ensuing dissolution of traditional ties, both familial and otherwise, would have far-reaching social ramifications. Most striking of all, perhaps, the loosening of legal restrictions and enforcement methods led to a boom in associational activity among Koreans, who joined hundreds of clubs, organizations, and other groups catering to countless interests and social identities.

These developments, together with the incorporation of thousands of Koreans into the colonial state, also engendered a reordering of the social structure by facilitating a dramatic rise in social mobility. The fundamental transformation and even overturning of Korean social hierarchy had begun in the late nineteenth century, but the colonial circumstances intensified these trends, particularly in urban centers. In these areas, the Korean social structure looked very different from that of a few decades earlier, as the diversification of the economy and occupations, together with legal reforms, further minimized the impact of hereditary status. Descendants of previously despised groups such as butchers and shamans organized campaigns to gain social acceptance, and many from secondary status backgrounds ascended to the highest levels of the new social elite. Most striking of all, perhaps, were the changes affecting women. From *kisaeng* courtesans and peasants in the countryside to the housewives and wage workers in the cities, females began to reshape the social landscape in a way unprecedented in Korean history.

KOREAN FEMALES IN THE NEW AGE

The most dramatic impact of the urbanization, industrialization, and increased availability of education in the 1920s might have been experienced by women. These changes affected mostly those females in the cities, but extended to the rural areas as well. In both environments, Korean females as a whole found room to explore new life paths and claim a greater role in determining their own lives. It marked the beginning of an unfolding of female subjectivity that, through its development in fits and starts the rest of the twentieth century, would leave a major imprint on how Koreans came to view gender roles in the modern era.

The most distinctive type of woman in the 1920s went by the terms "new woman" or "modern girl," a phenomenon visible in contemporary Japan and China as well. Concentrated in Seoul, these females shared a background of having been educated in the major cities (though often they had moved from the countryside), a strong consumerist orientation, and family connections to the new social elite, often through marriage to urban professionals. The New Woman appeared frequently in the contemporary literature, often portrayed in contrast—and not always flatteringly—to the more traditional women who still constituted the overwhelming majority, as an allegory on the choices and dilemmas presented by the rapidly changing world. They also appeared in articles, notices, and advertisements in the burgeoning publishing sector targeting their bourgeois lifestyles. These publications included women's magazines that dished out advice on everything from fashion to hygiene. Most of the readers were either students or graduates of the growing number of girls' secondary schools in the urban centers, and some could point to an experience of schooling abroad, especially in Japan, as the source of their worldly perspectives and tastes.

The urban, educated women not only appeared as emblems and consumers of the publishing world, but also as producers. Female authors, translators, essayists, and critics contributed to the construction of a distinctively modern Korean literary culture, the most formative period for which was the 1920s. New magazines and literary journals, such as *New Woman* (*Sin Yŏsŏng*), catered to women's interests and provided a forum for female writers. Na Hyesŏk, though known better for her paintings and essays, also expressed her ideals of female emancipation through poetry and short stories, the earliest of which was published in 1918. Renowned female contemporaries included Kim Iryŏp, who also founded in 1920 Korea's first women's journal, Kim Myŏngsun, whose novels explored the depths of female subjectivity, and later in the 1930s, Kang Kyŏngae, a realist storyteller whose works depicted the plight of Korea's underclass.

Korean women also made their mark in the realm of the arts. City dwellers eventually came to know of Yun Simdŏk, for example, the great singer whose concerts became lavish spectacles, and of Ch'oe Sŭnghŭi, the dancer who mesmerized audiences throughout the world before working as a propagandist for Japan's war effort in the 1940s. Na Hyesŏk was the third figure in this famed Korean triumvirate of female artists of the colonial period. Having demonstrated her precociousness as a school girl from a well-to-do Seoul family, she went to Japan in her late teens to enroll in a girls' art school. She returned to her homeland just in time to get caught up in the 1919 March First Movement, which derailed her career path as an artist, however briefly. After getting married under the condition—unheard of at the time—that she be allowed to continue her artistic career, Na developed her talents further by displaying her works in various exhibitions, including the solo exhibition of her own works in 1921. Motherhood and a brief move to Manchuria to follow her husband, who had become a diplomat in the Japanese empire, curbed her artistic activities somewhat. By the late 1920s, however, Na was on the move again, this time on a whirlwind tour through Europe with her husband, where in Paris she trained further in oil painting techniques. In Paris she also became involved in a scandalous affair with a well-known Korean nationalist figure, and within a year after her return to Korea in 1929, her husband divorced her, and she lost custody of her children. Although she experienced a few successes as a professional painter thereafter, her artistic career eventually suffered from a lack of public interest, and she lived out her life in obscurity, much of it in Buddhist temples, until her death in 1946.

The relatively small number of paintings attributed to Na Hyesŏk that can be considered reliably authentic today show indeed a master craftsman deserving of status as one of the accomplished Korean painters of her era, regardless of gender. But Na Hyesŏk's historical significance stems also from her opinions as a social commentator and chronicler, and from her own actions. Even in her student days in Japan she had expressed reservations about the prevailing "wise mother, good wife" model and insisted that females shape their lives in accordance with reason and self-confidence. In a 1921 newspaper editorial entitled "Painting and Korean Women," which provided a prelude to the opening of her single-artist exhibition, she deplored the social biases resulting in a lack of opportunities for Korean women to develop an interest and talent in painting. This stood in contrast to the visibility of female poets and writers, she noted. In a veiled reference to herself, Na proclaimed, "I am convinced that female painters can appear if only an effort arose to facilitate interest in painting among common women."

In her later writings, she expressed views that would have been considered radical even half-a-century later. In a long magazine essay entitled "Thoughts on Becoming a Mother," published in 1923, Na shredded the niceties of the motherly ideal and asserted that her experiences contradicted everything she had been taught. She wrote of the difficulties of pregnancy, childbirth, and child rearing, and of the resentments she built up against society, her husband, and even her baby for impinging on her career and personal freedoms. There must be an implicitly conspiratorial character to the social conventions that divided men and women into their respective roles, she wondered. Upon her return from Europe, she openly praised the model of gender relations that she observed in the West and even speculated that cohabitation before marriage, or a "test marriage," could allow women to become better informed before taking the plunge. After the failure of her own marriage, in writings such as "A Divorce Confession" she called for the liberation of women's sexuality, lamented the social and familial conventions that constrained females, and condemned the hypocrisy of typical Korean males regarding chastity. She even put into practice her calls for female empowerment by suing Ch'oe Rin, the nationalist activist with whom she had become involved in Paris, for "infringement on a woman's honor." She accused Ch'oe, in other words, of abandoning her despite his role in the events that led to Na's public disgrace and divorce, and she demanded monetary restitution. These actions failed to rehabilitate her artistic career or social standing, but Na Hyesŏk demonstrated that Korean women could aspire to new levels of assertiveness, even if society as a whole remained unaccommodating.

Like Na, most Korean women affected by the new era encountered definite limitations on their dreams and ambitions. The group of women who perhaps embodied these constraints the most were the thousands of young factory workers who "manned" much of the burgeoning manufacturing sector, in industries ranging from textiles to food processing. From having been nearly absent from enterprises at the turn of the century, women accounted for a fifth of the factory work force in the early 1920s and a third by the mid-1930s. Both the pull factors of regular wages and city life as well as the push factor of rural immiseration brought these girls, caught between puberty and marriage, into the factories. Their lives, however, were in many ways Dickensian: they were herded into tight and tedious working conditions and paid paltry wages. And despite the allure of the big city, they could enjoy at most one day a week off, and usually they spent this day in their cramped dormitories recuperating from their 12-hour shifts. These jobs also presented only meager opportunities for schooling, given the incessant work demands, and even for consumption, since whatever they earned in wages was usually sent directly to their families back home. The lives of these factory girls, then, fell far short of the glamorous existence of the "modern girl" lore. But their experiences offered them at least the foundation, however restricted, of self-determination through work and training.

This phenomenon also affected the countryside, though of course with differences in the scope and character of the changes. While most young women worked the fields or engaged in household work, unprecedented social forces, including the colonial government and private groups, gradually made possible educational and training opportunities—including, for a fortunate few, schooling itself. And here, too, women often stood at the forefront of generating the very changes affecting them as a group. An example comes from Ch'oe Yongsin, a rural educator whose life and activities were dramatized in a famous novel of the 1930s. After having attended a girls' high school in the 1920s, Ch'oe entered a women's seminary and thereafter used her newfound connections, in particular to the Korean YMCA, to engage in work to eradicate illiteracy and provide basic schooling to children in the countryside. Her close connection to church-sponsored activities exemplified the major role of religion, particularly Protestantism, in bestowing opportunity for rural women. Ch'oe was one of countless Christian women who served simultaneously as translators for foreign missionaries, as liaisons for outside educators, and as pastoral deputies dealing with people, especially females, who could not be easily approached. In turn, these women used this activity as a stepping stone to a higher calling, whether in religious or other kinds of work, and regardless of their social background.

RELIGION AND SOCIAL CHANGE

The connection between Protestant activities in colonial Korea and changes affecting Korean females bespeaks a larger issue of the relationship between religion and social change in the early twentieth century. This in turn compels us to ponder one of the great historical questions about modern Korea, namely, the cause of the unusual success of Christianity in Korea compared to other non-Western countries. And while Catholicism, as well as Buddhism, also experienced dramatic growth, the development of Protestantism is most notable. Foreign Protestant missionaries began their activities in the 1880s, having entered through a back door, in a sense, as attachments to the increasing diplomatic, educational, and commercial presence of North Americans. Through their unshakable aura of advancement, resourcefulness in employing the Korean alphabet, implicit promises of social liberation, and explicit promises of salvation in the afterlife, the missionaries found great success. Significantly, they counted among their converts many of the most influential social elites at the turn of the twentieth century. An early peak in Protestant growth was reached in 1907 through the Great Pyongyang Revival, a gathering of thousands in what quickly became the center of Korean Christianity, the northwestern region surrounding the city of Pyongyang.

In the colonial period Pyongyang came to be known as the "Jerusalem of the East," a designation pointing to its centrality in Korean Protestantism, but also to the incorporation of Protestantism in the city's self-identity as a beacon of freedom from the darkness of foreign rule. That the majority of the most prominent nationalists and independence activists of the early twentieth century were also Protestant could not have been a coincidence. Indeed many of these figures, including 16 out of the 33 signers of the March First Declaration of Independence, pointed to their Protestant faith as inspiring their work. Most conspicuous in this regard was An Ch'angho, from Pyongyang, who began his activities as an educator and independence activist in the first decade of the twentieth century, and soon became one of the first Korean immigrants to the US. Traveling to and from his home in southern California, which acted as a base for the early Korean American community, An organized and inspired efforts to achieve Korean independence throughout this period. His life and thought exemplified the role of both religion and nationalist activity as havens of collective identity away from the colonial state, and in turn as further examples of the forces of social change that marked the long 1920s.

18

. . . .

Nation, Culture, and Everyday Life in the Late Colonial Period

CHRONOLOGY

1925   Founding of the Korean Communist Party and KAPF
1931   Korean newspaper campaigns to eliminate illiteracy in the countryside
1931   Manchurian Incident and invasion of Manchuria by imperial Japan
1932   Establishment of the Japanese puppet state of Manchukuo
1936   Olympic marathon victory by Son Kijŏng, defacement of Japanese flag on
        newspaper picture of Son

THE DOCTORING OF A NEWSPAPER PHOTO OF
THE OLYMPIC MARATHON CHAMPION, 1936

The first evening edition of the August 25, 1936 issue of the Korean language newspaper, *Tonga ilbo*, had cleared the colonial censors. But just as the authorities had feared, a second evening edition quickly published thereafter caused quite a stir. On its front page was emblazoned the picture of national hero Son Kijŏng, who two weeks earlier had captured the gold medal in the marathon in the 1936 Berlin Olympics. The cause for alarm was not that Son himself, pictured solemnly on the medal stand, was prominently featured, but rather that the Japanese flag on Son's uniform had been rubbed out, leaving a black smudge in its place (see Image 18). Unbeknownst to their own editors and managers, a group of journalists had pulled off the stunt in a fit of emotion comprised of both pride and shame: pride that a Korean had reached a pinnacle of world sport, and shame that he had been forced to don a

Image 18　Son Kijŏng's photo, *Tonga ilbo* newspaper, Tuesday, August 25, 1936

foreign conqueror's flag. Not surprisingly, the ringleaders were fired, black-listed, even jailed, and the newspaper was shut down for almost a year.

This episode surrounding the picture of Son Kijŏng—or "Son Kitei," the Japanese pronunciation of his name through which he was officially known outside the peninsula—is commonly viewed as an act of nation-alist defiance. This is undoubtedly true, but the event also represents a window into the overarching patterns of culture and daily life in the late colonial period, with recurring exposure to each others' lives through mass culture strengthening a sense of commonality. The newspaper, in fact, played the central role in circulating these observations, impres-sions, and ideas. This prodded Koreans to contemplate and reconsider their collective identity, both through an active engagement with press-ing issues of nationhood and a more pedestrian pursuit of their lives.

EXPRESSION, WITHIN LIMITS

The brazen effacement of the Japanese flag on the picture of Son Kijŏng, in fact, epitomized the cat-and-mouse game Korean publications constantly played with colonial censors, as well as the ambiguities straddling the fine line between the overlooked and forbidden. The colonial state had itself unleashed the expressive energies of the Korean people through the "Cultural Rule" approach launched with great fanfare in the 1920s (Chapter 17). And Korean writers, artists, and journalists had no qualms about testing the limits of colonial censorship. After having nipped in the bud potentially disruptive movements throughout the 1920s, in the 1930s the colonial state, whether in print or in action, found itself having to deal with a more fully matured realm of social discourse and interaction. These challenges reached another level altogether with the Japanese invasion of Manchuria following the Manchurian Incident of September 1931, and with the establishment of the puppet state of Manchukuo a year later. Thereafter, Korea gradually turned into an industrial base for the Japanese Empire's advance into the Asian mainland.

Ironically, Korean newspapers had served unwittingly as propagandistic conduits for such Japanese designs, as reports about the Manchurian Incident and the imperial army's exploits fed a growing competition for readership. This was particularly important because reporting about these developments often included news on Korean settler communities in Manchuria. But Korean newspapers in the late colonial period also exhibited behaviors that deliberately fueled anti-colonial or anti-Japanese sentiments. Their coverage of Koreans in Manchuria, for example, included reports about the anti-Japanese Korean guerilla groups operating there. Back home, the newspapers and magazines that grew in circulation and influence served to transmit the Korean colonial experience, especially as windows into and mirrors of everyday life. They also stood as the authoritative forums for debates on the entire range of issues concerning life in colonial Korea. Most strikingly, the opinions, which often became heated, went so far as to condemn colonial policies, wonder about the justice of the colonial condition itself, and even promote specific steps toward independence. A full spectrum of ideologies, from anarchism to communism, found voice in these pages, although many of the most offending passages were excised by the censors before reaching the reader. The consequences for crossing the line often were severe—including dismissal and even, occasionally, incarceration—but this was not a totalitarian system, at least not until the 1940s wartime mobilization (Chapter 19); Koreans, including the elites of the publishing world who had the most to lose, were not brutalized for thought crimes.

Such a delicate equilibrium was sustained also by the fact that Korean newspapers and magazines found outlets for promoting national interests through more benign activities as well. For one, such publications were the canvasses for the most important intellectuals and writers of the time, who established in these pages the foundation for modern Korean literature and thought. Rarely did a full-length novel from this period, for example, first get published outside the established mode of serialization in newspapers or magazines. The publications, in particular the monthly journals whose circulation sometimes outpaced that of the newspapers themselves, also printed the reflections of philosophers and social commentators, the latest findings of scholars, and the works of budding poets. Consumers of the popular press in the late colonial period in turn constituted the first mass reading public in Korean history, and publishers grew powerful as purveyors of information, insight, and opinion.

The two major Korean newspapers of the time, though sometimes criticized by contemporaries as well as by later historians for a preoccupation with commercial gain, also displayed a Confucian sense of didactic social responsibility. To be sure, they benefited from their ties to the colonial authorities and often, even if unwittingly, furthered state interests. But they also were quick to promote national causes and laud Korean accomplishments, as exemplified by their leadership in public campaigns on behalf of Korean commercial products. Often the Korean press struck an unabashedly nationalist tone, as seen in the blaring headlines of "Hail the Global Triumph!" and "The Greatest Victory in All of Humanity!" in the *Tonga ilbo* newspaper's front page the day after Son Kijŏng's marathon victory. They furthermore pursued a spirited effort to curb illiteracy and expand educational opportunities among the overwhelming majority of Koreans still living in the countryside. They sent educated youth to the provinces to operate and teach in village schools on subjects ranging from hygiene to history, and of course to propagate the use of the Korean alphabet. One could suggest that this, too, was commercially driven—that the newspapers were simply looking to expand their readerships. But the newspaper companies were often harassed by the authorities on suspicions of inciting nationalism or simply of impeding the colonial government's own efforts at rural welfare, such as organizing agricultural cooperatives for water, fertilizer, and credit.

THE QUOTIDIAN BLOSSOMING OF MODERN CULTURE

Novels and short stories published in the newspapers and monthly magazines represented only a fraction of the totality of cultural production in the late colonial period that amounted, in hindsight, to the formation of modern Korean culture itself. Indeed, the very notion of a Korean culture to be explored and celebrated as a distinctive, self-enclosed civilizational entity reached full bloom in this era. That this feat was achieved when Koreans did not possess political autonomy constitutes a great irony, but this did not make Korea unique. Colonized or subject peoples throughout world history, if they could evade extinction itself, often forged a keener, sharper sense of collective self. In the modern world, this phenomenon resulted in the creation of wholly new nationalities or, as in the case of India (and Korea), a rejuvenated sense of national identity replenished by cultural enterprises now definitively identified with the nation.

In Korea, the project of creating modern culture through the combination of cultural production and systematic reevaluation of older cultural products had begun at the turn of the century, but it was not until the late colonial period that a critical mass of achievements appeared. The colonial authorities, while remaining on the lookout for explicit calls for independence, not only allowed these activities but actually promoted them. Japanese officials believed that such efforts would act as safe outlets for frustrations on the political front and even result in a reinforcement of the civilizational bonds between Japan and Korea. Regardless, Korean intellectuals began to engage intensively in research that they openly labeled "Korean Studies" (*Chosŏnhak*). Korean historical scholarship, helped in part by large-scale projects sponsored by the government, reached new levels of depth and sophistication, and it sometimes even challenged the validity of colonial rule. Some prominent people of letters, such as Ch'oe Namsŏn and Yi Nŭnghwa, turned their attention to incorporating the study of Korean religion into grand theories of Korea's place in Asian civilization. Still others took on the task of systematizing and standardizing the Korean written vernacular, which had enjoyed widespread use since the turn of the century but still suffered from a lack of usage standards. The Korean Language Society, comprised of many outstanding scholars of the time, took to fixing this problem by promulgating grammar and spelling rules and compiling an authoritative dictionary.

The emergence of a standard Korean vernacular resulted from several sources, including the work of linguists. Also playing a major role were the increasing propagation of common forms of mass culture and entertainment, and a shortening of distances through both communication and transportation technologies. And, notably, the lyric poetry of this era expanded the expressive potential of the Korean language, as shown by the three most renowned poets of the first half of the twentieth century: Kim Sowŏl, Han Yongun, and Chŏng Chiyong. Kim's best known poem, "Azaleas"—indeed the most famous and probably most popular poem in modern Korea—taps into the powerfully recurring theme in Korean folklore of sorrowful parting and unrequited love. This theme appears in everything from the *Tale of Ch'unhyang* to the semi-official national folk song of "Arirang," as well as in hit songs of this period such as "Tuman River, Full of Tears." It also is central to the title poem of Han Yongun's great collection of lyrics, *Silence of the Beloved*. While revealing himself a passionate nationalist and Buddhist reformer in his activities as educator and essayist, in his verse Han couched his concerns about the contemporary situation in allegories of love, lament, and reconciliation. Chŏng Chiyong, a Catholic and perhaps the most noteworthy stylist, painted serenely evocative images of nature and rustic life with breathtaking fluency. That Chŏng, who worked as an English teacher at a secondary school for the duration of the late colonial period, could consistently find outlets for publishing his poetry in various journals, including those he helped to edit, testified to the flourishing literary culture of this era.

Other forms of mass culture also enjoyed a major boom, helped by advances in technology and commercial development, including a thriving consumerism in the cities. Music and theater performances became popular events, and they featured both foreign and native works. Korean plays and musicals were offered through creative stagings of traditional folk tales as well as new works, and retellings of famous Korean stories not surprisingly became embraced by the early Korean cinema as well, the first "talkie" of which appeared in 1935. And in music a star system of singers emerged in the 1930s, with their most popular hits instantly becoming iconic treasures that remain in the popular consciousness today. These songs enjoyed distribution through the proliferation of phonographs among the upper and middle classes, but it was the advent of the radio that was most responsible for the widespread dissemination of popular music in the colonial period. Radio supplied people with news and education as well as entertainment, infusing the growing listening public in both rural and urban areas with a new sense of connection to each other and to the world at large.

Indeed the radio, specifically the regular live reports from Berlin, played a central role in igniting Koreans' interest in Son Kijŏng's great Olympic quest. When the day of the marathon came, Koreans huddled around their radios in the late hours of Saturday, August 9, 1936. Immediately following an update around midnight that Son had joined the lead pack about a third of the way into the race, however, the broadcast, in accordance with its regular schedule, cut off the coverage from Berlin. While the rest of the country had to wait until the next morning for the results, a group of people gathered just outside the *Tonga ilbo* headquarters received updates from a newspaper employee who had managed to establish telephone contact with Tokyo and Berlin. These people were the first to know when, around 2am, came finally the joyous announcement that, indeed, Son Kijŏng had won the Olympic marathon, and moreover, that another Korean, Nam Sŭngnyong, had taken the bronze medal. The following morning the country erupted in celebration, and a pervasive giddiness over this happy occasion would endure for months, even infecting the reporters at the *Tonga ilbo* enough, two weeks later, to alter Son's photo.

The newspaper workers behind this act were displaying an extreme example of the double duty that Korean reporters generally pursued in the colonial period—as eyewitnesses and chroniclers on the one hand, and as activists, opinion makers, and artists on the other. In fact, a great number of colonial period writers also had worked at one time as newspaper reporters. The line between observer and storyteller tended to blur—along with that between popular and high culture—through this connection and the serialization of novels in newspapers and periodicals. Furthermore, the themes explored by these literary works mostly focused on the here and now, and on daily events—as if, indeed, they were elaborations of newspaper reports. The first great concentration of canonical works in modern Korean literature emerged in the late colonial period and was suffused with the details of everyday life, from the tedious to the tragic.

Many of the most notable authors of novels and short stories won their renown through portrayals of daily, often mundane life in late colonial Korea. Ch'ae Mansik, known primarily for his masterpiece, the novel *Peace Under Heaven*, used his short stories to satirize, critique, and observe bemusedly the often dumbfounding dynamics of modern existence. His short story, "A Ready-Made Life," for example, depicts the legions of "petit bourgeois intellectuals" who, armed with an education and high tastes but no practical skills, drift about contemporary Seoul in search of jobs and meaning in their lives. The lead character, one such "ready-made life," rescues himself from his absurd destitution and desperation by returning to simple, indeed traditional, priorities. Another important chronicler of life in Seoul was Pak T'aewŏn, author of innovative narratives that at times dispensed with conventions, such as plot, for the sake of chronicling the pedestrian. "A Day in the Life of the Novelist Kubo" (serialized in 1934), for example, is an autobiographical stroll ("Kubo" was Pak's pen name) through Seoul relayed through streams of consciousness and snippets of observations, in a narrative style that often changes tenses and narrator in the same paragraph. Scenes of the rapidly modernizing capital city attract the attention of Kubo, who notes the goings on in theaters, restaurants, coffee houses, and that great symbol of high-class urban leisure at the time, the department store. What he finds in the teeming metropolis, however, often leads to aliena-tion and disenchantment. In the splendid Seoul train station, for example, he senses only a throng of lonely individuals: "Although the place is so packed with people that Kubo can't even find a seat to squeeze into, there's no human warmth. Without exchanging a word with those sitting next to them, these people are preoccupied with their own business, and should they happen to say anything to each other, it's only to check the train schedule or something along those lines." While the extraordinary pace and social impact of changes in the urban landscape are enough to devote an entire novella to the impressions of a curious observer, the novelties of modern life are not necessarily to be celebrated. Indeed, the effects are often lamented and feared.

Realist depictions of the underbelly of modern life and of the sad, sometimes brutal struggles of common people had appeared in the early 1920s, most notably in the works of Hyŏn Chin'gŏn. But the late colonial period witnessed an intensified politiciza-tion of literature through an explicit engagement with pressing sociopolitical issues. This trend was exemplified by KAPF, the Korean Artists Proletarian Federation, an organization founded in 1925 to rally authors toward the theme of class consciousness and the finer points of Marxism and historical materialism. KAPF also reflected larger social trends toward leftist activism, as seen in the founding of the Korean Communist Party in 1925, in the attempt to unify nationalist movements under the leadership of socialist activists in the late 1920s, and in the increasingly hostile agitation of factory labor movements and peasant unions well into the 1930s. Revolutionary leftist influence extended to the realms of social criticism, theater, cinema, music, and the fine arts, but had perhaps the most palpable impact on literature. The representative writer of KAPF was Yi Kiyŏng. After publishing several harrowing chronicles of struggling peasants in his short stories, Yi unveiled his great novel, *Hometown*, through serialization in the *Chosŏn ilbo* newspaper from 1933 to 1934. *Hometown* chronicles the attempts by a colorful cast of villagers—in effect, Korea's proletariat, given the relatively underdeveloped factory labor force—to adjust to the exploitative forces of early capitalism. It employs the ready tropes of proletarian literature, such as the heroic socialist intellectual in the role of the vanguard, but the success of this novel owed much to the compellingly lifelike characters and a grippingly melodramatic story that transcended conventions. Indeed, the work of KAPF writers moved even Korean authors who were not members, or even leftist in inclination, to infuse their works with a greater social consciousness and attention to the people's daily travails.

Whether through such literary works or via the new media of radio, phonographs, or cinema, culture in the late colonial period revealed to Koreans the countlessly variegated manifestations of each others' lives. Cultural production gave meaning, then, to the dizzying onset of industrial capitalism—the exploding proliferation of occupations and activities; the appearance of big machines, vehicles, buildings, and cities; and advances in transportation and communications, including especially the newspaper—that rendered contact with a greater world a recurring reality. By instilling a sense of collective plight and subjectivity, both as Koreans and as modern people, the revelation of larger society and the experience of daily life aroused a sense of transformation, modernity, and nationhood much more solidly than could calls to action and political movements. Even the occasional bursts of nationalist ardor served more as exceptions that reinforced the more powerful effects of the churning quotidian. The true historical significance of the Son Kijŏng photo incident, then, lies in its illumination of the centrality of newspapers in the unfolding process of modernity in the late colonial period. To be sure, debates about the propriety of colonial rule, ardent calls for independence, and enticing visions of a better, autonomous future continued to spark passions well into the 1930s. To the large majority of Koreans, however, life in the late colonial period remained firmly wedded to the here and now. Even to those who could afford to dwell on the grander issues, it was an open-ended time, and anything seemed possible. That soothing ambiguity would come to a screeching halt, however, once the colony became mobilized for war.

19
....
Wartime Mobilization, 1938–45

CHRONOLOGY

1935   Official order for school children and public employees to bow to the Japanese emperor
1937   Eruption of the (second) Sino-Japanese War
1938   Proclamation of wartime mobilization measures
1940   Shutdown of the two major Korean language newspapers
1940   Order to take Japanese names; organization of all Koreans into neighborhood patriotic associations
1942   Expulsion of Western missionaries
1945   Defeat of the Japanese empire in the Pacific War

THE VISIT BY AUTHORS YI KWANGSU AND CH'OE NAMSŎN TO JAPAN, 1943

Two of the foremost and best known Korean intellectuals of the colonial period, Ch'oe Namsŏn and Yi Kwangsu, made a discreet visit to Meiji University in Tokyo on November 24, 1943. This took place at the peak of the "Greater East Asia Holy War," so named by the increasingly strident propaganda effort that appealed for sacrifice from imperial subjects. Yi and Ch'oe traveled to Japan to assist this mobilization of manpower by urging a group of young Koreans studying in Japan to join the war effort as student soldiers. Afterward, the two writers gathered in a roundtable discussion with the event's host, another Korean author, to assess the reception and meaning of their message, and to expound on their motivations for their appearance. They also recounted their own experiences as young Korean students in Japan forty years earlier. Their lives thereafter had traversed the entirety of the period under

Japanese domination, during which they won recognition as two of the most pioneering and influential figures in Korean letters. That they found themselves in old age promoting the dissolution of Korean identity itself constitutes a profound if not tragic irony, as well as a microcosm of the final years of colonial rule as the country became swept up by war.

The experience of wartime mobilization left a pronounced imprint on Korea. It exposed Koreans to the horrific technologies of the most devastating war in human history, brutalized them through sexual slavery and forced labor, and stripped them of basic features of their ethnic identity, including even their names and language. Perhaps most significantly, these concluding years of Japanese rule came to dominate the prevailing perception of the colonial period as a whole, spawning a resentment, bitterness, and distrust among Koreans that would haunt their subsequent history. For despite the difficulties and extreme tensions of the wartime years, there remained a substantial minority of Koreans who took up the Japanese cause. Their numbers, in fact, likely were far larger than those of the celebrated independence activists, working mostly from outside the peninsula, whose impact proved greater in shaping Korea *after* liberation than in bringing it about. As with Yi Kwangsu and Ch'oe Namsŏn, the actions of these "collaborators" during the wartime mobilization period have ceaselessly challenged ongoing attempts to arrive at a reckoning of Korea's colonial experience.

INDUSTRIALIZATION AND STATE DOMINATION

Every society immersed in a modern war has faced the ferocity of mass mobilization, and in the ruthless spectrum that ranged from food rationing to Stalinism or the Holocaust, Koreans' experience during the Second World War likely sat closer to the latter. But while the litany of abuses can readily be dramatized to fit a narrative of unrelenting horror, the experience was uneven in its severity, depending on one's socioeconomic standing, geographical location, and, terribly for many women, gender. And while the hardships seem to have come in many forms and touched every facet of Koreans' lives, they mostly resulted from the intensification of two phenomena that had been growing for a couple of decades.

First was industrialization, which began sporadically in the early years of the twentieth century and received a major kick-start

Manchuria as a cauldron of modern Korea

The formative experiences of the two dominant Korean historical figures of the second half of the twentieth century, Kim Il Sung and Park Chung Hee, took place in Manchuria during the last decade of the colonial period. Kim Il Sung (b. 1912), who went on to rule North Korea for fifty years, grew up in Manchuria and eventually led the most successful of several anti-Japanese communist guerilla groups operating in tandem with their Chinese counterparts. In contrast, Park Chung Hee (b. 1917), long-time president and the person most closely associated with South Korea's accelerated economic development in the 1960s and 1970s, came of age as one of the few Koreans selected for training in the Japanese Military Academy in Manchuria. Though they both exploited nationalist sentiment to bolster their rules later, this strong contrast in their experiences as young men in Manchuria decisively shaped their respective destinies, and in turn those of their states, following liberation in 1945. In fact, throughout the first half of the twentieth century, Manchuria, both before and following the establishment of the Japanese puppet state of Manchukuo in the early 1930s, served as Korea's great frontier, the place to which Koreans could escape to forge a new life. In turn the forms of communal existence established there appear to have influenced significantly the social and political patterns back home.

Manchuria's pivotal role in Korean history was not a modern novelty, however. Since the ancient beginnings of state formation in northeast Asia, the peoples of Manchuria had supplied an impression of the (uncivilized) Other against whom Koreans conceived their own ethnic or national identity. As late as the seventeenth century, after the Manchus subdued Chosŏn on their way to conquering China itself, Manchuria continued to compel Koreans to sharpen their sense of self. The name for certain Manchurian tribesmen, *Orangk'ae*, in fact became synonymous with a common derogatory reference to the northern peoples—

⠀⠀⠀▮▮➤

whether Malgal, Khitan, Jurchen, Mongol, or Manchu—and turned into the default Korean term for "barbarian." This tendency also reflected the nostalgia for a mythical era when Koreans were said to have ruled this territory, and in turn the likelihood that Koreans, deep in their collective sub-consciousness, understood that they and these "barbarians" might have common origins. Japanese colonial rulers also promoted this idea by integrating their two conquered territories of Korea and Manchuria into a single extension of the Japanese homeland, claiming that this process reconstructed an ancient civilizational bond. Whether in spurring resistance to (Kim) or embrace of (Park) this process during the late colonial period, Manchuria's function as the cultivator of Korean leaders, and as the experimental cauldron of Korea's modern existence more generally, continued its long historical role of shaping Korean identity.

during the 1920s, and especially in the 1930s following Korea's transformation into a base for Japanese expansion into the Asian mainland. The economic growth that accompanied this shift had turned Korea's urban areas, especially Seoul, into centers of advanced consumer and popular culture. The colonial government's demand for industrial expansion and infrastructural improvements stimulated the cycle of occupational diversification, increasing expectations for economic opportunity, and urbanization. During the 1930s, and particularly in the wartime years, the mass movement of people extended beyond the peninsula as well, as peasants escaped rural poverty and followed work opportunities to Japan and Manchuria, where Korean capitalists even established factories. These mass migrations would present a major challenge to social stability following liberation in 1945.

The intensification of economic activity occurred throughout the 1930s. The most dramatic leaps in industrial output and the accompanying socioeconomic development, however, came with the shift to a wartime footing. Following the eruption of hostilities between Japan and China in 1937 and the formal proclamations of wartime mobilization measures in 1938, Koreans experienced a precipitous surge in the range and intensity of economic activity. The established sectors of early industrialization, such as textiles and food processing, were joined by the rapid growth of heavy industries catering to war: armaments, chemicals, machinery, and oil and gas. Factories churning out these products began to concentrate in special corridors along the west-central and north-eastern coasts, and the numbers of Korean factory workers and managers increased exponentially in line with equally enormous increases in industrial production. By the closing months of the war in 1945, industry accounted for nearly 40 percent of the total economic output in Korea, which a decade earlier had still been overwhelmingly agrarian.

For the most part, this remarkable expansion was not designed to improve the lot of the Korean people themselves. In Korea, the deprivation from mobilization for twentieth-century war was made worse by the colonial state's overbearing efforts to intensify both the economic *and* "spiritual" fortitude of its subject people. The colonial state, in short, instituted a relentless drive toward total war. This in turn reflected the state's development into an entity that actually surpassed industrial growth as an institutional force in the wartime years. In channeling the economy toward war, the colonial state forcefully blunted organized worker actions throughout the peninsula, even in the rural areas, where strikes by peasant unions had become increasingly vociferous. The searing trials of both urban and rural laborers undergoing these battles with factory owners and the state would contribute greatly to the creation of a proletariat in the concluding years of colonial rule.

The state's impact on the people's lives reached its comprehensive peak in the radical assimilation policies of the wartime years. Colonial authorities had always mouthed assimilation as a central goal, and indeed had explicitly stated this as a motive for annexation in the first place. But the irreconcilable reality of ongoing legal discrimination in the colonial system—from bureaucratic recruitment and compensation to segregation in educational and business opportunities—had marginalized this objective. Beginning in the latter 1930s, however, as war loomed in the air, the colonial state began to institute measures to coerce a psychological identi-fication with the Japanese empire—to turn Koreans into "imperial subjects"—that veered toward totalitarianism. In 1935 came a government order for Korean schoolchildren and public employees to begin their day with a ritual bowing toward the east in honor of the Japanese emperor, soon followed by orders for Koreans to make visits to Japanese religious shrines. These steps intensified the battle with Korean Christian groups that would end with the expul-sion of all Western missionaries from the peninsula in 1942. The authorities also began to prohibit children from speaking Korean in school. The two major Korean language newspapers were shut down in 1940. And as if to put a final stamp on the drive to suppress a separate Korean identity, in 1940 came the promulgation of what has often been considered the most egregious order, that to adopt Japanese names. The authorities instituted this measure more to streamline surveillance and mobilization of the subject people than to humiliate them, and disregarding this directive did not result in legal repercussions for everyone. But soon it became clear that, for anyone whose livelihoods depended on the colonial system—for example, professionals—taking a Japanese name was unavoidable. The harrowing tales of honorable Koreans forced to dishonor their ancestry by registering their new names tend to inflate the ultimate impact of this measure. Undoubtedly, however, the name-change law carried great weight as a symbol of the forced assimilation campaign, which continued to spread through slogans such as "Japan and Korea as One Body."

Also in 1940, a year before Japan escalated its conflict against China into a Pacific War that eventually embroiled the US, came the order for all Koreans to be organized into ten-family units of Neighborhood Patriotic Associations. This reflected the colonial state's quest to achieve complete control over human and material resources through penetrating surveillance and security. These neighborhood associations facilitated rationing and a comprehen-sive system of extracting "common good donations," of both food and materials, that forced people, especially in the last few years of the war, into desperate measures to feed themselves. Everything eventually became appropriated for war; indeed, the state even arrogated the choice of shoes and clothing that people wore. The term "total mobilization" ("soryoku," Kor. "ch'ongnyŏk") became pervasive, attached to a torrent of new regulations as well as to all kinds of groups organized according to occupation, region, and even religion.

For Koreans, it would be difficult to recall anything worse than the severe economic deprivations of the wartime mobilization period, especially in the countryside. However, two other phenomena would eventually rival rural immiseration both in terms of severity and in their impact on Koreans' memories of this period. The first was the descent of workforce mobilization into forced labor. Eventually thousands of Koreans, whether they were drawn by deceptive promises of employment or simply abducted, filled the labor shortages in Manchuria, Japan, and newly conquered Japanese territories such as Sakhalin Island. In munitions factories, shipyards, sweatshops, and mines, these Koreans led lives of unremitting toil amidst often dangerous conditions, with little food, no pay, few chances to escape, and diminishing chances of survival. Many of the descendants of those who did survive still live in Japan and Sakhalin Island, now part of Russia. The other, and by now the most publicized wartime atrocity, was the roundup of thousands of young women into the "Comfort Corps" forced prostitution rings servicing imperial soldiers on the battle fronts throughout the expanding Japanese empire. As with those Koreans who eventually found themselves in coerced labor conditions, these females were either kidnapped or lured out of their villages with promises of economic opportunity. The extraordinary horrors that they experienced in these brothels can hardly be imagined. But beginning in the 1990s, as they neared the close of their lives, survivors gradually came forward with wrenching stories recounting their ordeals, following a lifetime of hiding what they deemed an unspeakable shame. These accounts incriminate the collusion of colonial authoritarianism with the long-held nexus of sexual vulnerability and social status, a practice that readily fell prey to the depredations of wartime mobilization.

RESIGNATION, COLLABORATION, AND
MODERN IDENTITY

Given such harm inflicted on the Korean culture and people, how, one may ask, could there have been so many Koreans who collaborated with Japanese colonialism during wartime, and indeed actively promoted the efforts at extreme mobilization? At one level, it is not that difficult to answer: many Koreans earned their livelihoods or otherwise benefited from the colonial system. And many of them, as well as others, sincerely believed that the best outcome for the Korean people—not necessarily for Korea's status as a politically autonomous nation-state, which might have been less important—was incorporation into and support for the Japanese empire's pursuit of war. This would explain the thousands of civil servants, businessmen, intellectuals, artists, educators, and other professionals who publicly encouraged fellow Koreans to contribute to the war effort and renounce their Korean loyalties. Even more confounding is that central figures in the formation of modern Korean identity later came to advocate its obliteration. This is why the case of Yi Kwangsu and Ch'oe Namsŏn is so compelling.

It would be no exaggeration to call Yi Kwangsu and Ch'oe Namsŏn the two most influential intellectuals of the early twentieth century, and indeed perhaps the two seminal figures in the formative period of modern Korean culture itself. Yi, author of what is considered the first modern novel (and possibly still the most famous one), *Heartless* (1917), became the standard-bearer for Korean fiction writing in the colonial period. And Ch'oe, a pioneering poet and publisher whose innovations, beginning with his poems "Song of the Seoul-Pusan Railroad" and "From the Sea to the Boys," along with his literary journal, *Boys*—all unveiled in 1908—established the stylistic foundation for modern Korean poetry. But these two figures' influence extended beyond literature, as both played active roles in educational campaigns, scholarship, and, most intriguingly, causes for Korean independence. Ch'oe Namsŏn, in fact, authored the stirring March First Declaration of Independence of 1919. His turn into a vocal supporter of the Japanese war effort, then, would be akin to Thomas Jefferson's joining the British forces in the

War of 1812. Granted, Ch'oe shunned political activism and even demurred from actually signing the Declaration of Independence, but he also produced foundational works of scholarship on Korean history, religion, and language. Yi Kwangsu, for his part, published essays that adamantly called for reforming Korean customs and character to prepare for eventual autonomy. He also idolized his mentor, the celebrated independence activist An Ch'angho, who died in 1937 while recovering from a prolonged bout in a Seoul prison.

In their roundtable discussion following their November 1943 speeches to a throng of Korean students studying in Japan (see Image 19), Ch'oe and Yi rehashed the by-then familiar arguments calling for Koreans' support for the war effort: that Korea had a great deal to gain from Japanese tutelage; that the real enemy was the Anglo-Saxon civilization that threatened to destroy the East Asian one; that it would be an honor for the individual, family, and nation to sacrifice one's life for this great cause. Interestingly, Ch'oe Namsŏn also alluded to the findings of his historical research, noting that in ancient times—before Korean civilization had become "soft" through a preoccupation with literary pursuits under Chinese influence—Korea was much like Japan: militarily oriented. Indeed, Ch'oe notes, these ancient Koreans who had migrated to Japan were likely the ancestors of the samurai themselves!

Image 19   Ch'oe Namsŏn, Yi Kwangsu, and children's author Ma Haesong at the roundtable discussion in Tokyo, November 1943. (Courtesy of *Sŏjŏng sihak.*)

For his part, Yi, who appears in the transcript through his Japanized name, betrays an anxiety that his message should have been better received by the Korean students, who still seemed overly attached to their Korean identity. As if to accentuate such a naive innocence of youth, Ch'oe and Yi spend the rest of the discussion recounting their own formative years, starting four decades earlier, as students in Japan. This experience, they note while praising each other, had provided the springboard for their major accomplishments in developing Korea's modern literary culture.

It is somehow fitting that these two giants took an intellectual stroll through the entire colonial experience. Much more had emerged than modern Korean literature and culture; the colonial period in many ways had stood as the intensive cauldron of modern Korea as a whole. Within a relatively short span of three decades, Korea had experienced nearly the full spectrum of changes that took one-and-a-half centuries to take hold in, say, colonial India: urbanization, industrialization, state-led development, nationalism, communism, social restructuring, and so on. By the early 1940s much of Korea, especially the urban areas, looked fundamentally different than in 1910, and throughout the country a pervasive feeling of permanence arose regarding Japanese colonial rule. Even the dislocations of wartime mobilization reinforced the sense that Koreans were simply cogs in the wheels of the Japanese empire. For many Koreans, then, resignation, not "collaboration," was almost unavoidable and equated simply to accommodation with the inexorable changes of modernity.

What complicates matters is that the wartime mobilization included the excesses of forced labor and sexual slavery, as well as the horrors of wartime combat itself for many caught outside the peninsula. In other words, the ultimate judgment on the so-called collaborators cannot escape consideration of the colonial period as a whole, which in turn cannot disregard the crimes of the wartime years. Given what happened in the subsequent Korean War, it is not difficult to believe that, had Korea remained independent, the wrenching trials of modern change would have resulted in horrors of one kind or another, either among Koreans or committed by Koreans on other people. The terrible events, however, cannot be detached from the reality that Korea was ruled by a foreign power, and this makes fingering and condemning Korean collaborators almost inevitable, however simplistic. The suffering of Koreans was one thing, but for Koreans to assist the Japanese colonial system in committing abuses invites outrage. As in France's periodic soul-searching regarding its Vichy past, the complicity to horrific crimes (in the French case, the Holocaust) is almost overshadowed by the more facile condemnation of national betrayal—collaboration with a longtime foreign rival turned hated ruler. In this sense, to most Koreans today, the wartime mobilization period represented a fittingly ignoble end to the despicable enterprise of colonial rule as a whole. To forgive the Korean collaborators from the wartime mobilization period would be as unfathomable as acknowledging any positive results from the colonial experience.

THE GRAND NARRATIVE: INDEPENDENCE MOVEMENTS

The most ready alternative to a more forthright engagement with the issue of collaboration in the wartime era, and indeed of the colonial period itself, has been to focus on the celebrated efforts by Koreans to fight for their independence. These are well known, hailed as evidence of a resilient national spirit. Among the renowned leaders was Syngman Rhee, who spent most of his lifetime in the US trying to use his patchy connections to the Washington elite in order to influence American foreign policy. There were also Kim Ku and Kim Il Sung, who fought alongside the Chinese nationalists and Chinese communists, respectively, in the common struggle against Japanese imperialism. By the 1940s, in fact, Kim Ku acted as the *de facto* leader of the Korean government in exile that had originated in the spring of 1919. He even formed a Korean Restoration Army from his base in China, with hundreds of soldiers ready to charge into the peninsula. There are several problems with the traditional focus on these movements, however: first, these organizations were all operating outside the peninsula; second, they were splintered and commanded little cooperation from each other; finally, and not unrelated to the first two issues, these movements had little to no effect on actually bringing about liberation from Japanese colonial rule.

The heroizing of these freedom fighters is understandable, given that they at least made great sacrifices for the cause of independence, and given the demands of constructing the modern narratives of nationhood; indeed, the North Korean political system has always been utterly dependent on this story. But their historical significance lies more in understanding the history that followed than the history for which they are honored. That their role in achieving Korean liberation was far greater in legend than in actuality bespeaks the complexities of the colonial experience as a whole.

20

....

The Liberation Period, 1945–50

CHRONOLOGY

1945 August	Liberation from Japanese colonial rule
1945 September	Formation of the Korean People's Republic
1945 September	Start of the Soviet occupation in the north and American occupation in the south
1945 October	Return of Syngman Rhee and Kim Il Sung to Korea
1945 December	First Soviet–American Joint Commission, announcement of trusteeship
1946 October	Mass general strike in southern provinces
1947 April	Dissolution of the Joint Commission
1947 July	Assassination of Yŏ Unhyŏng
1948 April	The Cheju Island Uprisings
1948 May	Elections for members of the National Assembly in southern Korea
1948 June	Syngman Rhee elected president of southern government by National Assembly
1948 August	Proclamation of the Republic of Korea (South Korea)
1948 September	Proclamation of the Democratic People's Republic of Korea (North Korea)
1948 October	Yŏsu-Sunch'ŏn Rebellion
1948 December	Passage of the National Security Law
1949 June	Promulgation of the South Korean land reform
1949 September	Dissolution of the Committee for Investigating Anti-National Behavior

THE MAY ELECTIONS IN SOUTHERN KOREA, 1948

On May 10, 1948, in southern Korea, people formed long lines waiting to do something they had previously only heard about: choosing government officials in a national election. These first-time voters were electing legislators for the provisional National Assembly that would be charged with devising a constitution for the Republic of Korea. These citizens were responsible, then, for helping to establish a new Korean government. That this government would come into being three years after the end of Japanese colonial rule, and that its jurisdiction would cover only the southern half of the peninsula, encapsulated the uneasy circumstances leading to this momentous event. The jubilation that had greeted liberation from thirty five years of Japanese colonial rule in the summer of 1945 had quickly shifted to a more somber realization that freedom from Japan did not mean freedom from foreign rule. Indeed the division of the peninsula into separate northern and southern occupation zones headed by the Soviet Union and the US, respectively, turned the peninsula into the first Asian theater of the emerging rivalry between these Second World War allies: the Cold War.

For Koreans in the southern zone, the American occupation would bring forth greater political and economic freedoms than the Japanese colonial period had, but an almost equally repressive stifling of their aspirations for autonomy. The unremitting clashes between American priorities and Korean goals, American disregard for Korea's internal dynamics versus Korean ignorance of geopolitics, and often bitter divisions among Koreans came to dominate the "liberation space" in the southern occupation zone. This tense five-year period between liberation in 1945 and the Korean War in 1950 brims over with historical significance, primarily because it must be viewed in relative terms: unable to escape the foreshadowing of the Korean War, but also bound inescapably to the colonial legacy. One can consider the liberation space a transitional period from colonial subjugation to national division, a short-lived interregnum between two devastating wars, or a wasted opportunity to reset Korea's modern historical trajectory. In any case, what took place at this time would cast long, dark shadows over the rest of Korea's twentieth century, and indeed frame the perspective on Korea's modern experience as a whole.

THE PRIMACY OF POLITICS: A MULTI-LATERAL DYNAMIC

Korea's modern history appears to be dominated by politics, so intense and rapid have been the political changes and their repercussions. The intrusion of politics into every other sphere of existence was never more acute than in the post-liberation period. Political interests and conflicts, from village disputes over property and ideology to the geopolitical rivalry between the Allied victors-turned-occupiers, seem to have overwhelmed everything else. Complicating the situation even further were the constant shifts in the political forces arrayed against and alongside each other: the two occupation armies and governments, the various Korean organizations of all ideological stripes, the emigrant workers and independence activists returning to their homeland, those who benefited from as well as those victimized by the colonial wartime mobilization, and so on. There simply was little room in the liberation space for much else beyond politics.

This reality seemed far-fetched during the enormous celebrations that spilled into the streets beginning on August 16, 1945, the day following the Japanese emperor's proclamation of unconditional surrender that had been heard by some on the radio. The joyous news spread like wildfire, and for several days Koreans marched up and down urban boulevards shouting and waving placards and makeshift symbols like the Korean flag. For some, however, this was not a surprise. A few days before liberation, the Japanese colonial leaders had asked the man they considered the *de facto* Korean leader still in the country, Yŏ Unhyŏng, to form a provisional governing organization. Yŏ, a moderate leftist, consented to this request and quickly formed the Committee for the Preparation for Korean Independence (CPKI). Scarcely could he have known that, upon the signal for Koreans to exercise their new freedoms, a host of other political groups would emerge to push a variety of interests and ideologies. This was a portent of things to come.

By early September the CPKI gave way to the Korean People's Republic (KPR)—like the CPKI a coalition of ideological and political interests—which served as the central governing institution connecting the hundreds of "people's committees" that sprang up around the country. The people's committees lie at the heart of a great historical debate concerning this period, namely, whether the Korean population in the south, aroused by the destabilizing demobilization of wartime society—including the return of those

Koreans who had been abroad—sought a leftist social revolution. Despite their name, however, the people's committees and even the KPR appear to have represented diverse concerns of disparate localities. Indeed the most pressing, common item on their agenda was to secure local order and ensure a rectification of the traumas caused by the wartime dislocations, the first steps in the great challenge of decolonization. To be sure, many of the people's committees quickly fell under the sway of the promises and prowess of Korean communists emerging from their underground existence, but clearly most of the participants themselves had little inkling of the larger communist program. Indeed the KPR's original platform called for nothing more radical than standard labor laws and the redistribution of ill-gotten gains. There was hardly a set ideological agenda in this preparatory period of flux.

The KPR leaders, in fact, chose as their chairman a right-wing nationalist, Syngman Rhee—by far the best-known independence activist—who still was making his way back to Korea from a decades-long exile in the US. With the American government's help Rhee arrived in Seoul in mid-October, ready to pursue his long-held dream of leading Korea's first independent government. His homecoming, however, came a few days after that of Kim Il Sung, the former leader of a communist guerrilla band in Manchuria, who accompanied the Soviet army into the northern zone and was introduced by the Soviet authorities to cheering crowds in Pyongyang. In late November, the final major independence activist from abroad, Kim Ku, a right-nationalist who had led the Korean Restoration Army and Provisional Government in China, made his triumphant return. All three figures returning to the peninsula would ultimately exert far greater power than their domestic counterparts.

That foreign-based Koreans came to dominate the post-liberation political space, a somewhat discomfiting reality in hindsight, had much to do with the fact that the Allied forces, and not Koreans themselves, liberated Korea. And, as the agents of liberation, the two Allied powers determined the ultimate fate of the country, which meant that they were also the immediate agents of national partition. Well before the end of the Pacific War, in fact, the Soviets and Americans had agreed on an allocation of wartime responsibilities that would place the Soviets in a prime position in the northeast Asian mainland, while the Americans would be busy with Japan. When the Americans suddenly realized in August of 1945 that this would likely result in the Soviet Union's occupation of the entire Korean peninsula, they proposed a split occupation. Surprisingly, the Soviets accepted, even though the Red Army could have easily driven down the entire length of the peninsula, and even though the thirty-eighth parallel dividing line placed Seoul in the American zone.

Thereafter the two occupations determined what was politically acceptable in their respective occupation zones. The Soviets, as unaware and unprepared for their occupation as the Americans were, had to deal with a strong right-nationalist and Christian tendency in the populace, particularly in the northwest. It recognized the Korean People's Republic and the people's committees while ensuring that Kim Il Sung and other Korean communists would gain the upper hand in political struggles (see Chapter 22). Americans in the south, for their part, found their situation even more complicated and harried. Much of this difficulty arose because, as they had desired, the Americans controlled the capital of Seoul, the major stage and prize of political contestation. From the perspective of Korean political actors vying for influence in Seoul, the American occupation would constitute the dominant factor in their struggles against each other. The two occupations, in turn, used this intra-Korean strife to further secure their own favored political outcomes in their respective zones.

This complex dynamic became apparent almost immediately, with the announcement by the superpowers in late December of 1945 of a five-year trusteeship over Korea, an idea originating from Allied summits during the war. This promptly triggered vociferous opposition from just about everyone in the country. The communists, though, quickly changed their stance to support the trusteeship, and thus began the most conspicuous, though not necessarily the most important, source of division among Korean political interests. Henceforth the right wing solidified itself around opposition to the trusteeship, which became a convenient bogeyman for excluding and suppressing leftist opponents, who could be tarred for taking a treasonous stance. The United States Army Military Government in Korea (USAMGIK), with its own set of concerns about the Left, assisted this effort, maintaining its role as primarily an enforcer of anti-communism and cultivator of pro-American political forces. The de-classified military intelligence documents from the very beginning of the southern occupation demonstrate clearly the premises, suspicions, and ignorance that colored American perceptions of Korean actors. And various stripes of right-nationalist Korean interests were keen to goad the occupiers into reckless actions.

IMPLANTING THE SOUTHERN SYSTEM

Anti-communist autocracy, then, became the hallmark and bulwark of the American military government, and of South Korean political rule for another forty years. The southern system took hold, however, not only by matching the American occupiers' inclinations—including, ultimately, the acceptance of a separate southern government if necessary—but also by eliminating rival political forces. The communists and other leftists were dealt with most harshly (see below). Even moderates, however, who pursued a coalitional solution to the great challenge of establishing a unified government amidst rival superpower occupations, faced constant harassment and pressure. Syngman Rhee and Kim Ku, the two right-nationalists with the largest followings, maneuvered incessantly to block any outcome that might incorporate moderates in a power-sharing arrangement. The most conspicuous victim of this dynamic was Yŏ Unhyŏng, the widely revered leader who had led the earliest Korean governing order in the summer of 1945. Yŏ was assassinated in July of 1947, just as he appeared as the only viable alternative to the far right. The rightists had recognized this, and they eliminated Yŏ from the scene. As it turned out, with him died any chance for moderates to survive in this volatile political atmosphere.

The American occupation, too, did its part in ensuring the victory of the immoderate right wing. One of the first major steps taken by the American leadership after marching into Seoul in the fall of 1945 was to declare illegitimate the people's committees in the south, absurdly suspecting this vast collection of disparate groups as uniformly left-revolutionary. Afterwards, USAMGIK paved the way for the triumph of the Right, not by intervening in the disputes among political leaders as much as by clamping down on any popular or mass activity the occupation deemed too close to communism. Beginning in the spring of 1946 and over the course of the three-year occupation, the American military and rightist constabulary forces incarcerated thousands of leftist activists and killed hundreds of them. This intractable American orientation was sufficient to prohibit leftist politics from vying for any realistic influence in Seoul. As for its dealings with the Soviet occupation through the occasional gatherings of the Joint Commission, which sought to work out a unified governing solution, USAMGIK, like its Soviet counterpart, was never prepared to countenance any Korean government that smacked of the opposing occupation. After yet another failure to come to terms in the spring of 1947, it became clear that the deadlock had only tightened. Thus the Americans sought to shift responsibility to the United Nations while promoting the formation of a provisional governing council in the south. Headed by Syngman Rhee, this council purged leftists and combined various militias and paramilitary groups into a policing force that would carry out a thorough, often brutal cleansing of political opponents from the scene. As for the UN, it declared its first priority to be the holding of a UN-sponsored election for a new Korean government. Given that the Soviets refused to participate in this effort, in effect the elections would establish a government for only southern Korea.

The United Nations forged ahead with these plans even after being refused entry into the northern occupation zone in early 1948. And so, over increasingly vocal resistance, on May 10, 1948, elections were held to choose representatives for the National Assembly, the first concrete step toward establishing a separate southern state. By all accounts, the people demonstrated great enthusiasm, as voters waited patiently in long lines for this new privilege of electing their political leaders. Those so chosen gathered in Seoul at the end of May and selected Syngman Rhee as the Assembly's speaker, then voted promptly to implement a presidential system over a parliamentary one—clearly a reflection of Rhee's increasing hold on power. On June 20, Rhee was elected by the Assembly as the new president, establishing a pattern for indirect presidential elections frequently used later in South Korea to maintain dictatorial rule. Indeed, despite the outwardly liberal constitution of the new Republic of Korea, what was inaugurated on August 15, 1948—on the third anniversary of liberation—was a South Korean government that would use its dogged claims of jurisdiction over all of Korea to justify repression. (The separate North Korean government, formally established a few weeks later, would be no different.)

Little wonder, then, that throughout the liberation period in the south, anti-state and anti-imperialist sentiment grew, as people became aware that liberation from Japanese colonialism was not leading to independence or even to national unity. The discontent was exacerbated by rampant inflation, unemployment, and poverty in the first year of the occupation. This in turn fed the swelling labor movement stirred by leftist interests, and in the fall of 1946 a massive general strike that began in the southern industrial city of Taegu shook the nascent southern system. The resulting crackdown by police and military forces resulted in the deaths of hundreds of strikers, policemen, and officials. The other major group of resistors in the south were the so-called *ppalch'isan* ("partisan"), communist guerrillas who, while under constant siege, still managed to wage resistance campaigns in the spring of 1948 after the separate southern elections were announced. They also appear to have instigated the eruption of a major uprising on Cheju Island off the south coast, as protests against the southern elections turned into a major insurrection by hundreds of combatants. The response by the south's paramilitary forces, though, was excessive, sweeping, and horrific, as whole villages were wiped out indiscriminately and tens of thousands of innocent bystanders were killed. Later in the fall of 1948, some members of these militia forces themselves rebelled against the southern system in the cities of Yŏsu and Sunch'ŏn on the south-central coast. The rebels, quickly joined by communist guerillas holding out in the surrounding mountains, managed to capture many towns in the region before being chased back to the hills by the military. As with the Cheju Island episode, the government response was brutal, and over half of the captured instigators, numbering in the hundreds, were summarily executed by firing squad. The Yŏsu-Sunch'ŏn Rebellion would be the originating backdrop for the acclaimed multi-volume novel (and later, film), *The T'aebaek Mountains*, which depicted people already caught up in the ideological polarization, political violence, and terrible recriminations that would soon mark the Korean War itself.

A TROUBLING HISTORICAL SHADOW

Notwithstanding its short duration, so much importance is attached to the liberation period between 1945 and 1950 that it constitutes a fulcrum of modern Korean history. Lodged between the long colonial ordeal and the Korean War that solidified national division, the abbreviated liberation space has chronically tugged at contemporary South Koreans' sense of self, an uncomfortable reminder of what might have been. What if the Allies had left the country alone following the end of the Second World War? What if the Americans had supported the moderate elements that sought a coalitional solution to the political divisions? What if Yŏ Unhyŏng had lived? And, what if decolonization had truly been achieved, when it appeared most people considered this the most pressing issue?

Beyond political autonomy, so the thinking goes, decolonization would have addressed above all the injustices and severe hierarchies of the late colonial period, hence overturning the economic and political privileges associated with Japanese colonialism. The American military government, ever wary of Soviet influence and communist ascendance, cracked down on the people's committees and left in place the police and high officials of the colonial system as a way of ensuring stability. For similar reasons, the right-nationalists such as Syngman Rhee and Kim Ku found the American preoccupation with communism a convenient facilitator of their own political aims. The landed and business interests, though sometimes in contentious relations with Rhee, would have been the targets of any purge of late colonial elites, along with the police and high bureaucracy, and hence these groups in the end had to throw in their lot with Rhee. Rhee helped to salvage their privileges in late 1948, when he implemented the National Security Law, the all-purpose tool of the state's suppression of political opposition down to the present day. In the summer of 1949, a land reform to address the inequities from the colonial period (achieved in northern Korea in early 1946) was finally promulgated, suggesting that the landed elites were in danger of losing their most entrenched advantages. But later, in the fall, Rhee, under the pretext of anti-communist cleansing, forcefully dissolved the year-long criminal court investigating the most notorious pro-Japanese collaborators.

The historical narratives of responsibility for both national division and the Korean War are thus dramatically complicated by the reality of multiple divisions among Koreans and the unsavory behavior of many influential actors. In the search for what went wrong, the overarching impact of the superpower occupations, of course, cannot be discounted, but ultimately the actions of Koreans themselves must be, and recently have been, the focus of attention. Even if southern Korea in the liberation space was not really on a path toward leftist social revolution, what did happen in the southern zone has cast a troubling historical shadow over South Korean state and society: the uneasy examples of ready complicity with another foreign occupier, the brutal suppression of political opponents and innocent bystanders alike, and the preservation of late-colonial sociopolitical privileges, the vestiges of which remain powerful today.

21

· · · · · · · ·

The Korean War

CHRONOLOGY

1948–49	Training of North Korean troops in China
1950 January	US Secretary of State Acheson's declaration of American defense perimeter
1950 June 25	Outbreak of the Korean War; Northern army pushes Southern army south
1950 September	General MacArthur's "Inchon Landing"; Allied forces drive back northern army
1950 October	Chinese intervention in the Korean War on behalf of the North
1953 July 27	Armistice to end the war

THE CHINESE ENTRANCE INTO THE KOREAN WAR, OCTOBER 1950

The Chinese military had intervened in peninsular affairs several times before the twentieth century. In the late nineteenth century alone, the Chinese thrice helped put down Korean rebellions—first an insurrection by a group of Korean soldiers in 1882, and then in 1884, when radical enlightenment activists attempted a coup. Finally, in 1894, Chinese troops arrived to assist the Chosŏn government in quelling the massive Tonghak Uprising, a move that would launch the 1894–5 Sino-Japanese War and bring an end to China's preeminent standing in Korea. In earlier Chinese interventions, the stakes were even higher: the Ming dynasty's assistance in saving Korea from the Japanese invasions of the late sixteenth century; and the Tang dynasty's alliance with Silla to conquer the two other kingdoms on the peninsula in the seventh century, which led to the first unified Korean polity. The lone Chinese military intrusion of the twentieth century, that of October of 1950, would also play a crucial role in the founding of a Korean state, but this time, in the context of the emerging Cold War, the beneficiary was not Korea as a whole, but rather a part.

The flooding of the battlefront by hundreds of thousands of Chinese soldiers brought about a startling turn in the tide of the Korean War, which by the closing months of 1950 had been approaching a decisive victory by the US-led United Nations forces. The Chinese soldiers, along with their North Korean allies, quickly pushed the front down to the middle of the peninsula, where the Korean War had started a half-year earlier, and where it would be waged for another two-and-a-half years, with tremendous bloodshed, until the Armistice of July 27, 1953. By then, Chinese intervention had been integral not only to the Korean War, but also to the emerging Cold War order that engulfed the Korean peninsula, and indeed the entire East Asian region.

CIVIL WARS AMIDST THE COLD WAR

The Korean War that began in 1950 is commonly cited as the first "hot war" of the Cold War, the confrontation between the capitalist and communist blocs that dominated the second half of the twentieth century and still leaves Korea divided today. One could argue, however, that this designation should apply to an even earlier conflict, the Chinese civil war of 1945–9 between the communists, with the backing of the Soviet Union, and the nationalists, who were supported by the US. Having cooperated for the common anti-Japanese cause in the Pacific theater of the Second World War, the rival Chinese parties almost immediately turned their guns on each other after the Japanese defeat in 1945. After four years of fighting, the communists under Mao Zedong drove Chang Kai-shek's nationalists to Taiwan. The nascent polity of North Korea might have played a small role in the Chinese civil war. Kim Il Sung's ties to China from his youth and his contemporary bonds with fellow communists led to a contingent of North Korean troops training under, and perhaps fighting for, the Chinese communists. This relationship, which was subsequently highlighted by both sides, might have provided valuable experience in forging a crack North Korean fighting unit.

The opposing forces leading to Korea's civil war originated in the colonial period and were dramatically incited by the reoccupation and division of Korea in the immediate post-liberation period (see Chapter 20). These same forces would render the conflagration unleashed by these crack North Korean troops almost an inevitability by the first half of 1950. Syngman Rhee himself, the South Korean president, clearly agitated for a US-backed move toward forcible reunification, and his soldiers along the increasingly fortified frontier with North Korea came close several times to sparking a full confrontation. The North Korean troops returned the hostility in kind with their own provocations. These skirmishes reflected the bitter divide that had arisen, amidst the pressures of superpower rivalry, out of an array of interests in the first few years after liberation. As in China, while one must not lose sight of the profound divisions among Koreans that constituted the core factors leading to civil war, the geopolitical context framed the outbreak and progress of the conflict.

Kim Il Sung's decision to launch the Korean War, in fact, required adherence to the pecking order of the communist bloc. Recent research from de-classified archives and other sources have pointed to the strained efforts of the North Korean leader to gain permission and assurance of support from the heads of the Soviet Union and China. For this, Kim played the two leaders, Josef Stalin and Mao Zedong, off each other. Stalin first had to consent to Mao's returning thousands of North Korean troops left over from the Chinese civil war. Kim then found it relatively easy to convince Mao that the North Koreans should proceed with a communist-led military reunification of the fatherland, just as Mao had done. Mao, though wary of American involvement, even offered Kim Chinese military assistance, but Kim Il Sung was convinced that such help would not be necessary, so quickly and decisively would the North Koreans overwhelm their southern counterparts. Plus, American Secretary of State Dean Acheson had flatly stated in early 1950 that South Korea lay outside the US defense perimeter, suggesting strongly that the Americans likely would not get involved. Still, a cautious Stalin, while begrudgingly permitting Kim to seek his desperately sought unification and providing North Korea with strategic and material assistance, required that traces of Soviet involvement be eliminated. And with such assurances came the go-ahead for the invasion.

6–25

"Six-Two-Five" (*Yug-i-o*) is the simple, powerful term for the Korean War among Koreans, in the same way that "Nine-Eleven" suffices for Americans in reference to their signal moment in recent history. At dawn on June 25, 1950, the Korean People's Army launched a full-frontal assault over the thirty-eighth parallel border and, despite the saber-rattling that had been going on for months, this attack came as a major surprise. The South's lack of preparation showed clearly in the Northern army's easy rampage to Seoul, which it captured in two days, trailing just behind the massive flight of refugees streaming southward. Koreans throughout their history had experienced these sudden invasions that turned their world upside down, but never from their own national brethren. There was no advantage of local knowledge in fending off the invaders this time.

Indeed, as the Northern army chased the refugees and the Southern forces southward and quickly captured most of South Korea within a few weeks, it was joined by the leftist guerillas holding out in the mountains, as well as by communist sympathizers hiding within South Korean society. Together they instituted a swift revolutionary change in the occupied territories: land was redistributed, leftist political prisoners were released, and prominent local leaders, intellectuals, and businessmen were arrested, killed, or taken up north. The Southern army, for its part, took little care to discriminate between possible northern collaborators and regular citizens as it committed atrocities on its southward retreat. So began the cycle of recriminations and reprisals that would victimize hundreds of thousands of mostly innocent bystanders and constitute one of the greatest tragedies of the Korean War. The brutal cleansing of suspicious elements and radical restructuring of social relations emulated, in telescoped fashion, the North Korean revolution itself from 1945–50 (see Chapter 22), and it set the stage for reciprocity once the tide of the war changed and towns were reoccupied by the opposing side. The people of Seoul, which the North Korean leadership had claimed to have "liberated" in June 1950 and went on to change hands four times in the first half-year of the Korean War, would bear some of the worst retributions in this truly vicious cycle.

The first major turning point of the war took place while the "Pusan Perimeter," the roughly forty-mile radius around the south-eastern port city, held off the North Korean siege long enough for the United Nations to organize an American-led recapturing of the South. In September of 1950, through the famous "Inchon Landing," just to the west of Seoul, the American forces, led by General Douglas MacArthur, attacked the North Koreans on the backside as UN reinforcements were sent into the south. This in effect squeezed the Northern forces through a pincer movement. The retreat of the Northern army up the peninsula thereafter was almost as swift as its sweep down the peninsula a few months earlier. The combined US-ROK forces recaptured Seoul and within a few weeks had chased the People's Army out of Pyongyang as well. In its flight northward, the North Koreans made sure to destroy both the property and persons that might assist the Southern forces. These horrific sights failed to deter the American military commanders' push up the peninsula, all the way to the border area with China, in their determination to take a complete and quick victory, which, by late 1950, seemed well in hand.

CHINESE INTERVENTION AND THE STALEMATE

It was not as if the American army failed to foresee the potential intervention by the Chinese People's Liberation Army on behalf of the North Koreans, as reconnaissance flights showed columns of Chinese troops assembling close to the border. Apparently, however, the American commander, General MacArthur, believed the Chinese would never engage American might. (There remains speculation that MacArthur might actually have sought to provoke a wider confrontation as a way of overturning the communist victory in China. If so, he badly miscalculated both the formidable military challenge presented by China as well as the degree of support he would enjoy back in Washington.) When the Chinese did enter the war beginning in early November 1950, the sheer scale and suddenness of the invasion delivered nothing less than a stunning blow, as hundreds of thousands of Chinese troops chased the joint US–ROK forces back down the peninsula. Only after the joint Chinese–North Korean forces recaptured Pyongyang, then briefly even "re-liberated" Seoul, did the UN forces put a halt to the southward advance and press the front just to the north of Seoul, where it would remain for the next two-and-a-half years.

The stalemate of the rest of the war from early 1951 to mid-1953 refers to the lack of movement of the battlefront itself, which shifted little until the Armistice of July 1953 and ultimately left the country divided along the same thirty-eighth parallel where the war had started. This was the Korean War of the American film and TV series *M*A*S*H*. But the notion of a stalemate should not lead us to consider these two-and-a-half years a respite, for the relentless destruction of this period led ultimately to the greatest tragedy of all in the Korean War: the decimation of the population and landscape, with ultimately little to nothing accomplished other than millions of deaths and a bitterness and distrust singed into the memory of all actors. To North Koreans, the stalemate brought constant siege in the form of American bombs, napalm, and other carriers of devastation that left the North, by the summer of 1953, with few major buildings remaining standing. This is also the memory of the war that the North Korean leadership has sustained and incited as a reminder of American brutality, and thereby also as a reinforcement of its own legitimacy. To the Chinese, the Korean War is remembered as the conflict in which Chinese "volunteers" bravely kept American imperialism at bay. Today, the sacrifice of thousands of these Chinese soldiers prompts the grief of Chinese tourists who visit the site of a major battle of the war in the border town of Ch'ŏrwŏn, just south of the Demilitarized Zone separating the two Koreas. Ch'ŏrwŏn in fact remains an open-air museum, with artifacts from the Korean War battles displayed in plain view as a

Image 21   The shelled-out headquarters of the South Korean Communist Party from the Korean War, left intact in Ch'ŏrwŏn, South Korea, near the border with North Korea. (Author's photo.)

reminder of South Koreans' own sacrifices and need for vigilance (see Image 21).

As it had done throughout the course of Korean history, China once again played a key role in determining the character and fate of the Korean nation. The hyper-nationalist historical narrative in North Korea has deleted China's contributions toward preserving the country during the Korean War, just as Chinese assistance in fending off the Japanese invasion of the sixteenth century has been officially forgotten. But the replay of historical motifs is striking. Chinese intervention in the Korean War arose first and foremost from its own interests, this time to maintain a buffer against American domination of East Asia. As was often the case in the long history of Chinese–Korean relations, Chinese influence framed the place of Korea in the larger East Asian regional order—politically, economically, and culturally. China's participation in the Korean War also symbolized the peninsula's distinctively modern entanglements as well. Indeed, Korea remains one of the few places on the globe where the Cold War still has powerful remnants. In fact, while the stage has changed dramatically, the primary geopolitical actors in the early twenty-first century affecting the peninsula are the same as those during the Korean War: the US and China. And given the increasing ties today between China and South Korea as well, Chinese actions likely will affect significantly the ultimate fate of Korea in the near future, just as they did in 1950, and just as they have done throughout much of Korean history.

22

....

Early North Korea

CHRONOLOGY

1945 August	First Soviet incursions into northern Korea; liberation from Japanese colonial rule
1945 September	Soviet Central Administration established; Cho Mansik asked to head a coalitional governing body
1945 October	Kim Il Sung introduced by Soviet occupation to cheering crowds in Pyongyang
1945 November	Massacre of Christian nationalists in Sinŭiju
1946 Spring	Initiation of comprehensive land reform in the northern occupation zone
1946 November	Elections for the interim northern legislature
1947	Establishment of the People's Army
1948 September	Formal establishment of the Democratic People's Republic of Korea
1950–53	Korean War
1955 December	Kim Il Sung's speech introducing the concept of *Juche* to party propagandists
1956	Failed attempt to oust Kim by Soviet-backed Korean communists
1957	Beginning of the *Ch'ŏllima* heavy industrialization campaign
1962	Purge of novelist Han Sŏrya, the leading propagandist for Kim Il Sung's personality cult
1968	North Korean seizure of the *USS Pueblo*

KIM IL SUNG'S "JUCHE" SPEECH, 1955

To an audience of propaganda officials of the North Korean Communist Party in late December of 1955, Kim Il Sung delivered a historic speech that introduced the concept of "Juche" (*Chuch'e*), the ideal of

213

self-reliance that would become the country's ruling ideology. Kim's emphasis, as it would be for the *Juche* concept itself, lay in forging a distinctively Korean path to socialism through a focus on national history and customs. The mistakes made thus far in North Korea, he claimed, stemmed from an excessive dependence on external models, particularly those of the Soviet Union. Not coincidentally, this speech came amidst a purge of Kim's political rivals, targeting especially those Soviet-Korean communists who had come to the country as Soviet occupation advisors. Indeed, despite the outward appeals for achieving "peaceful reunification" by presenting a stellar model of Korean socialism in the north, this historic speech and its political context pointed directly to the solidification of Kim's political power. It encapsulated the core elements in the politics, economy, and culture of the early northern system and launched the dominion of *Juche* as North Korea's ideological justification for Kim's absolute rule.

North Korea's comprehensive transformation in the first two decades of its existence, beginning in 1945, laid the groundwork for its more familiar late-twentieth century form. By the early 1960s, Kim Il Sung stood as the undisputed source of political authority, and the country had embarked on a heavy industrialization campaign that would speed the North past its southern counterpart in economic development. Furthermore, the reordering of society into categories that reflected this political and economic collectivization, a process that had begun in the post-liberation period, was by now well in place. Kim's speech in 1955 outlining the basic principals of *Juche*, which nourished the idea of self-reliance with a fierce nativism and wariness of the outside world, also demonstrated his regime's preoccupation with history—history as knowledge, but also as an ideological tool. As it turned out, this obsession with historical orthodoxy constituted a cover as well as a corrective for dependence.

LIBERATION SPACE NORTH KOREA

There remains considerable debate about the Soviet impact on northern Korea during the liberation period from 1945 to 1950. The more that previously classified Soviet documents have become accessible, however, the more it appears that Soviet influence was paramount and indeed decisive in determining the political outcome in the northern occupation zone. This should be expected, but such a revelation goes completely against the North Korean historical orthodoxy as well as substantial scholarship that has forwarded a dominant role played by domestic forces in shaping the northern system. The stakes are as high as they are for South Korea (Chapter 20), for this issue gets to the heart of North Korea's historical legitimacy and purported independence, touted by *Juche* ideology as the foundation of North Korean existence.

The Soviet occupation, however, faced almost as much difficulty in bringing about its desired outcome in North Korea as the Americans did in the southern occupation zone. Like the Americans, the Soviets, who entered Korea as combatants a week before the end of the Pacific War on August 15, 1945, were unprepared to administer the country and utterly ignorant of their new territory. The Soviet Central Administration (SCA), the makeshift governing organization of the Red Army in Korea, stumbled onto a complex scene, with a diverse population characterized by ideological differences that overlapped with socioeconomic, religious, and regional ones. The regional characteristics of northern Korea, deeply rooted in history and shaped considerably by the colonial experience, showed that while the northeastern region had conditions conducive to communist growth, the northwestern part of the country—where Pyongyang lay—was a stronghold of Korean nationalism.

The nationalists in this area tended to be landed, with strong business influences, and Christian. All of these strains were embodied in the most respected and well-known figure in the north, Cho Mansik, a Presbyterian elder who had steadfastly resisted colonial assimilation and mobilization efforts. He was, in this sense, the northern zone's counterpart to Yŏ Unhyŏng, the left-moderate who commanded a great following in the south before his assassination in 1947. Cho was not killed until 1950, but the SCA, after turning originally to him in September of 1945 to head a Soviet-friendly coalitional governing body, found him recalcitrant in opposing communism and any hint of national division. He was arrested by 1946, but the Soviet occupation's difficulties with him reflected the bitter divisions in northern Korea that had developed between Protestant nationalists and Soviet or communist elements. An early outbreak of violence in this struggle took place in November of 1945 in the border city of Sinŭiju, on the Yalu River, when a Christian protest against the Soviet occupation sparked a massacre of dozens.

One of the great ironies of North Korea is that Kim Il Sung, this country's dominant communist figure, came from a typical Protestant household in Pyongyang. The Soviet occupation officials' fateful decision, in October of 1945, to promote Kim as the prospective Korean leader came only after their failure to win over Cho Mansik, whose anti-communism stemmed from his religiously-inspired nationalism. Unlike Cho, Kim wielded little influence over the populace, despite his being known to some as a famed guerilla leader from the 1930s who had managed to escape the Japanese hunt for him. After four years of living quietly in the Soviet Union from 1941 to 1945, the period when his son, Kim Jong Il, was born in Siberia, Kim accompanied the Soviet army's entrance into his home city in late September, 1945. In a large mid-October rally in Pyongyang staged to celebrate the Soviet occupation, Kim was introduced to a cheering crowd as one of several featured Korean leaders, including even Cho Mansik. But through cunning, ruthlessness, charisma, considerable political skill, and a lot of luck, Kim gradually won enough confidence from the Soviet authorities to take, step-by-step, the reigns of the native political system in northern Korea.

Henceforth it became difficult to separate Kim Il Sung from the fate of the northern communist party, for the two grew together in stature and authority under Soviet auspices. Beginning at the end of 1945, the Soviets gradually placed Kim in the leading party positions and provisional governing structures, which took increasing responsibility over administration in the north. And the northern communist party eventually superseded the Seoul-based party in the southern zone—acting, in fact, like a typical Soviet government. The election for an interim northern legislature in November of 1946 was a classic Soviet-style, single-candidate ballot. By late 1947, a separate northern regime, backed by a powerful People's Army, was effectively in place, along with the usual accoutrements of a Stalinist state. Even the personality cult surrounding Kim was on early display in the enormous celebrations in Pyongyang on August 15, 1947, the second anniversary of liberation. In a scene that would become familiar later, film footage of this event shows Kim, firmly entrenched on his perch and flanked by Soviet officials, overlooking the adulatory spectacle, much of which is devoted to hailing him (along with Stalin). Large portraits and statues of Kim also appeared around the country well before the Korean War.

We should be careful, however, before dismissing Kim Il Sung and the communist party as creatures solely of Soviet favor. By most indications, there was substantial popular support for the actions taken by the northern political authorities, and Koreans themselves directed key components of what became a quick and true social revolution—systematic, indeed totalizing, in scope and ambition. By the first half of 1946, a comprehensive land reform stripped large landowners and others deemed social enemies, such as colonial period officials, of their property and redistributed it to the peasantry. The intensive reorientation of the economy and culture followed suit, making life in the north uncomfortable, if not dangerous, for landlords, businessmen, professionals, and colonial-era bureaucrats. To the northern leaders, the mass exodus of these former social elites southward to the American occupation zone represented good riddance, allowing the northern regime to consolidate power with relatively little competition (and bloodshed). What remained was a northern society and culture primed for shaping by a determined communist party controlling an ambitious, and in many ways typical, communist state. The strength and military prowess of this state, in particular, was on full display in June of 1950, when it launched the Korean War.

THE FORMATIVE FIFTIES

North Korea's recovery from the complete devastation of the Korean War began immediately, and with a flourish: An intensified effort not only to rebuild, but to reconstruct society from the ground up, quite literally, through political integration, ideological discipline, cultural uniformity, and accelerated industrialization. However, while the post-Korean War 1950s represented the most formative period of North Korean history, this process did not start from scratch, despite the decimated landscape. A strong foundation for the developments of the 1950s had been laid in the post-liberation period, the most critical element of which was Kim Il Sung's political ascendance.

Kim had garnered the Soviet and Chinese go-ahead to launch the Korean War, for which he acted as the North's chief military commander. As was the case in South Korea with Syngman Rhee, the Korean War served ultimately to solidify Kim Il Sung's grip on political power. But also like Rhee, Kim found himself still facing challenges to his absolute rule, which the December 1955 address to the communist party's propaganda officials attempted to overcome. This so-called *Juche* Speech indeed emphasized self-reliance, autonomy, nativism, and absolute national unity— the pillars of the comprehensive *Juche* ideology that later came to be identified with North Korea. In a tacit rebuke of the war effort, Kim claimed that the overt dependence on foreign models and ideas, including even the international communist movement itself, had hindered North Korea's progress. And hence the party workers must turn to a focus on Korean customs and conditions, in particular Korea's distinctive historical experience. "Only when we educate our people in the history of their own struggle and traditions can we stimulate their national pride and arouse the broad masses to revolutionary struggle," he exhorted. This is what constitutes the spirit of *Juche*, he noted—an overarching approach, more than a term, that considered Korean realities before "mechanically copying" external forms.

The flip side of this Korea-first theme was a diatribe against some internal political forces, whom he accused of toadyism. Indeed Kim called out the guilty parties by name, including Pak Hŏnyŏng, who had been executed just a few days earlier on charges of being an American spy. Pak had been the leader of the domestic Korean communist movement at the time of liberation, but he soon found himself in the wrong occupation zone, that of the south. Following his move to the northern sector in 1947, he gained some appointments to high posts, but ultimately his fate mirrored that of the domestic communists themselves—that is, he lost out in the intra-communist struggle for power. By the mid-1950s, Kim Il Sung actually found the greatest challengers to his own faction, the former guerillas from Manchuria, to be not the domestic communists but rather the Soviet-Koreans, who stood as embarrassing reminders of his own dependence on the Soviet Union. These Soviet-Koreans attempted, in fact, to oust Kim in 1956 through a targeted campaign of open criticism and appeals to the Soviet Union, but Kim, thanks partly to the groundwork laid by the 1955 speech, outmaneuvered and eliminated them from the scene. This might have been a signal moment in North Korean history, a potential turning point that was not to be. The last rival group remaining toward the end of the 1950s, the Chinese-based Korean communists, also met their fate, though not without considerable struggle.

These purges of Kim's political rivals, then, required a shift in the North Korean system itself from a Soviet-sponsored state to one of greater autonomy. But in fact, aside from the ousted figures themselves, the Soviet ways of doing things were still preeminent; indeed the methods of eliminating political opponents—from the show trials to the trumped up accusations of espionage, anti-party activity, and "factionalism"—displayed Kim's reliance on the Soviet template. Kim in fact was moving North Korea toward a firmer Stalinism just as many other communist states, led by the Soviet Union itself, began to repudiate it following Nikita Khrushchev's famous speech in early 1956 denouncing the Stalin personality cult. Kim also owed a considerable debt to Mao Zedong, the Chinese communist leader whose espousal of paternalistic, even Confucian, dictatorship as the way to gain maximum subservience provided Kim a blueprint for his own efforts. Kim even appropriated from Mao many ideas related to cultivating a blend of nationalism, communism, and personality cult.

These strands of foreign influence were also on prominent display in the great effort, called "Ch'ŏllima" (after a legendary flying horse of Korean folklore), to collectivize and industrialize the North Korean economy beginning in the late 1950s. The nationalization of industry, along with other economic measures such as currency reform, had begun in the years just preceding the Korean War by exploiting colonial period infrastructures, especially in hydroelectric generation and mining. The *Ch'ŏllima* campaign completed this process and launched a mammoth effort focused on heavy industries, such as construction, steel, and agricultural and military machinery. It required—and gained, it appears—a tremendous mobilization of labor, which resulted in a substantial increase in North Korea's economic output and living standards. The campaign was contemporaneous with and similar to the doomed agricultural collectivization effort in Mao's China, the Great Leap Forward, but it avoided China's mass starvation—mostly because North Korea's agricultural mobilization was limited in scope. Still, the foreign connections continued to play a central role: the promulgation of Soviet-style fixed-period development plans; the contributions of Soviet-Korean experts; the major impact of the Chinese troops stationed in North Korea until 1958 in terms of security and reconstruction; and the ongoing economic aid coming from China and especially the Soviet Union that paid for many spectacular North Korean gains. By all accounts, that is precisely what allowed North Korea's economic growth to outpace that of South Korea from the late 1950s through the 1960s.

Such a collective fervor for reconstruction manifested itself in cultural mobilization as well, as culture became thoroughly politicized into a form promoting nativism and the Kim Il Sung-led state. This process had already developed considerably in the post-liberation period, as music, theater, literature, paintings and sculptures, and cinema became immersed in revolutionary state-building. As in communist societies elsewhere—and ironically, given the Marxist emphasis on the material basis for historical development—ideological and cultural training was perceived as paramount in fortifying mass support for the sociopolitical system. Divergence into "frivolous" or "empty" expression, the coded terms for art that was not goal-oriented toward a display of "socialist realism," came under attack in the 1950s. Aesthetics had to service ideology. Cultural practitioners who had originally moved to or stayed in North Korea as a haven for their leftist ideals soon found themselves at the mercy of political developments, none more potent than the ongoing solidification of Kim Il Sung's authority. The novelist credited with devising the aura of Kim's personality cult, Han Sŏrya, became the most prominent and powerful figure in North Korean literary circles, himself leading many of the 1950s purges of suspect writers. But tellingly Han, too, eventually fell victim to the whims of politics and was purged in 1962, never to be heard from again.

JUCHE, HISTORY, AND LEGITIMACY

Perhaps the most dramatic and enduring ideological outcome of this intense political concentration and mass mobilization came in the shaping of a new historical perspective. As Kim indicated in his 1955 speech, the most urgent task for propaganda workers—and presumably for society at large—was to focus on the essential lessons of Korean history. As elaborated upon later but clearly present already in the 1950s, the self-reliance constituting the core of *Juche* ideology could not be divorced from a strong consciousness of Korea's historical experience, in particular the suffering from foreign intervention. North Koreans were taught that, throughout the nation's history, including the most recent experiences of colonization and the Korean War, the outside world had consistently brought harm. But under the revolutionary leadership of Kim Il Sung, Koreans could finally escape this destructive pattern. At the most simplistic but comprehensible level, this narrative made tremendous sense. One can understand, then, why the North Korean people could have found this message of confidence and optimism appealing, especially in tandem with real gains in their standard of living and with a redress of grievances grounded in the inequities of the recent past.

The fabrication of historical details to shape this grand narrative began in the post-liberation period and gained momentum through the propaganda activities of intellectuals like Han Sŏrya. All of Korean history eventually came to be seen as an unrelenting

The Pueblo Incident

To put a cap on the economic recovery, social stability, and political consolidation achieved by the mid-1960s, in the summer of 1966 North Korea's national soccer team stunned the world by defeating heavily favored Italy in a World Cup match. As if this triumphant event emboldened the North Korean regime amidst the increasing volatility in northeast Asia at the time, over the next three years it aggressively challenged its sworn enemies, the US and South Korea, through a series of incidents that together appeared as resumption of unfinished business from the Korean War. The most notable such provocation was the so-called Pueblo Incident, in reference to the North's capture of the American naval intelligence vessel *USS Pueblo* in early 1968.

Just a couple of days before this event, on January 21, 1968, a group of thirty North Korean commandos had attempted a raid on the South Korean presidential compound, resulting in the deaths of nearly all the assassins and scores of South Koreans. Apparently, however, news of this event had not reached the *Pueblo*'s officers, who continued their surveillance off the peninsula's east coast in what the US considered international waters. Speedy North Korean boats, claiming American infringement on North Korean territory, attacked the *Pueblo*, boarded the ship, and took into custody its crew of over eighty. Thereafter the crisis surrounding the fate of those sailors preoccupied a segment of the American government for the rest of the year. After months of negotiations behind the scenes that resulted in a formal apology from the US for having entered North Korean waters, the crew was released. Immediately thereafter, upon learning of the abuse and torture that the sailors had endured while held in captivity, the American government retracted its apology. But the damage had been done.

The Pueblo Incident was followed by the hunt for a large group of North Korean soldiers who had landed off the east coast of South Korea in the fall of 1968. In the spring of 1969, North Korean fighter jets shot down an American naval surveillance plane, killing a crew of over thirty. To the US and South Korea, these incidents presented proof of the need to maintain vigilance; to North Korea, they reinforced the chronic sense of threat from American imperialism as well as from its South Korean "puppet." Today the *USS Pueblo*, presented as a tourist attraction while docked on the banks of the Taedong River in Pyongyang, continues to serve the interests of the North Korean regime's legitimation narrative, just as it had done in 1968.

Image 22   The captured ship *USS Pueblo* on display on the banks of the Taedong River, Pyongyang, 2003. (Courtesy of Tae Gyun Park.)

struggle against harmful external forces and exploitative internal elements, such as those Koreans who collaborated with the Japanese colonialists and American occupiers. In service to Kim's political ascent, his colonial period struggles against the Japanese in Manchuria underwent transparent inflation, even gaining credit for having achieved Korea's liberation in 1945. The Soviet Union's precipitous fall in significance in the historical orthodoxy thus paralleled its descent in political influence in the 1950s. Indeed, in the 1950s, as the North Korean regime's legitimacy became more firmly hitched to Kim's credentials as an independence fighter, his official biography gave him another boost, this time hailing him for saving Korea from American imperialism as well. Kim lashed out at the US for having launched the Korean War, seeking world conquest, and desiring to "enslave" the Korean people. For evidence, he noted, one needed only to look at what had happened to South Korea since liberation. The strong implication behind this emerging North Korean historical orthodoxy was that only a great historical figure—namely, Kim Il Sung himself—could rally the people to learn from their experiences. This self-serving narrative sought to instill a dependency on Kim by equating him with the fate of Korean civilization itself.

The historical irony was inescapable, compelling, and, given North Korean history as a whole, tragic: this narrative stemmed from efforts to hide Kim's dependence on, as much as to tout his resistance to, outside forces. The Soviet occupation put him in power in the first place, and then China's intervention in the Korean War preserved the nascent state itself. The lofty *Juche* rhetoric of fierce autonomy and nativism that accompanied the North's increasing isolationism in the early years, then, compensated for the fact that North Korea the country, and Kim Il Sung the leader, began with and were sustained by external assistance.

23

....

1960s South Korea

CHRONOLOGY

1960 March 15	Rhee government rigs election for vice president; protests against Rhee in Masan
1960 April 19	Outbreak of student demonstrations and violent crackdowns around the country
1960 April 26	Resignation of Syngman Rhee
1960 June	Establishment of the Second Republic, a parliamentary system of government
1961 May 16	*Coup d'état* engineered by Major General Park Chung Hee
1961–3	Rule by the Supreme National Reconstruction Committee, headed by Park
1962	Promulgation of the First Five-Year Economic Development Plan
1963 September	Election of Park Chung Hee in presidential election, start of Third Republic
1964 March	Student protests against prospective Normalization Treaty with Japan
1965 May	Dispatch of first contingent of Korean troops to Vietnam
1965 June	Signing of the Normalization Treaty with Japan
1967 May	Re-election of Park; establishment of Pohang Iron and Steel Company and Kuro Industrial Park
1969	Mass opposition to constitutional amendment allowing a third presidential term for Park

DEMONSTRATIONS AGAINST THE NORMALIZATION OF RELATIONS WITH JAPAN, SPRING 1964

In the spring of 1964, as throngs of young people in Britain and the US were enraptured by Beatlemania, their counterparts in South Korea also filled the streets for mass gatherings, but for a far less joyous occasion. With news that the South Korean government was close to reaching an agreement to formally reestablish diplomatic ties with Japan, Korean students exploded in protest. To them, the shameful period of Japanese colonial occupation, especially the horrors of wartime mobilization, remained a contemporary event. They could not fathom why the South Korean government, under the direction of President Park Chung Hee, would even consider such a thing. Their demonstrations reached a crescendo in June of 1964, when tens of thousands of students disrupted campus life throughout the country and invited a government crackdown as well as the imposition of a state of emergency. Such a back-and-forth between students and state power would act as defining moments for much of the 1960s, just as they did in other parts of the world.

It turned out that Park Chung Hee had authorized secret negotiations for this breakthrough agreement with Japan not long after he came to power through a military coup in 1961. Park considered the normalization of relations, in particular the capital investment and technology transfer that it would bring, a cornerstone of his plan to modernize the nation's economy. Historical judgment has largely looked favorably upon the "miraculous" economic development that marked the second half of the twentieth century in South Korea, and the 1960s, under Park's direction, is considered the take-off period for this stunning phenomenon. But as the student protests and other forms of resistance against governing authority indicated, the particular pattern of economic growth institutionalized in the 1960s—driven by the combination of a military government and big business—faced significant resistance. These challenges, too, would characterize the 1960s, and indeed, much of the subsequent history of South Korea.

DICTATORSHIP, DEMOCRACY, AND REVOLUTIONS

Student demonstrators, in fact, had acted as the catalyst behind the major event that opened this decade. When Syngman Rhee, whose presidency in the First Republic descended into despotism and corruption in the post-Korean War 1950s, attempted to steal another election in the spring of 1960, the unrest that followed led to his overthrow. The occasion this time was his government's blatant rigging of the polls for vice president, with examples of massive fraud such as ballot stuffing conducted in the open. Rhee was perhaps emboldened by the fact that his own electoral opponent for the presidency had died shortly before the election—interestingly, the second Rhee opponent to die under such circumstances (and still another being executed for treason in 1956). The anti-Rhee protests gained momentum initially in the southern coast, and with the discovery of the body of a student protestor killed by a tear gas canister in the city of Masan, students in Seoul rose up, only to be met with a brutal crackdown themselves. On April 19, 1960, this led to the explosion of student demonstrators hitting the streets throughout the country, with the most furious clashes with the police coming in Seoul and reaching a scale of mass protest not seen since the immediate post-liberation period. Hundreds of demonstrators were killed before Rhee, under pressure from a wide range of political and social sectors, including university professors, agreed to step down and go into exile in Hawaii (where he died in 1965). Even at the time, this series of events was referred to as a "revolution," for it brought down a dictatorial system and displayed the power of popular action.

What followed the April Student Revolution was Korea's first experiment in full-fledged democracy. The pronouncement in June 1960 of the Second Republic, a parliamentary system with the president merely serving as a figurehead, unleashed creative energies and accompanied a spike in civic cooperation and volunteerism, along with a dose of optimism. Chang Myŏn, selected as the prime minister, ruled through a coalition of mostly conservative elites who had grown weary of the Rhee dictatorship. In addition to the eradication of blatant corruption at the top of the government, some major policy shifts took place under Chang's leadership. One of these reforms was the extension of electoral democracy to the provinces. In December 1960, for the first time in Korean local elections—which did not reappear until the 1990s—people went to the polls to directly elect provincial governors and the mayor of Seoul. This, too, constituted a revolutionary step.

Naturally, with the loosening of the state's grip came the license also for people to protest their conditions more freely, which intensified a re-polarization of politics. Large-scale unrest starting in late 1960 reflected a worsening economy, especially high unemployment, although the situation had actually improved compared to the end of the Rhee era. The Chang Myŏn government responded with the implementation of public works programs, including the construction of a nationwide transportation infrastructure. Such episodes represented the natural growing pains attendant to any such experiments in electoral democracy, and they did not necessarily constitute a threat to the nascent system. But what might have tipped the scales toward placing this democratic experiment in a precarious state were student demonstrations in early May 1961 calling for immediate reunification with North Korea. Such a step, the students claimed, represented the true spirit of the April Student Revolution. The military, ever sensitive to any softening regarding communism, responded swiftly. On May 16, 1961, troops under the command of Major General Park Chung Hee occupied government offices and immediately pronounced another revolution that emphasized first and foremost the need for anti-communist vigilance. It represented the third "revolution" in thirteen months, and another shift in the long historical arch of struggle between students and dictatorships in South Korea.

PARK CHUNG HEE

No person is more associated with South Korean history than Park Chung Hee. For good and bad, in the pervasive historical perspective on the second half of the twentieth century, he is inseparably linked to the combination of authoritarian state-making and rapid economic development. That he remained as the apex political figure for almost two decades, from 1961 to his assassination in 1979, naturally explains his historical prominence, but this endurance also reflects Park's long-term approach to South Korea's pressing needs. As with most dictators, he convinced himself of his continuing indispensability. Such a mindset began to appear with greater clarity toward the end of the 1960s, setting the stage for the descent into iron-fisted rule in the 1970s.

Park's compelling background reveals much about his world view and actions once in power. Born into a poor rural family in the south-central part of the country in 1917, he experienced first hand the decay of the countryside, a theme that would preoccupy him in office. Gifted and ambitious—his hero as a boy was Napoleon—he took advantage of all the opportunities made available by Japanese colonialism to escape his conditions. Following a stint as a school teacher in his native region, in the early 1940s he became one of the few young Koreans selected to receive training in a Japanese military academy in Manchuria. There, and later in the metropole itself, he imbibed the lessons of the rapid modern transformation of Japan, in particular the military's preeminence in the Japanese approach to governing. As with many of his compatriots who came of age in the late colonial period, his affinity for Japan, or at least the Japanese model, did not subside, even after liberation. He developed a fierce nationalistic streak as well, and that perhaps explains his brief participation, as an ROK officer, in the anti-American, anti-Rhee resistance in the late 1940s following liberation. He was captured and implicated, in fact, in the Yŏsu-Sunch'ŏn Rebellion of 1948, and only the intervention of an American officer on his behalf—Park had become entangled in his brother's more explicitly leftist guerilla activities—spared his life. For the Korean War and the rest of the 1950s, Park retreated to the South Korean military, gradually ascending the ranks and cultivating a following among officers that would prove decisive later.

Although he spent most of the 1960s as a civilian president, his approach to rule throughout the decade was militaristic, from the way he gained power through a coup to the regimentation of politics, society, and economy that his reign implemented. The Military Revolutionary Council and then the Supreme National Reconstruction Committee through which Park ruled the country from 1961 to 1963 set in motion the mobilization of society along militaristically disciplined lines. His "revolutionary" government in 1961 immediately set out to clean up the streets by eliminating blight and seedy social elements—rounding up and putting to work street kids, vagrants, and even gangsters, for example. To maintain surveillance and control over such unsavory elements and, later, opposition political figures, the notorious Korean Central Intelligence Agency (KCIA), the internal security apparatus of the military government, was also established in 1961. For most of the public, however, "reconstruction" became the all-encompassing word on people's lips, a shorthand for the comprehensive changes that would require destruction as much as construction: destruction of the old ways of thinking that led to corruption and decay, of the legacy of Korea's sad history that produced weakness and tragedy, and of the impoverishment that made the country an easy target for communism. As it did under Syngman Rhee's regime, anti-communism became a mainstay of Park's claims to legitimacy and method of rule. In the latter part of the 1960s, sensationalistic incursions by North Korean commandos and spies further stoked the government's anti-communist campaign.

Such a heavily military bent to the polity and society, and even to the economy and culture, actually complicates any general assessment of politics in the 1960s. Although it is common simply to label the entirety of Park's rule from 1961 to 1979 as an era of "military dictatorship," in the 1960s, at least, the military facet of rule outstripped the dictatorship. On the occasion of the formal transition to civilian government in 1963, Park shed his officer's uniform to run in the presidential election, which he narrowly won, but much of the cabinet and Park's top advisors came from the military. His re-election in 1967 was a more comfortable affair (over the same opponent, coincidentally) but, throughout the 1960s, Park had to deal with constraints imposed by the formalities of republicanism, including opposition from national assembly members, activists, workers, and especially students.

ECONOMIC TAKEOFF

Park made it clear that his highest priority throughout his first decade of rule was to lift the country out of poverty and set it on the path to economic modernization through industrialization. For the most part, he accomplished both of these goals, although it took the entirety of the decade, and the economy encountered problems with periodic shortages. Borrowing an approach found in communist systems, Park deployed the model of the "Five-Year Plan" for national economic development, with clear-cut goals and blueprints for pursuing a growth strategy managed by skilled bureaucrats. Park's government promulgated the First Five-Year Plan in 1962, the same year that it also designated the city of Ulsan on the southeastern coast a special industrial development zone. Ulsan would become the home region of the Hyundai Corporation's manufacturing juggernaut. By the end of 1966, the final year of the plan, there were indeed signs of major infrastructural and urban growth, as well as of the drive for exports gaining full force. One of the most visible transformations had taken place in 1964, when some areas in the country were the first to experience twenty-four-hour electricity provision, engendering a dramatic lifestyle change by expanding the scope of night time activity. Indeed, materially and otherwise, especially in the urban areas, conditions continued to improve, and the people's perspectives on the world, especially those of the youth, widened with greater exposure to foreign cultural and material products.

The Second Five-Year Plan, beginning in 1967, more explicitly targeted export-oriented growth as the primary goal, which would lay the foundation, in turn, for a shift toward heavy industry. That year the government finalized plans to establish a nationally-owned steel venture, the Pohang Iron and Steel Company, or POSCO. POSCO became incorporated the next year and went on to supply the major industries of shipbuilding, auto manufacturing, and construction through which South Korea became an industrial power. 1967 also witnessed the creation of a special export manufacturing zone in southwestern Seoul, the famed Kuro Industrial Park. With its concentration of toiling workers producing everything from shoes and clothes to machinery, the Kuro Industrial Park eventually turned into a symbol of the sacrifices and lives of the South Korean labor force. Korean workers, the economic miracle's backbone that the state and big business exploited for the comparative advantage of cheap labor, suffered conditions not unlike their counterparts throughout the modern world. Many South Korean workers fiercely resisted this heavy-handed state control and even won significant legal concessions through union actions, but prodded by calls for national sacrifice and the promises of material gain, they too mostly fell in line with the larger industrialization drive. This inclination, together with a dedication to education and training, made the work force the most indispensable element of the South Korean success story.

The biggest beneficiaries of the state-led, export-oriented industrialization drive, however, were the family-owned conglomerate companies, the so-called *chaebol*, a mostly pejorative term meaning "financial clique." Some of the best-known of these conglomerates today, such as Samsung and LG, began as small enterprises in the colonial period, while others, such as Hyundai, began shortly after liberation. By the 1960s, the government selected well-performing companies for targeted export-oriented production, rewarding them with cheap and big loans, easy licenses, tax benefits, and government guidance. The result was the astonishing growth of many of these companies into the "octopus"-like entities that came to dominate the South Korean economy. The families that controlled the conglomerates came to be followed as national celebrities, though not always flatteringly, and the tycoons who began these enterprises won listings in the pantheon of national heroes. Hyundai presented a prime example. Begun by Chung Ju Yung, a man from the east coast of what is now North Korea, as a transport service supplying the American military, Hyundai became perhaps the most celebrated beneficiary of government largesse in the 1960s. Hyundai's first major industry, construction, jump-started its rise through foreign building contracts in southeast Asia in the mid-1960s, while at home it won major infrastructural projects, including construction of the main national artery, the Seoul-Pusan Expressway, completed in 1970. Its second major industry, automobile manufacturing, began in 1967 with an agreement to build a Ford model in its plant in Ulsan. By the 1970s, Hyundai would produce and export its own car, the Pony, and by the 1980s it would penetrate the largest car market in the world, the US. Hyundai eventually expanded into shipbuilding, for which it became a global leader, as well as cement, chemicals, and even electronics. Today, like the other well-known *chaebol*, Hyundai is commonly seen as a standard-bearer for Korean industrial prowess, and even for Korea itself.

A final major factor in the 1960s economic takeoff, though one not easily discerned, can be deemed "association with America." The US affected the South Korean economy in several ways. Its dozens of military bases and tens of thousands of soldiers stationed around the country injected capital into the consumer economy. The American government's direct aid in the form of grants and loans provided the South Korean regime great leverage, through its control of the lending practices of major banks, in getting industry and labor to fall in line behind state-directed planning. There was also the considerable impact of American "soft power"—the widespread influence of American popular music, fashion, movies, and enter-tainers, some of whom, like Louis Armstrong, actually performed in Korea. These examples of soft power helped set trends and increase demand for American items, both cultural and material.

A more pronounced impact came from South Korea's troops sent to the Vietnam War, which, beginning with over 17,000 soldiers sent in 1965, came to comprise the second largest foreign contingent in Vietnam after the Americans. South Korea's participation stemmed from its service as a dutiful American ally, but the economic benefits also were enormous: in addition to gaining favorable treatment from the US government, South Korea became a major supplier of American military provisions, which added further to the national coffers supporting export-oriented industrial growth. Korean entre-preneurs, many as soldiers, flooded Vietnam, some making a fortune, with others sending smaller amounts back home, and still others using their Vietnam entrepreneurial experience as the basis for businesses and careers after their return. The total economic impact of South Korea's involvement in the Vietnam War in the 1960s, as with the Japanese investment of capital and technology, is difficult to measure, but proportionally it was far more significant than it was for the US. To the Korean youth, in fact, the image of Vietnam as a great opportunity for adventure and money making tended to over-shadow any anxiety.

YOUTH AND ANGST

Although both the participation in Vietnam and the normalization of relations with Japan played significant roles in South Korea's economic push in the 1960s, the youth culture displayed a starkly contrasting response to the two ventures. While many of the South Korean elite who had come of age in and benefited from the colonial period, like Park Chung Hee, might have viewed the prospect of reestablishing Japanese ties pragmatically, university students and other younger Koreans fiercely resisted this as a betrayal of the nation. Park himself made his first official visit to Japan in November of 1961, just half a year after seizing power, and his advisors engaged shortly thereafter in secret negotiations to reestablish formal diplomatic ties and attract an infusion of Japanese capital and know-how. When these quiet maneuvers were revealed and word spread in March of 1964 that the two governments were on the verge of an agreement, thousands of students spilled into the streets, engaging in clashes with riot police and even entering into mass protest fasts. By June, over ten thousand student demonstrators had risen up, inviting the promulgation of a state of emergency in Seoul. The spirit of rebellion was further fueled by a hit film released that year, *Barefooted Youth*—Korea's answer to *Rebel Without a Cause*—which portrayed the anxious and directionless existence of a younger generation falling victim to the constraints of customs and authority. Whether so intended or not by the filmmaker, Kim Kidŏk, this movie was taken as tacit support for the students protesting the prospective treaty with Japan. Alas, the delay in finalizing this treaty caused by the protests did not last long, and by June of 1965 the treaty was signed, followed by easy ratification in the government-controlled National Assembly later in the fall. The heavy-handed ratification process compelled the mass resignation of opposition politicians and the eruption of more student protests, which the government suppressed through a military occupation of college campuses.

These protests against the Normalization Treaty with Japan represented both the confluence and conflicts of economic, political, and cultural forces that drove the spirited decade of the 1960s.

While the strong state and big business moved the country in one focused direction, less powerful sectors of society, embodied especially in the students, pushed back, or at least demanded a reorientation of priorities, a reconsideration of consequences. This dynamic reappeared in 1969, as politicians and students rose up to block the prospective constitutional amendment that would allow Park Chung Hee to run for a third consecutive presidential term. Once again, universities were shut down and opposition political figures were stifled as the constitutional amendment, like the Normalization Treaty, was railroaded through the National Assembly before being approved in a national referendum. With this, the turbulent 1960s came to a close, setting the stage for the somber 1970s.

24

. . . .

Culture and Politics in 1970s South Korea

CHRONOLOGY

1970 April	Proclamation of the New Village Movement by Park Chung Hee
1970 May	Publication of Kim Chiha's narrative poem, "Five Bandits"; Kim's arrest
1970 November	Protest through self-immolation by young labor organizer Chŏn T'aeil
1971	Re-election of Park Chung Hee to third consecutive presidential term
1972 Summer	Joint declaration of reconciliation by the two Koreas
1972 October	Suspension of constitution; proclamation of the "Yusin" constitutional dictatorship
1973	Global oil shocks; kidnapping of opposition politician Kim Dae Jung
1974 April	Roundup of dissident students and activists, sentencing of many to execution
1974 August	Assassination of Park's wife
1977	Achievement of $10 billion in value of South Korean exports
1979 October	Assassination of Park Chung Hee; end of Yusin system

PUBLICATION OF KIM CHIHA'S "FIVE BANDITS," MAY 1970

Kim Chiha, a budding poet laden with personal travails from the 1960s, published one of his earliest major works in 1970, and was promptly arrested. His alleged crime, and that of his publishers, was violation of the Anti-Communist Law, although the poem in question, "Five Bandits," made no mention of support for North Korea or communism. It simply satirized the gross inequalities in South Korean society due to corruption, though in an unmistakably condemnatory and mocking fashion. For continuing to protest the political and economic injustices of the increasingly autocratic and rapidly industrializing South Korean system, Kim Chiha spent most of the 1970s in jail, even receiving a death sentence in 1974. Kim was not alone in lobbing criticisms of the dramatic changes that Korean society was undergoing, for the primary thrust of cultural expression in this period carried a political undertone. But Kim Chiha, through his connections and impact, can be seen as the embodiment of the watershed decade of the 1970s, the memory of which continues to be colored predominantly by the term, "Yusin," in reference to the constitutional dictatorship forcibly implemented in 1972.

Those who arose to counter and call attention to the abuses of the Yusin system included writers like Kim, artists, publishers, musicians, and religious leaders, in addition to the students and laborers who maintained their vanguard role. Indeed the 1970s witnessed the emergence of many major historical figures who would dominate lasting perceptions of South Korean history, and none more so than in the arenas of politics and culture. Whether explicitly or not, the most notable cultural developments of this decade, which reflected and affected broader historical currents to an extent unseen since the colonial period, were tinged with politics.

THE YUSIN DECADE

Not everything in 1970s South Korea was shaped by the Yusin system; it just seemed that way. Even the continuation of the remarkable economic growth through export-led industrialization and domination by conglomerate companies appeared to have been a handmaiden of politics. As is the case eventually with most dictators, Park Chung Hee became convinced of his indispensability and conflated his power with the people's welfare, although the country—partly due to the success of his policies, ironically— was very different in the early 1970s than a decade earlier. The October 1972 imposition of the so-called *Yusin* ("revitalization") constitution prohibited political dissent and in effect rendered Park president for life (which turned out to be true). The official justification for this move—which amounted to his second *coup d'état*, this time of a system that he was already heading—was to solidify the path toward reunification. Forced into a response to the Sino-American *détente* in 1972 that cast doubt on America's security commitments, the two Koreas had achieved some stunning breakthroughs in reconciliation talks, at least publicly, earlier in the summer that year. But the dictatorship clearly came amidst signs of growing dissatisfaction with Park's rule, as reflected in his less-than-convincing re-election in the 1971 presidential election. And soon after the inauguration of the Yusin system, the global oil shocks beginning in 1973 and the killing of his wife by an assassin in 1974 added further to Park's growing siege mentality. By the fall of 1979, amidst unmistakable indications of widespread, impassioned opposition to the dictatorship, Yusin came to an end with that of Park's own life at the hands of his own internal police apparatus. By then, the Yusin system had intensified the autocratic political approach of the 1960s and extended it to suppress all forms of dissent through a constitutional dictatorship that bordered on absolutism.

Such an ostensible comfort zone of total power provided Park the capacity to push through a state-led revamping of the countryside. The New Village Movement (*Saemaŭl undong*), which in some ways emulated the North's *Ch'ŏllima* movement in the 1950s, began in 1970 through a personal directive from Park. The New Village Movement quickly became the general catch-phrase for all efforts to improve the countryside and even was applied to an overarching spirit of reform that the government encouraged in urban areas as well. The mobilization of state resources focused first on improving the rural communities' basic infrastructure and appearance—removing, for example, the blight of thatched roofs, for which Park was said to have had a particular disdain. By the middle of the 1970s, the New Village Movement became a comprehensive effort, driven by a systematic, large bureaucracy that directed money, labor, and expertise to mechanization, irrigation, road construction, electricity, and the provision of consumer items. The goal was to improve agricultural output, to be sure, but also to close the gap in living standards between the city and countryside. Some historians view the New Village Movement, which continued in revised form into the 1990s, as having been more of a political ploy to divert excess materials, such as cement, and thereby tamp down any potential restiveness among the rural populace. But without a doubt the material welfare of rural Korea improved dramatically. The gains in agricultural efficiencies, however, did little to stem the steady stream of migration out of the countryside, and in fact might have accelerated it.

This movement of people to the cities and factories fueled the explosive growth of metropolitan areas, especially in and around Seoul, as well as of the major conglomerates, the family-controlled enterprises that expanded through the government-guided export drive. These companies propelled the industrialization of the South Korean economy to an emphasis on heavy industry and high technology, the products of which supplied the dramatic increases in the size of both the domestic and foreign markets. Companies like Samsung Electronics and LG (Lucky-Goldstar) produced a bevy of consumer products such as televisions and microwave ovens, while Hyundai and Daewoo manufactured big-ticket items such as automobiles and supertankers designed primarily for export. These and other enterprises also facilitated the remarkable mobilization of expertise and workers, in the tens of thousands, for large-scale construction projects overseas, especially the Middle East, to build power plants, water treatment facilities, roads, bridges, and big buildings. Such efforts resulted in the achievement, with great fanfare, of the $10 billion mark in the annual value of South Korean exports in 1977, an extraordinarily feat given that, at the beginning of the decade, the figure was barely $1 billion.

Needless to say, the clearing of such economic benchmarks reflected and induced dramatic changes in the lives of South Koreans everywhere, especially in the urban areas. There, a robust consumer culture arose, spurred by the increasing supply of goods and buying power as well as by the extension of communications and transportation networks. In the first half of the decade alone, in fact, South Koreans witnessed the opening of the Seoul-Pusan Expressway and other major highways, the inauguration of the first subway line in Seoul, and the sizeable expansion of the capital city to many areas south of the Han River. Not everyone, however, was benefiting equally from these advances. The agitation of the growing working class, which manned the factories that made these developments possible, in fact continued to remind everyone of the underbelly of rapid industrialization: gross inequality, poverty, and exploitative, even dangerous, working conditions. Tellingly, the Yusin decade had begun with one of the most memorable moments in South Korean history, one that compelled attention to the plight of laborers: in late 1970, a young man named Chŏn T'aeil, who had unsuccessfully attempted to improve the conditions of his fellow workers in a typical sweatshop, committed ritual suicide by setting himself on fire while clutching a book of labor laws that the government had failed to enforce.

LITERARY RESISTANCE

Kim Chiha proclaimed to speak for such downtrodden victims of Korean society, and in later works such as "Cry of the People," he invoked the memory of Chŏn's self-immolation in his calls for revolutionary action. As for the work that thrust Kim into the public spotlight, "Five Bandits" (*Ojŏk*) was published in the May 1970 issue of the journal *Sasanggye* ("Realm of Ideas"), then soon again in the organ of the main opposition political party. The government immediately shut down both publications and arrested their editors and publishers. Kim Chiha himself was booked on charges of violating the Anti-Communist Law, a generic tool for silencing political opposition. Kim likely knew what would happen—indeed, he even anticipated his arrest in the balladic poem's preamble—for he bore the battle scars of struggle against the anti-communist system. As a college student he had participated in the demonstrations to overthrow Syngman Rhee in 1960, led the reunification efforts that had alarmed Major General Park Chung Hee into seizing power in 1961, and joined the huge student protests against the Normalization Treaty with Japan in 1964 (Chapter 23). He had spent most of the latter part of the 1960s trying to fend off both severe illness and government surveillance, a pattern that would also characterize his life in the 1970s. Indeed he spent most of the decade either in jail or under house arrest, and was briefly sentenced to death in 1974 after being nabbed in a sweep of activists and students on fabricated charges of sedition. He was fortunate to escape with his life, for eight others in this roundup were quickly executed following sentencing in a kangaroo court. His resilience in the face of hardship, including torture, inspired a persistent, concerted movement to win his freedom that became a *cause célèbre* in literary and intellectual circles far beyond Korea. Kim Chiha served, then, as the counterpart figure to Park Chung Hee as the symbol of 1970s South Korea, and it had all begun with a brilliant, biting poem.

"Five Bandits"—a title in unveiled reference to the "Five Traitors of 1905" (*Ŭlsa ojŏk*) who had signed the protectorate treaty leading to the Japanese takeover (Chapter 16)—is a narrative poem suffused with the lyrical elements of local dialect and the singing quality of shamanistic rituals. Its story revolves around a contest between five bandits—a contest in corruption, that is, among representatives of the five most privileged and powerful groups of people in South Korean society at the time: tycoons of conglomerates, national assemblymen, high-ranking bureaucrats, generals, and cabinet ministers. Each of these five bandits takes turns to outdo the other in debauchery, ostentatious wealth, and venality, and before the poem ends with heavenly retribution, a sixth class of miscreant emerges, a clueless public prosecutor who ends up joining rather than indicting the bandits. The message could not be clearer: the system itself suffered from a comprehensive miscarriage of social justice that divided the populace into the parasitic and exploited. And while Park Chung Hee himself escapes direct mention, "Five Bandits" unmistakably targets him. In the poem's accounting of the five bandits' contest, for example, they joyously recall that they had originally gathered "ten years ago" to begin their collective efforts to rob the people. The bandits' affinity for Japanese ways and brutality, and the fact that one of the five bandits is actually a general, all point to Park. Kim also makes no attempt to hide his own personal connection: the poem's poor, suffering peasant who makes an appeal to the prosecutor has come to Seoul from Kim's home region of Chŏlla province.

While not so brazen in their condemnation of the South Korean system, other great writers of the 1970s, too, came to be marked by a pervasive social consciousness in their works. One was Ko Ŭn, who led a campaign in the literary world to bring about Kim Chiha's release from jail and himself was arrested for his political activities. Like Kim originally from Chŏlla province, Ko Ŭn had spent his twenties as a Buddhist monk, and this Buddhist sensibility infused his perspective on social injustice and the means to overcome it. His breakthrough work came in 1974 with a narrative poem, "To Munŭi Village," which described and decried the desolate winter landscape in a rural area, and took the snow as a cover for and of death. A social consciousness is only hinted at here, but in later poems Ko exuded a clearer anti-government voice. In "Arrows" (1977), for example, Ko calls on those fighting for democracy to let go of all of their possessions, accomplishments, and even "happiness" for the singular purpose of "becoming arrows and advancing with all our might" toward a bloody struggle. Ko would later establish himself as Korea's most revered contemporary poet through his epic narrative verse, especially the "Genealogy of Ten Thousand Lives" (*Maninbo*) that recounts his encounters with people both contemporary and historical. His most stirring expressions, though, came in the cauldron of the 1970s.

Many of the great South Korean novelists also made their mark in this decade. Interestingly, three of the most renowned writers— and not only as authors of anti-establishment, social commentary fiction—all made their literary debuts in the same year, 1970, as the publication of "Five Bandits." Hwang Sŏgyŏng, considered by some Korea's greatest contemporary novelist, entered the literary scene in 1970 with a short story with the Korean War as the backdrop (Hwang had just returned from a tour of duty in the Vietnam War). But his big splash came the following year with "Kaekchi." "Kaekchi," roughly translated as "strange land far from home" in reference to the story's focus on struggling factory laborers who had migrated from the countryside, established Hwang as the foremost practitioner of what came to be called "people's literature," or *minjung munhak*. In later works, Hwang would display a remarkable versatility in topics and settings, but always through a concern with the stifled voices of the oppressed. 1970 also was the year Cho Chŏngnae debuted with the first in a string of novels that discerned the impact of modern Koreans' historical experiences on their current circumstances. Cho would later expand his literary canvas in the 1980s and 1990s as a prolific producer of the multi-volume historical novel. The best known such work was *The T'aebaek Mountains*, which featured the same connection between historical and contemporary conditions by reimagining the Korean War from a more balanced rather than the conventional anti-communist, Cold War perspective. Finally, the 1970s witnessed the flowering of literature by female novelists, and none more prominent than Pak Wansŏ, who debuted with a novel published in 1970, *The Naked Tree*. In later works such as *A Hobbling Afternoon*, Pak combined a probing rumination on Korea's historical experiences, especially that of national division, with a critique, through a distinctly female sensibility, of the emerging middle class existence.

A final author who embodied this charged world of 1970s literature was Pak Kyŏngni, a towering figure who combined Pak Wansŏ's prioritization of the female voice with Hwang Sŏgyŏng's attention to the Korean underclass within Cho Chŏngnae's sweeping historical flow. Though she was already well established, it was through the serialized unveiling of her masterpiece, *Land* (T'oji), in the 1970s that Pak Kyŏngni—coincidentally, Kim Chiha's mother-in-law—came to be perhaps the nation's representative literary voice. An epic at once sprawling and intimate, *Land* traces a family over several generations as its members, and the community around them, adjust to dramatic developments on the south coast of the peninsula from the late nineteenth to the mid-twentieth centuries. In using this family's story as an allegory for the turbulent experience of modern Korea itself, Pak calls attention to the mighty accumulation of quotidian changes through a focus on the lives and perspectives of the main female characters. While not set in the author's contemporary times, *Land* epitomized the scratchy realm of literary production in the 1970s, when almost everything, whether intended or not, alluded to the ominous restlessness of the times.

MASS CULTURE UNDER THE YUSIN

During the darkest periods of the Yusin experience, beginning around 1974, free expression became suppressed to an extent that would be unfathomable to younger South Koreans today, and in fact was not far removed from the conditions up in North Korea. Indeed the Emergency Measures issued by the Park regime criminalized all manner of actions, and by the time Emergency Measure Number 9 came around in the spring of 1975, the government proclaimed a power to arrest people summarily for any expression or behavior deemed anti-state. The atmosphere of intimidation also stemmed from the regime's mobilization measures to prevent any potential outbursts of anti-government sentiment in broadcasting, films, music, and publishing. But these areas also reflected the expanding connections of social life and access to information through the dissemination of technological advances. Television viewing, for example, became widespread, and while government censorship kept programming fairly tame, television's capacity to act as a mirror of society kept it a potentially subversive element.

The start of South Korea's television age

In 1969 just over 200,000 television sets were in operation in South Korea. Ten years later, the number was almost 6 million, meaning that in the 1970s the number of televisions in use increased nearly thirty-fold, from penetrating 6 percent of households to nearly four in five. Amidst the political strife, the Yusin period opened the age of television in South Korea and witnessed the emergence of familiar patterns of television broadcasting and viewing that remain today. In this decade, for example, the Korean Broadcasting System (KBS) went from being a government broadcaster to a public television corporation much like the British Broadcasting Corporation, and another company,

MBC, founded in 1969, became a private national network and competitive alternative to KBS.

In terms of programming, however, broadcasters faced definite limits from the Yusin censors. Furthermore, in this age of black and white TV (color would come in the 1980s), the government restricted not only television's content but also its style, issuing a decree in the mid-1970s, for example, prohibiting the appearance of male personalities with long hair. Programming was mostly limited to censored news, soap operas, variety shows, educational programs, sports, and foreign, especially American, shows. Even the amount of broadcasting itself was curtailed, shutting down in the afternoon and late-night. (Indeed twenty-four-hour programming was only introduced in the new millennium.) Still, television had a major impact in the 1970s, especially with soap operas that hooked large audiences and became a cultural phenomenon. These programs came under heavy fire from social critics for their alleged portrayal of frivolous, decadent, and immoral lifestyles, but clearly, at a certain level, these shows provided a much-need escape from the atmosphere of political tension.

Not everything, though, could be so tightly controlled as to prevent any injection of untidy politics. A shocking example of this came on August 15, 1974. As often was the case for the national holiday celebrating liberation from Japanese colonial rule (August 15, 1945), the anniversary was to be marked by a major occasion, this time the formal opening of the first subway line in Seoul. The day started, as usual, with a public address by the president to an assembled audience in a public hall, carried live on television. Very few people could have foreseen what happened next: as Park Chung Hee was delivering his speech, a man came running down the aisle firing a gun in the direction of the stage. The assassin, ostensibly aiming for Park, instead hit the first lady, Yuk Yŏngsu. After she was carried away to the hospital (where she died) and the commotion died down a bit, an equally remarkable thing happened: Park continued with his speech! Perhaps nothing better captured Park and the spookiness of Yusin—as anyone watching television could see.

The government crackdown also aroused dissent in mass culture that otherwise might not have formed. One example of this came in popular music, which had earlier become a ubiquitous entertainment medium and powerful cultural element. In the 1970s, the Koreans' innate affinity for socialization through music turned some popular songs into expressions of anti-government sentiment. The ballad "Morning Dew," released in 1971 by the singer Yang Hee-Un, for example, resonated with its lyrical tribute to inner strength and determination in the face of hardship. Young people caught in the constraints of the dictatorship found in this message a stirring call to resistance, and when the Yusin regime caught onto this possibility and banned the work, "Morning Dew" only grew in popularity and eventually became the anthemic "movement song" for a generation. The ballad's composer, folk singer Kim Min-ki, became a champion of the anti-Yusin artists' movement and continued to churn out protest music.

The realm of publishing also grew into a potent voice of opposition in the 1970s. In addition to *Sasanggye*, the magazine that published "Five Bandits," other intellectual journals, political organs, and newspapers served as forums for provocative analysis and criticism of Yusin society. Among literary journals with an activist bent, most notable was perhaps *Creation and Criticism* (*Ch'angjak kwa pip'yŏng*), a publication begun by academic Paik Nak-chung with modest aims in the 1960s but which, by the 1970s, had become an indispensable player in the social discourse. While continuing to remain wary of censors, *Creation and Criticism* published seminal works of literature, literary scholarship, and social commentary, and hence became an arbiter of not only great literature but also of political debate. Finally, the maturation of the "Hangul generation"—the first South Koreans raised in the postcolonial practice of disseminating information printed primarily in the Korean alphabet, or *Hangul*—also contributed greatly to the growth of publication activity.

The higher literacy rate and publication activity were likely related to another phenomenon in mass culture that came to define the Yusin decade, the social standing and influence of organized religion. While dramatic religious growth was a story that continued throughout the twentieth century, not since the 1910s had religions and the religious establishment exerted such a pronounced impact on society and polity as in the 1970s. As noted above, Buddhism inspired the social criticism of Ko Ŭn, and the same could be said for Catholicism's role in the work and actions of Kim Chiha. Indeed much of Kim's Catholic inspiration came from his being mentored by Bishop Chi Haksun, who in the 1970s stood at the forefront of the Catholic Church's steadfast opposition to the Yusin system, suffering arrests and beatings but unbending in his criticism. The same could be said for the Catholic politician Kim Dae Jung, who, like Kim Chiha, was raised in the city of Mokp'o on the south-western coast. Kim Dae Jung had been the opponent who nearly pulled off the miraculous victory over Park Chung Hee in the 1971 presidential election. For this offense and his continuing opposition to the regime—much of it inspired by his Catholic faith—Kim was kidnapped while in Japan and came close to being executed before international pressure forced Park to relent. It is little wonder, then, that the Catholic clergy in South Korea developed a stout reputation for social justice that endures to this day.

The same does not apply to Protestantism, which for the most part—despite, or perhaps because of, its enormous growth in followers—remained mostly an anti-communist and pro-government stalwart. But there were eminent exceptions, including Mun Ikhwan, a Presbyterian minister who headed numerous organizations in the 1970s, religious and otherwise, that publicly resisted the Yusin dictatorship, for which he was arrested and constantly harassed. The most acclaimed Protestant figure of this period, though, was actually a Quaker, Ham Sŏkhŏn. Unlike most of his fellow Protestants originally from the north who were driven by their hostility to communism, Ham sought to mobilize senti-ment for major issues such as reunification through a focused push against dictatorship. Ham, already well-established as a renowned activist from the colonial period, began publishing a monthly in 1970, *Ssial ŭi sori*, which perhaps can best be translated as "voices of the people." In the ensuing ten years, this journal became the mouthpiece for Ham's calls for ecumenism, non-violent resistance, and human rights, and cemented his moniker as the "Gandhi of Korea." Ham became, then, among the most renowned symbols of the long journey toward democratization in modern Korea, a breakthrough in the 1980s that would not have been possible without the trials of the 1970s.

25

········

Monumental Life in
North Korea

CHRONOLOGY

GROUNDBREAKING FOR THE RYUGYONG HOTEL, 1987

The construction of Pyongyang's Ryugyong Hotel, a massive, pyramid-shaped building over 100 stories and 300 meters tall, began in 1987 amidst the ongoing battle for prestige in advance of the Seoul Summer Olympics the following year. The North Korean regime believed this mammoth edifice would symbolize the advancement, power, and pride of North Korea. But after construction was halted in 1992 and left it an empty shell for over fifteen years thereafter, the Ryugyong Hotel became a national monument for all the wrong reasons. Like North Korea itself, and especially its regime, the structure originated in visions of grandeur, depended on foreign assistance, was built on the backs of the mobilized masses, and

249

stalled in the face of cold reality. In 2008 construction of this colossus was revived, but it remains to be seen whether it will ever function as originally intended, or rather endure as a symbol of the decay, mystery, and tragedy of recent North Korean history.

THE HISTORICAL CHALLENGE

Anyone attempting to understand North Korea faces a host of obstacles, beginning with the difficulties of accessing reliable information about this notoriously secretive land. This problem is compounded when pursuing a historical examination, for the temptation is to focus on North Korea as an immediate, present object of concern. We tend to ask about current conditions without wondering how they might have gotten that way, which is as misguided as to view North Korea only through the lens of the country's effect on the outside world. The task, then, is to comprehend North Korea as a product of its unique, mostly internal historical circumstances.

The lack of unfiltered information has not stopped the emergence of a major publications industry on North Korea. In the West, and particularly the US, the demand for knowledge has stemmed from the chronic sense of threat from the North Korean nuclear program. In South Korea, the recent lifting of the long-standing official insecurity, bordering on paranoia, regarding information from the North has allowed the southern citizens a glimpse of their compatriots through North Korean television broadcasts and newspapers. What the South Koreans have found, however, is, to put it mildly, not very exciting, mostly due to the monotony and transparent propaganda in this content.

The attempt to decipher the realities of North Korean society and history based on what flows out from the tightly controlled sources of information, then, must be grounded on an analysis of what the official reports might be hiding as much as revealing. One must of course also rely on accounts from defectors, refugees, the occasional visitor, and other observers. But in all instances, the picture that emerges from both the official and unofficial sources should serve to demystify North Korea and its people, and to move beyond caricatures and the easy condemnation of its ruling system. The other major historical challenge is to treat North Korea on its own terms and to integrate it into Korean history, overcoming the temptation to dismiss the country's history as somehow an aberration. Only then can we can attempt a sincere understanding of North Korea's development within the larger historical context—not just that of the recent or modern periods, but of Korean civilization a whole. We can then find strong parallels to premodern patterns, which are essential to understanding North Korea today, and come closer to solving that most demanding of all historical questions about modern Korea: how did North and South Korea diverge so dramatically out of common origins?

HISTORICAL PATH, 1970s TO 2000s

Notwithstanding these lessons, it is difficult to avoid a consciousness of South Korea when tracing the North's history, and vice-versa, for in part the radical departures in the two states' development resulted from their strenuous efforts to contrast themselves with each other. For both, the rivalry drove their self-perceptions and actions. By the turn of the 1970s, both countries had completed their post-Korean War recoveries and established strong foundations of industrialization and military autocracy. Whereas South Korea continued to undergo dramatic change in comprehensive fashion thereafter, however, in the North the post-war economic growth hit a wall, and politically the leadership demonstrated a disturbing recidivism, a lapse into primal Korean forms and values. It was as if North Koreans had nothing to do, and nowhere to go, but to reassure themselves of their specialness. The echo chamber, however, resulted in an ongoing tragedy of modern Korean history.

Like many countries, North Korea squandered its relative plentitude in natural resources, such as hydroelectric capacity, coal, and even oil. The industrialization of the 1960s and 1970s made available many advances in material comfort, especially in the urban areas, where citizens enjoyed modern amenities. Even in the agricultural sector, where growth from collectivized farming appears to have been inconsistent, production was sustained sufficiently to allow the country even to export grains into the 1980s. The following decade, however, was one of unremitting economic catastrophe, beginning with the collapse of the Soviet Union and end of the Cold War, and hence the halt of cheap fuel and other subsidies. This was soon compounded by the disastrous floods, then drought, of the mid- and late-1990s, which resulted in the famine that likely killed more than half a million people (with some estimates reaching 2 million) and robbed the country of an entire generation to malnourishment. Though endowed with a relatively solid economy by communist standards toward the end of the 1980s, within a decade North Korea entered the new century a basket case, with its people suffering from rationed food, lack of power and heating, and general misery. How much of this downfall can be attributed to natural disasters, and how much to deficiencies in the economic system itself, will have to await further judgment; but on another level, of course, this is a moot point, for the system was responsible for placing the people in such a vulnerable position in the first place. The decade of the 2000s witnessed somewhat of an economic recovery, including thorough efforts to attract South Korean investment in the tourism and manufacturing sectors. Private markets even sprouted around the country. But the steady flow of refugees showed that this liberalization failed to overcome widespread privation—or more likely, that the economic conditions continued to be dramatically uneven within the country.

According to visitors' accounts, the people of the showcase capital city of Pyongyang and of some other urban areas such as Kaesŏng, for example, appeared anything but impoverished. This simple reality offered a reminder of how this self-identifying socialist paradise developed into a society dependent on starkly unequal access to privileges and resources. While the revolution of the immediate post-liberation years had permanently flipped over the pre-1945 order, as time passed tight control over social interaction led to a startling regression to the premodern Korean patterns of hereditary hierarchy. Ancestry, in short, was paramount and, as in the dynastic eras of the past, much of the "purity" of one's blood was determined by the political circumstances of the founding of the regime. Below the royal family, the Kims, the aristocratic elite were the party leaders whose ties to Kim Il Sung extended back to the Manchurian guerilla days. After the descendants of party cadres, top bureaucrats, and army brass, North Koreans with peasant backgrounds came to occupy the commoner middle class. A despised or stigmatized population, meanwhile, was comprised of descendants of political criminals and colonial-era elites and landlords. A bureaucracy that investigated the lineage background of individuals in prospective marriages maintained this bizarre transplantation of premodern patterns.

Such a social hierarchy reflected, of course, the distribution of political power as well. But as time passed, evidence surfaced that the regime, despite its outward appearance, stopped short of becoming a monolithic structure, particularly after the death of Kim Il Sung in 1994 following half a century (!) of rule. Even before this staggering event, the military, party leadership, individual bureaucracies, and local agencies appear to have established their own power bases that relied upon corruption, black marketeering, and international trade for funding. The divisions and rivalries between these power centers might have played a role in the circumstances surrounding Kim's death and will likely resurface stronger than ever upon the death of his son Kim Jong Il. Kim Jong Il, who was officially introduced as the successor in 1980 while in his late thirties, in fact always relied on his association with the army. His preferred official title as the military's supreme commander was bestowed upon him just three years before his father's death, and later he was commonly referred to as "The General" despite having no military background. And the public proclamation of a "Military First" state policy beginning in the 1990s appeared as a tactic to ensure the support of this powerful institution. Despite his ostensibly unquestioned supremacy, Kim Jong Il never enjoyed the same aura of authority as his father. Kim Jong Il's own successor, whether a son or someone else, will face even greater difficulties in establishing legitimacy, for legitimacy was always based on the recognition of Kim Il Sung's personal heroics.

Even more daunting for the next regime will be to maintain its delicate balance in foreign relations. While people outside of North

Korea have prioritized this regime's impact on the outside world in attempting to understand the country itself, more illuminating is the question of how external forces or, more precisely, the perception of these forces, have determined the internal workings of North Korea. On the one hand, of course, the regime exercised stringent control over its people's exposure to the larger world, for it depended on the belief, within the country, of North Korea's relative superiority. Here, ignorance was a powerful tool. On the other hand, the regime found the threat of foreign forces useful in reinforcing the foundations of its rule. The everlasting Korean enmity for Japan was stoked whenever necessary, for example, given that it served as the basis of Kim Il Sung's historical claims, and hence the state's claims to legitimacy.

The US, too, readily served as a bogeyman for North Korea's constant vigilance, based on the populace's grim memories of the Korean War and occasional skirmishes with the US military in Korea thereafter (Chapter 22). In the mid-1990s, this chronic hostility suddenly reached the level of an emergency, as American detection of North Korean activities to reprocess nuclear fuel at a plant in Yongbyon triggered a crisis. The response of the North Korean regime to international calls for inspections was to withdrawal from the Nuclear Non-Proliferation Treaty and to intensify the public vilification of American intent. Just as tensions in the summer of 1994 reached the stage of imminent military confrontation, former American President Jimmy Carter traveled to Pyongyang and came away with an agreement, which was eventually signed later in the year as the Agreed Framework. The Agreed Framework's call for North Korean allowance of inspections in exchange for fuel and food aid, however, failed to stop the nuclear program, mostly due to the regime's attempts to stall indefinitely while extracting as many concessions as possible. But the Americans shared the blame. Indeed North Korea's relentless push to develop nuclear weapons was historically fated to prick and preoccupy the US, for the genuine fears of an interventionist American military drove much of its nuclear ambitions. American leaders who engaged in juvenile name-calling of North Korea while remaining painfully ignorant of these larger circumstances only exacerbated the North's fears and therefore strengthened the effects of the regime's propaganda for internal consumption.

And finally, South Korea, the so-called American puppet, was steadily condemned as a prime example of the shame of foreign domination, despite the occasional breakthroughs in reconciliation such as the 2000 summit in Pyongyang with South Korea's president, Kim Dae Jung. What outsiders called North Korea's isolation, then, was touted internally rather as a manifestation of the country's fierce independence. Following the famine and economic collapse of the latter half of the 1990s, however, the country had to open up sufficiently to entice foreign capital and know-how, including, as noted above, from South Korea. Even Internet and cell phone traffic was made available to a privileged few. But the wariness of the slippery slope potentially leading to the collapse of the system itself remained, and this delicate balance between too much exposure and too much hardship promised to suffer even greater stresses.

MONUMENTAL LIFE

One begins to understand, then, the paramount significance of maintaining the impression of North Korean superiority, and hence also the extraordinary lengths undertaken to enforce this narrative. This furthermore accounts for the eerie monumentality of life in North Korea that developed in the closing decades of the twentieth century: the mind-numbing proliferation of over-the-top propaganda, gigantic memorials and construction projects, and ever-stupendous claims about the country and regime. In a classic case of overcompensation, such grandiosity and myth-making that lay at the core of North Korean existence, in which everything was said to be "perfect," seemed to intensify the more it diverged from reality. North Korea, and in particular Pyongyang, turned into not only an Orwellian society, but an uncannily precise realization of Orwell's vision in the novel *1984*. All the elements were there, including the viral surveillance, the double-talk and absolute control of information, the relentless vigilance and incapacity to turn off the propaganda, the erasure and fabrication of history, the ritualized hatred of a bogeyman enemy, the submission of the self into the mass, brutal punishment for nonconformity and political crimes, and, of course, Big Brother.

The cult of personality quickly reached absurd proportions and eventually went beyond the scale of other totalitarian regimes in its attribution of extraordinary powers to both the father and son, but especially the latter, who was not only showered with adulation but credited with superhuman intelligence. There is evidence that Kim Jong Il viewed this narrative, much of which he himself probably crafted, more soberly, and repeated the explanation of other North Korean officials in rare moments of candor: the lessons from Korean history, especially in the modern period, required resolute mobilization for the cause of preserving national independence and dignity, and a heroic leader was necessary to rally and properly channel this energy. Tellingly, however, the personality cult in North Korea, as well as political rule itself, also took on a hereditary nature, an understandably rare occasion for communist regimes subscribing officially to an ideology, socialism, with pretenses to perfect rationality. While some commentators detected an unmistakably Christian tenor in the droning public worship of the father–son tandem, the most common and plausible explanation was to observe simply that the North Korean ruling system revived the Korean kingship. In addition to preserving power within a given family, the North Korean monarchy tapped into a basic longing for stability, national pride, and autonomy (however imaginary), as well as for a symbolic leader whose leadership was expressed in familial overtones.

But this kind of mythology required constant reinforcement, especially as reality intruded upon it. Hence the erection of enormous monuments celebrating the system, its ideology, and especially its leader. The round-numbered anniversaries of Kim Il Sung's birthday of April 15, 1912 seem to have triggered the most memorable memorials. In 1972, on the occasion of his sixtieth birthday, a 20-meter bronze statue of his most majestic pose was unveiled close to the banks of the Taedong River. His seventieth birthday in 1982 brought forth a staggering trio of monuments that still dominate the visitor's impression of the city: the Arch of Triumph, a little taller and wider than the one in Paris after which it was styled, in celebration of Kim's struggle against Japanese colonialism; the Tower of the Juche Idea, a paean to the official ruling ideology of self-reliance that has simply been called "Kim Il Sung-ism," so transparently did it serve to rationalize the Kim monarchy; and the splendid Grand Study House of the People, a public library that still stands as the largest building in the traditional Korean architectural style.

It was hoped that the Ryugyong Hotel (see Image 25) would be completed in time for the next super-great birthday celebration, Kim Il Sung's eightieth in April 1992. Groundbreaking for this one-of-a-kind structure, towering over 100 stories, took place in 1987, at the height of the feverish competition over which Korea could outdo the other in presenting itself to the world ahead of the 1988 Seoul Summer Olympics. In addition to planting a bomb in 1987 that destroyed a South Korean airliner with over a hundred souls on board, the Northern regime prepared its own international sports festival, for which the world's largest stadium, with a seating capacity of 150,000, was actually completed. The Ryugyong Hotel, however, ran into troubles, and construction stopped midway in 1992 due to astronomical costs and, as widely suspected, problems

Image 25   Ryugyŏng Hotel in Pyongyang, 2003. (Courtesy of Tae Gyun Park.)

257

in the building's structural integrity. Thereafter it remained an unsightly skeleton, a 300-meter hollow pyramid of concrete. Visitors to Pyongyang remarked, though almost never flatteringly, on its unavoidable presence, visible from just about everywhere in the city. Some observers described it as "hideous" or "monstrous," while one American magazine dubbed it "the world's worst building." Others, however, found the superstructure a tremendous curiosity and remarked on its distinctive shape with three extended wings, each grounded by a smaller pyramid at the base. The hotel, then, appeared to mimic the layout of the Egyptian pyramids of Giza, although many commented that it looked like a giant rocket ship ready to launch. After a fifteen-year dormancy, construction on the hotel was revived in 2008, this time targeting for completion April 2012, the hundredth anniversary of Kim Il Sung's birth— or Year Juche 100, according to the North Korean calendar.

In the meantime, the unfinished Ryugyong Hotel turned into the unwitting symbol of North Korea itself: the fantastical and megalomaniacal ambitions, economic bankruptcy, and disabling stagnation, waiting only for collapse itself. And as with North Korea's historical development and ultimately its survival, the Ryugyong Hotel project became a matter of utter will, dedication, delusion, and mobilization. Like the Ryugyong Hotel, North Korea passed the turn of the new century an empty shell, a testament to misplaced priorities (and funds) for the sake of preserving a fantasy. The problem, of course, was that this historical experiment, while grounded in Korea's past, harmed millions of people.

As noted above, it is difficult to gage how the people of North Korea actually led their lives, as so much that foreign visitors observed was carefully staged. But sufficient evidence suggests that, at least in the 1970s and 1980s, the modicum of economic development and political stability produced enough to eat as well as a modern lifestyle, at least for Pyongyang and the cities, not terribly different from that of other communist societies. People pursued their routines of work and family life, followed long-established modes of social interaction, enjoyed leisure and play, engaged in romance, and in keeping with traditional Korean passions, often went picnicking, singing, and dancing. They also partook in popular culture by revisiting traditional tales such as the "Tale of Ch'unhyang" through grand theatrical, musical, and filmic productions. With the collapse of the Soviet Union and famine of the 1990s, however, came deprivation and resignation, and an intensified dulling of the senses from the relentless monotony and closure to the external world. Exposure to the outside was the purview of the privileged minority who had the most to lose in any dramatic change: the elites of the army and Communist Party, who grew dependent on the system of permanent exploitation and radical difference between the haves and have-nots. For the rest of the country's people, existence might have been occasionally satisfactory but likely debilitatingly hollow—intellectually, psychologically, and spiritually. In the face of the overarching primacy of formality in the ruling *Juche* ideology, correspondence to reality was less significant than the collective will to forge an ideal.

Above all, then, North Korea became a historical tragedy, and "tragic" ultimately rang more true than the other adjectives that immediately came to mind: weird, unknowable, evil. While those labels were readily applied to the regime, the greater concern could only be the North Korean people, victimized by the disastrous turns taken by their history. An investigation into the manner by which the regime came to hold such destructive sway over the populace must be balanced by an inquiry into how the people came to find themselves in such a position in the first place. Here a consideration of the greater historical context is inescapable. One cannot deny that the obsessive fear of external domination was rooted in the painful memories of the colonial period, the post-liberation occupation, and the devastation of the Korean War. One also cannot deny the allure of a fierce nationalism for North Koreans—indeed, Koreans as a whole—given the lessons of the modern experience. The Soviet occupation determined the Cold War orientation of the North's political system, but understandably a charismatic strongman touting himself as the savior from foreign intervention found resonance. The effects of the colonial experience, furthermore, were not just oppositional: the colonial state's militaristic and industrializing mobilization of the populace provided a model and foundation for such a system to arise after liberation. And the reception of traditional forms of monarchical authority, paternalistic leadership, and hereditary social hierarchy also made perfect sense.

In short, North Korea was an unmistakably direct product of its history, including the history that it had in common with South Korea before 1945. That these two states and societies eventually diverged so drastically as time passed suggests not that North Korean history was somehow an aberration or illegitimate, but rather that the two Koreas served as counter-factual examples to each other: each a logical, if perhaps extreme, outcome of a shared past.

26

South Korean Democratization

CHRONOLOGY

1979 October	Assassination of Park Chung Hee
1979 December	*Coup d'état* engineered by General Chun Doo Hwan
1980 May	The Kwangju Uprising
1987 June	Mass pro-democracy demonstrations in Seoul; "June Declaration" of direct presidential elections
1987 December	Election of Roh Tae-woo as President
1988	Summer Olympics in Seoul
1992	Election of President Kim Young Sam
1997	Economic crisis; election of President Kim Dae Jung

THE JUNE DECLARATION OF 1987

Tear gas again filled the streets of downtown Seoul and other major cities in June of 1987, just as it had so often in recent South Korean history in response to civil unrest. This time, however, the number, determination, and makeup of the demonstrators portended something on another level altogether. Anger and frustration against the Chun Doo Hwan dictatorship among the students and workers had been a given for many years, but in June they were joined by increasing numbers of white collar workers, representing the burgeoning middle class. These soon swelled the ranks of the protestors to upwards of a million people throughout the country. They called for the immediate revocation of plans to hand over the presidency to Chun's designated successor, Roh Tae-woo, which had appeared as a clear intent to continue the dictatorship in defiance of the popular will. Chun was inclined to proceed with a harsh crackdown on these enormous demonstrations that would have brought chaos and great bloodshed. When he became aware, however, that such a move, coming on the eve of the Seoul Olympics to be held the following year, would garner little support from the bureaucracy, his American allies, or even the military, he acceded to demands for a direct presidential election.

This "June Declaration" of 1987 began the formal breakthrough to a permanent and stable democratic governing system in South Korea. But to suggest that democratization itself began in 1987 would errone-ously diminish the long and painful struggle of South Koreans against the forces of both political and economic domination—a struggle that, as in 1960–1, even attained formal success occasionally. Narratives of the political history of South Korea have, understandably, tended to focus on state actors. But as time has passed a counter-narrative of democratiza-tion as the central feature of South Korean political history has emerged, a storyline that views 1987 more as the culmination, not outbreak, of popular yearning and sacrifice for democracy.

THE PRELUDE: KWANGJU, MAY 1980

One could argue, in fact, that the single most important event in South Korean democratization did not happen in 1987, but rather in 1980: the Kwangju Uprising, normally called simply "5–18" in reference to the date, May 18, of its beginning. The incapacity to account for this bloody episode denied the South Korean regime of the 1980s any lasting legitimacy. Likewise, the memory of Kwangju drove the intensifying struggle against dictatorship until it burst forth irrepressibly in June of 1987. It is safe to say that, without Kwangju, the breakthrough to formal democracy would probably have taken much longer, if at all.

The Kwangju Uprising itself stood as the culmination of resist-ance efforts in the 1970s against the "Yusin" system that Park Chung Hee instituted in 1972 to stifle all dissent and keep himself permanently in power (Chapter 24). As the end of the decade approached, a tense national atmosphere emerged from the combi-nation of many factors: Park's inaccessibility and siege mentality, which steadily deepened following the assassination of his wife in 1974; a deteriorating economy hit by the worldwide oil shocks; a heightened crackdown on opposition politicians who had gained a plurality in the December 1978 National Assembly elections; and the escalation of popular protests. On October 26, 1979, in the midst of the largest mass unrest to date exploding in the southern coastal cities of Pusan and Masan, Park was assassinated by, ironically, the head of the Korean Central Intelligence Agency, the internal security apparatus that had muzzled political dissent throughout his reign. During his trial, this man, Kim Chaegyu, insisted that he had been motivated by a desire for democracy.

Following their initial shock, the Korean people, too, could justifiably expect, after almost two decades of Park's rule, an opportunity finally to establish a fully democratic order. As with the euphoria following the overthrow of Syngman Rhee in 1960, the national mood entered an expectant stage with the cancellation of Park's state of emergency, the release of political prisoners, and the selection of a new president, Choi Kyu-ha. The man appointed to lead the investigation into Park's assassination, General Chun Doo Hwan, however, had other ideas. On December 12, 1979, Chun engineered a coup by arresting the country's top military commander. Henceforth, despite the nominal political authority vested in President Choi, it was Chun's group of officers who held real power. The awakening to this reality fueled the "Seoul Spring" of 1980, when laborers and students staged large demonstrations calling for an end to Chun's control, a lifting of martial law, and a concerted effort to establish a functioning democracy. The peak of these demonstrations came on May 15, when a hundred thousand mostly student protestors gathered in the plaza of Seoul Station. They retreated the following day to their classrooms, but another crisis would emerge on May 17 with the extension of martial law to the entire country, the shutdown of campuses, and the arrest of opposition leader Kim Dae Jung. Chun was solidifying his grip on power.

The Kwangju Uprising that erupted the next day, on May 18, 1980, started in a conventional way, with students gathered at the gate of a university for a rally. But the shockingly brutal response by the government troops—in this case, paratroopers sent down to quell any such disturbances—sparked the intensification of the conflict from a student protest to a civil uprising involving a considerable portion of the region's citizenry. Over the years scholars and observers have cited many factors that might have contributed to the stunning phenomenon of crack troops trained to fight North Koreans unleashing their fury on the very citizens whom they were supposed to protect: the suspicion fed by misinformation on the presence of North Korean elements; regional antipathy toward Chŏlla province, where Kwangju lay; and even the drugging of the paratroopers. Whatever the precise combination of causes, the result, after ten days of the uprising, was a total of more than 200 people killed, many more hundreds injured, and a deep wound in the national soul that would take decades to heal. The city of Kwangju itself functioned as an autonomous, almost pristinely primitive collectivity following the retreat by government troops from the city center on the fourth day. When the soldiers returned to re-take the Provincial Hall building at dawn on May 27, many of these citizens, knowing full well their fate, chose to take up arms against the troops in a final act of defiance.

These victims of the Kwangju Uprising were not aiming for a hallowed place in the annals of Korean history, but rather expressing outrage and insisting on their dignity in the face of barbarity. The citizens of Kwangju, however, came largely to embrace the popular judgment that their sacrifices represented an indispensable element in the path toward democratization. In fact the Kwangju Uprising took on even greater historical significance: as the explosive climax of the buildup of wrenching divisions in South Korean society; and as the origin of many other defining features of South Korean politics and society thereafter, including radicalization, regionalism, anti-Americanism, and, of course, democracy. It was, then, truly a watershed event, and if popular culture was any indication, the Kwangju Uprising remained a source of fascination and contemplation. Novels, television dramas, documentaries, and feature films over the next three decades continued to explore its multi-faceted significance.

THE DEMOCRACY GENERATION

The greatest and most lasting impact of Kwangju, however, was felt by the first generation to come of age following the uprising. To these young Koreans, news about what happened in Kwangju came through the thriving underground networks of first-hand written accounts, art work, photos, and even video footage smuggled into the country from the foreign reporters who had witnessed the event. Chun's consolidation of power through the Kwangju bloodbath rendered the validity of his regime null and void, but it was enough to instill an atmosphere of official silence about what really happened during the so-called Kwangju Incident. Intellectuals, students, laborers, and other activists, however, maintained the memory of Kwangju, which they eventually used also as the chief rallying cry for the drive to overthrow the Chun regime in the 1980s.

These activists also employed Kwangju as the springboard for further refinement of the *minjung*, or "people's," movement that pervaded the anti-government resistance circles in the 1970s and 1980s. This was a movement in the sense not of a coherent organization, but rather of a powerfully enveloping mood that framed the perspective on Korean politics, culture, foreign relations, and, in particular, history and national division. From the *minjung* perspective, the Korean people had been stripped of their primacy in recent Korean history by authoritarian and corrupt government, big business, and foreign powers that all conspired to divide the Korean masses and suppress their will. The *minjung* movement sought to regain the people's autonomy and subjectivity by expressing itself not only in anti-government activity, but also in popular culture, patterns of public life, and academic inquiry. The primary practitioners, furthermore, were those who came of age in this era, mostly as university students.

In the 1990s, when the *minjung* movement faded away, these people would be referred to as the "386 generation" (a play on the name of a well-known computer chip): those who were in their thirties, went to college in the 1980s, and were born in the 1960s. By the middle of the twentieth century's final decade, they could look back on their formidable influence in the 1980s, when they represented the shock troops behind the democratization movement. By subsequently entering the workforce and the comforts of middle class domesticity, they had found themselves concerned with matters other than politics, but their intense experience in the struggles for democratization would maintain its grip on their outlook. Indeed, when many of them, in their late thirties and forties, reached the top circles of political power in the opening years of the new century, they showed that issues of historical justice remained uppermost in their concerns.

THE 1987 DECLARATION AND ELECTION

However essential this group of young people was to the democratization cause, the breakthrough of 1987 would have not occurred without the massive show of support from the growing middle class. To understand this phenomenon, we must return to the core problem of the Chun Doo Hwan dictatorship: its lack of legitimacy. Following his consolidation of power from late 1979 to late 1980, Chun instituted a rule that largely continued the 1970s *Yusin* patterns of state surveillance, suppression of dissent, and the encouragement of state-directed economic growth dominated by the family-run conglomerates. The US and other major governments recognized his regime soon after it began and, for a while at least, economic growth continued apace. While these developments might have helped in procuring the right to host the 1988 Summer Olympics, they could do little to garner recognition from the South Korean populace. When the economy started to slow down and an atmosphere of corruption and brutality emerged around the Chun junta, the bitter memories of 1980 brought forth an entrenchment of resistance to his rule. This sentiment went far beyond the semi-permanent base of anti-government activists. Indeed, when the long-reigning dictator of the Philippines, Ferdinand Marcos, was overthrown by a popular uprising in 1986, South Koreans felt emboldened to take steps that would ensure the imminent end to their own humiliating condition of chronic dictatorship.

Unsurprisingly, then, protests erupted when, contrary to the expectations of most people, Chun Doo Hwan announced in June of 1987 that the end of his "term" later that year would be followed by a parliamentary, not popular, election of the next president. This blatant move would ensure that his hand-picked successor, Roh Tae-woo, would take office, but it also triggered an outpouring of anger that spilled into the streets and begat the largest mass protests, with upwards of a million demonstrators throughout the country, in South Korean history (see Image 26). The students who initiated these efforts had little idea that they would soon be joined by salary workers, managers, housewives, and others. Unlike in the past, when political dissent remained the purview of students and hard-core activists, this time the middle class flooded the streets and expressed their support for the protests in numerous other ways as well. The Chun regime had grossly miscalculated the degree to which the people would succumb to the latest machinations of dictatorship. As revealed later, the regime also overestimated its support from the military and bureaucracy for a potential crackdown

Image 26 Clash between protestors and police in the city of Kwangju, June 26, 1987. (Courtesy of Noonbit Publishers.)

on these demonstrations. A certain catastrophe would have ensued, and it would have marred the much-anticipated hosting of the Summer Olympics in Seoul the following year. So feared also the American ambassador to South Korea, who in a private meeting with Chun relayed his government's strong warning that no violent moves be made to force the demonstrators off the streets.

The final, major actor to intervene in order to avert disaster was the man picked to be Chun's successor, Roh Tae-woo. Roh understood that any crackdown would severely stain his reign, just as Kwangju had marked Chun's. With Chun's grudging consent, Roh issued a declaration on June 29, 1987, calling for a direct presidential election and a new constitutional system that would make permanent an entire range of democratic reforms. The Sixth Republic that this new constitution ushered in continues to this day. Even with this concession, however, Roh was not prepared to forego his political ambitions, and he placed himself as the presidential candidate from the ruling party in the direct presidential election to be held at the end of the year. Given the distaste of much of the public for Chun's stewardship, Roh should not have anticipated electoral success, but the two leading politicians in the democratic resistance since the 1970s, Kim Dae Jung and Kim Young Sam, failed to reach a compromise to select a single opposition candidate. The result, to the dismay of so many who had waged the democratization struggle, was the election of Roh with a plurality of less than 40 percent of the ballots, as the Kims split the opposition vote.

Kim Young Sam and Kim Dae Jung would eventually get their turn at the coveted prize of the presidency in the 1990s, with each new president, and each new peaceful transfer of power, further consolidating the democratic political culture. Notwithstanding, or perhaps due to, his historical baggage, Roh made no attempts to reverse the democratization process. He even overturned long-standing national imperatives through his "Nordpolitik" strategy of establishing diplomatic relations with China and the Soviet Union (soon Russia), which led to the further isolation of North Korea just as the Cold War came to a close. Kim Young Sam's election in 1992, which came about after he joined hands with Roh in order to procure conservative support, represented the first popularly-elected civilian presidency since the early 1960s, following three decades of rule by military leaders. The election of his successor in 1997, Kim Dae Jung, constituted the first peaceful transfer of power to the opposition candidate in South Korean history.

Both Kim presidencies, while deeply wounded by a shroud of corruption surrounding the president's confidants and family members, also advanced national healing from the battle scars of democratization. Kim Young Sam's administration, in fact, revisited Kwangju, this time to officially vindicate the citizenry and launch a prosecutorial investigation into the circumstances, from October 1979 to May 1980, that led to the massacre. In the process the country stood transfixed at the stunning sight of the two main figures in these events, Chun and Roh, being tried and found guilty for their illegal grab for power over this period, as well as for the astronomical slush funds they had accumulated as presidents. Their respective sentences of death and life imprisonment were eventually commuted, and Kim Dae Jung, as the new president in 1998, formally pardoned them for the sake of achieving national reconciliation amidst an economic crisis. That the South Korean people successfully weathered this storm spoke volumes about the health and reparative capacity of their nascent democracy.

27

· · · · · · · ·

South Korea in the New Millennium

CHRONOLOGY

QUARTERFINAL MATCH VERSUS SPAIN IN THE 2002 WORLD CUP FINALS

As the South Korean people entered the new century they were still recovering from what they called the "IMF period," when the economy fell into a foreign exchange crisis in 1997 and had to be rescued by a colossal loan from the International Monetary Fund. But following the election of longtime dissident Kim Dae Jung as president at the end of that year, citizens rallied to recover from this shock. Not only did the government repay the IMF loan ahead of schedule, but the weathering of this crisis, as well the 2000 summit between Kim Dae Jung and Kim Jong Il of North Korea, instilled a widespread sense of a new historical era: South Korea had matured past the growing pains of rapid industrialization, dictatorship and democratization, and even the Cold War. Behaviors and technologies, often devised by Korean companies, that exploited the endless possibilities of the Internet and the mobile phone turned South Korean society almost overnight into a futuristic urban space where identities could be readily mixed and reinvented. Mass culture also reflected this newfound confidence and determination, establishing the basis for the "Korean Wave" (*Hallyu*) in pop culture that swept through Asia in the first decade of the new millennium.

The 2002 World Cup Finals, hosted jointly by South Korea and Japan, served as perhaps the most potent symbol of this new era. The unanticipated success of the national team on the field corresponded to the extraordinary energy of the citizenry in demonstrating its collective support, as seen in the throngs of people in the streets when the national team played a game. The peak in the mass euphoria might have come in the moments following the stunning victory, in an overtime shootout, by the national team over Spain in late June, 2002. This sent the upstart South Koreans to a wildly improbable birth in the semi-finals, an achievement never before reached by any World Cup team outside of Europe and Latin America. Indeed, the ecstasy of the entire World Cup month served as the emblem of the continuing "coming out party" of sorts for South Koreans. They reveled in their awareness of a new era epitomized by their national team, by the Korean Wave, and by their experience in overcoming the national emergency of just five years earlier. The new millennium allowed South Korea to start anew, and to enter a postindustrial age economically that coincided with rapid social and cultural changes.

ECONOMIC GROWTH: A RECONSIDERATION

Even before the crisis of 1997–8, throughout the 1990s South Koreans had a creeping sense that not all had gone well with the extraordinarily rapid economic growth they had traversed over the previous three decades. Perhaps the pace had been too quick, or that government oversight had not matched its policy ambitions, but whatever the causes, the construct of the economic miracle began to come apart at the seams. The roads were constantly clogged by too many cars on too little space, and even relatively simple structures seemed unstable. In 1993 a rail line collapsed over an illegal tunnel project in Pusan, killing scores of people, and the next year, a section of one of the major bridges spanning the Han River in Seoul gave way, plunging many to their deaths. In the spring and summer of 1995 came the biggest such disasters: an explosion at a subway construction site in the city of Taegu that killed hundreds, and the sudden collapse of an five-story luxury department store, which took the lives of over 500 innocent shoppers and workers. In the latter case, it turned out that the shoddy construction pursued on the cheap by yet another would-be tycoon had been permitted to pass, through bribes, by government inspectors, some of whom suspiciously failed to show up to work the day following the accident. Such unethical collusion led Koreans to wonder aloud whether, in the relentless pursuit of development, they had lost their soul. This type of national hand-wringing and reflection had a long history, and in fact had intensified following the Kwangju Uprising of 1980, but now it seemed as if the country was being bombarded with material evidence for this sense of malaise.

The worsening mood continued through the final year of the Kim Young Sam presidency in 1997, and the revelations of corruption surrounding his son only magnified the unpopularity of his administration. The final blow to Kim's reputation hit in late summer of 1997, just as the presidential election campaign for his successor started to intensify. What began as a precipitous depreciation of currencies through a speculative run in Southeast Asia soon hit South Korea, which suffered, like these other countries, from runaway growth and foreign debt that left it vulnerable to fluctuations in the currency markets. More ominously, the spreading financial crisis in Asia exposed a Korean economy with serious structural problems, such as mountains of under-performing loans—many government-sponsored—to enormous conglomerates that had taken this unending supply of easy credit to expand without restraint. Like the roads, bridges, and buildings of the preceding years, the edifice of the Korean financial and economic system came down like a house of cards. This resulted in the rapid depreciation of the Korean *won*, a dive in the Korean stock markets, and worst of all for the populace, the bankruptcy of thousands of firms both big and small. The collapse and down-sizing of companies and the massive wave of layoffs struck the country like a punch in the stomach, victimizing workers both blue and white collar alike. The social dislocation and deeply bitter despondency that ensued were exacerbated by the national humiliation suffered, from the Korean perspective, at the hands of the International Monetary Fund (IMF). The IMF rescued the South Korean government from insolvency by arranging a $57 billion bailout, but only according to strict conditions for economic restructuring and reforms. Koreans still refer to this crisis as the "IMF period," as if the lords of world capitalism were responsible for a problem that Koreans had brought on themselves.

In licking their wounds, however, Koreans soon demonstrated that the worst of times could also bring out the best in people. They found the bitter medicine of restructuring and sacrifice in every major sector of the economy—the conglomerates and state-controlled banks as well as labor unions—a bit easier to swallow by a strong sense of national resolve. This collective conscious-ness suffused the social fabric, made visible in everything from telethons to locally organized campaigns to help laid off workers and contribute to the repayment of the IMF loan. The stunning sight of Koreans bringing their jewelry, family heirlooms, and wads of cash to the collection centers pointed to the power of national identity, as well as perhaps to the thoughtful reflection on their recent history that began well before the financial collapse. In the midst of the most serious crisis to hit the South Korean economy since the Korean War, the people demonstrated a resolve that would lay the foundation for national rebirth.

The IMF loan was repaid far ahead of schedule, and the reforms demanded by the IMF, while not going so far as to permanently shake the influence of the major conglomerates, cleared the slate for the construction of a postindustrial economy. This economy would be built largely on information technologies that turned South Korea into the most wired country in the world. Some of the same technological, social, and cultural factors converged to transform South Korea quickly into one of the most wire-*less* countries as well, as much of social interaction came to be centered on the mobile phone. Such a revival corresponded, in the political arena, also to a fundamentally different approach to the relationship with North Korea. The famed "Sunshine Policy" of President Kim Dae Jung, who won election in late 1997 with the slimmest of victory margins and promptly shepherded the country through the economic crisis, sought to engage the North through a focus on reconciliation and assistance. This shift led to the historical summit meeting in Pyongyang in the summer of 2000 between Kim Dae Jung and Kim Jong Il. It was discovered later that this agreement had included a massive, secret payment of direct aid to the Northern regime. This revelation tainted the historical judgment on these efforts as well as on Kim Dae Jung's Nobel Peace Prize, which he won later that year partly as a result of the Sunshine Policy. But despite these setbacks, symbolically the summit signaled an array of changes in South Korea as the country reemerged from the financial crisis to face the new millennium.

WOMEN AND FAMILY: SEISMIC SHIFTS

One of the areas that underwent the most striking transformations involved the social and familial standing of women. The suddenness and scale of changes along these lines said more about the relatively slow pace of progress in gender relations before the 1990s, especially in the broader areas of customs and family law. In fact, until the closing decade of the twentieth century, family law had remained the legal realm that had most successfully resisted de-Confucianization, despite the many and rapid developments in political rule and socioeconomic conditions over the course of the modern era. But the industrialization and urbanization of the late twentieth century compelled the legal system to account, finally, for very different circumstances. In 1990, a major series of family law reforms was enacted to provide greater rights and authority to women. These included the possibility for women to succeed a descent line as family head, the legal recognition of children born out of wedlock, and equal rights for divorced women in child custody and property struggles. But as the strengthening voices of women's organizations made clear, these steps only partially addressed the realities of family life for females, and through these groups' influence another major set of legal reforms was passed in the middle of the 2000s. These provisions attacked the last major vestige of traditional family law, that of the household registration system. They abolished the centuries-long prohibition of marriage between two people of the same "clan" identity, eliminated the six-month delay before divorced women could remarry, allowed children of divorced parents to take the surname of the mother or stepfather, and legally recognized the relationship between divorced mothers and their biological children.

As these moves suggest, the increasing incidence of divorce stood out as one of the most conspicuous phenomena in South Korean society. In fact, within a decade after the mid-1990s, South Korea became marked by one of the highest divorce rates in the world, which was probably not unrelated to other extraordinary changes: a precipitous drop in the birth rate, and an equally stark increase in the number of females who either did not get married or declined to have children after marriage. While traditionalists decried these developments and saw the legal reforms as only exacerbating the problem, many citizens perceived these measures as a reflection of social realities and as a release for women from the unequal burdens of Confucian family customs. Furthermore, these developments, so went the argument, represented only a portion of the larger phenomenon of Korean women belatedly gaining the freedom to pursue interests, careers, and family arrangements long enjoyed by modern Korean men.

The seemingly sudden emergence of prominent South Korean women in many social realms—with big business a conspicuous exception—seemed to support such a sentiment. Beginning in the late 1990s, but especially in the opening years of the next decade, Korean women took high-profile, leadership positions in academia, broadcasting, and government, with the realm of politics, in particular, accounting for a surprisingly large number of prominent females. Riding a wave of new female lawmakers and high government officials, a woman emerged as a top deputy to the successful presidential candidate of 2002, around the same time that the daughter of Park Chung Hee, Park Geun-hye, began to make her mark in the conservative opposition party. In 2007, Park barely lost the primary election of this party, the Grand National Party, to the eventual president-elect, Lee Myung-bak, but she remained a powerful political figure. Finally, Korean women made a major splash in sports. Long having succeeded in international competition in archery and Taekwondo—well-established traditional sports—and, of all things, short-track speed skating, Korean women, in the most striking development of all, began to dominate international golf. Starting with the breakout of Pak Se Ri in 1998 through her victories in two major championships, Korean women flooded the upper ranks of professional golf. This sensation, while in many ways a testament to Pak's influence, also defied easy explanation, since the sheer number of top players and their victories, given Korea's short history in this sport, was staggering. But these remarkable developments also suggested that Korean women in the new millennium were poised to put their stamp on many more social sectors.

Popular culture, too, reflected the rapidly changing standing of women in South Korea. Much of the mass culture industry was driven by female consumers, although the portrayal of Korean women in films and television dramas often depicted a shallow preoccupation with material and consumer interests, especially among urbanites. But these depictions also showed the contradictions that tugged at the Korean female: economic limitations as well as consumerist freedom, familial duties as well as individual desires, social controls as well as opportunities. What the portrayals and consumption patterns of popular culture had in common was their reflection of a very different world for Korean women at the turn of the millennium. The perennially popular television historical dramas also reflected these changing circumstances. In revisiting familiar historical figures and imagining others, these dramas showed a strikingly *modern* Korean female in settings dating back centuries or even millennia—characters who came across as intelligent, savvy, and determined to overcome life's limitations instead of being consumed by social constraints or fatalism. Perhaps the most representative of such a depiction was the lead character in "Jewel in the Palace" (*Taejanggŭm*), a tale of a sixteenth century woman who began as a palace servant and, through her wit, skills, and perseverance, rose to the position of royal physician and chef. This television series, when exported to other Asian countries, became an international hit, attesting both to the sophistication of the Korean entertainment industry behind the Korean Wave that washed over foreign shores, as well as to the social changes affecting women.

TOWARD A NEW ERA

While perhaps most conspicuous in their impact on women, the dramatic and rapid socioeconomic developments pervaded the country as a whole, which became increasingly driven by the lifestyles and perspectives of the younger generations. Until the 2007 presidential election, the generational divides of the new century proved most pronounced in electoral politics, as the so-called Generation X of twenty-somethings, as well as the 386-generation in their thirties and forties (see Chapter 26), together displayed a decidedly different perspective on a wide range of issues. The Gen-X youth, with their unprecedented spending power and cultural influence, often set the trends not only in consumer behavior, but also in the expansive realms of politics, civic movements, and national consciousness. Largely unbound by conventional imperatives, they proved deft in negotiating disparate cultural norms, social behaviors, and group identities. They were much more cosmopolitan than their elders, as South Korea's Internet revolution placed the world at their fingertips, and as they were increasingly composed of people normally not even considered Korean. Indeed, the continuing rapid influx of migrants from other parts of Asia came to constitute a major component of any understanding of South Korea in the new millennium, and their impact on Korean society—from marriage patterns and social welfare to a reassessment of what it means to be Korean—promised to increase dramatically.

Such an eagerness to reconsider longstanding norms accounted for much of the extraordinary displays of both national pride and group behavior during the 2002 hosting of the World Cup. The unofficial fan club of the national team called itself the "Red Devils," and red shirts and other paraphernalia emblazoned with "Be the Reds" and other phrases in awkward English could be seen everywhere. Whether originally intended this way or not, the sentiment spread that this choice of nickname and slogan deliberately defied the association of the color red with North Koreans and communists from the days of anti-communist authoritarianism. The South Korean youth could thus been seen as proclaiming an identification with their northern brethren. More importantly, they were appropriating the symbols of the past to craft a new identity, even national identity, that moved well beyond the Cold War confrontation and forged a greater awareness of Korea's ties to the larger world. As the national team—managed, significantly, by a Dutch coach—performed far beyond expectations, and as the streets filled with increasing swarms of people eager to partake in the euphoria, it became clear that these enormous gatherings were about much more than soccer; they were about the overwhelming desire to experience directly a new mode of social connection as it was being invented.

When the national team, a heavy underdog, beat Portugal, one of the World Cup favorites, to advance to the round of sixteen, these crowds erupted, and they grew even bigger for the next game against Italy, another perennial power. At the start of this game, the Red Devils constructed a gigantic sign on one end of the stadium reading "Again 1966". This referred to the last time an Asian team shocked the soccer world with a win over an established World Cup power: North Korea's astonishing victory over Italy in 1966. Alas, the South Korean team achieved a hard-fought, stunning overtime win over an exhausted Italian team, and the crowds erupted again. For the next game, the quarterfinal match against Spain, what seemed like a phenomenon that could not get any bigger did exactly that, as now millions of Koreans filled city plazas, parks, and other designated areas to channel their collective spirit to the national team. The game ended in regulation time with a scoreless tie, but the Korean team had escaped some close calls and seemed, finally, overmatched. When the extra period achieved no resolution, however, the game entered the penalty kick shootout stage, when psychology is said to be more decisive than skill. Playing in front of a raucous home crowd in the city of Kwangju, the Korean team proved this aphorism true, as the team captain, Hong Myung-Bo, booted the ball past the Spanish goalkeeper for the game-winner. This moment, magically captured in a famous photo of Hong gliding with his arms outstretched to celebrate his kick, would represent the high point in the annals of Korean soccer, for South Korea would fall to Germany in the semi-final match, then lose again in the third-place match against Turkey. But the national team had taken the country on a rapturous journey over a four-week span, a symbolic capstone to South Korea's revival from the depths of despair just five years earlier.

It is likely that the youth-led euphoria of the World Cup also played a role in the election later in 2002 of Roh Moo-hyun as the next president. Roh, the "liberal" candidate who came out of nowhere to gain the ruling party's nomination, had faced long odds of winning. The people had grown weary of Kim Dae Jung's administration, which was mired in corruption scandals, and the conservative opposition party's challenger was a highly-respected, well-known figure. But, in addition to overwhelming support from the younger generations, who were cultivated and mobilized through an innovative Internet-centred campaign, Roh also rode the cresting wave of anti-American sentiment in 2002. When two school girls were accidentally run over by an American military vehicle in the spring, fierce protests and large-scale candlelight vigils arose to demand punishment of the soldiers involved. Even before this incident, one of Roh's central campaign platforms had been a reconsideration of the American alliance, including greater assertiveness of South Korea's autonomy and interests. That such a pledge enjoyed widespread support spoke to the way anti-Americanism, a very complex phenomenon that developed from many factors, continued to resonate among many Koreans. Still, it was never known with any degree of probability that Roh would pull out the victory, and when he did, South Korea witnessed the first transfer of power from one liberal administration to another.

Roh became the standard-bearer of the 386-generation's ideals and interests, even though he himself did not belong to this generation, and his broad appeal to younger, progressive Koreans generated a passionate following. In his governing approach, however, Roh, an inordinately introspective and intelligent man, also came across often as arrogant and aloof to both his political foes and the citizenry. This ensured that many of his signature reform efforts, which on the whole were targeted at greater socio-economic equality and the "rectification" of historical imbalances, would not succeed. He was even impeached for abuse of power by the opposition-led National Assembly, though this transparently political move was quickly overturned by the Constitutional Court. His biggest failure, perhaps, was the defeat of his efforts to move the administrative capital from Seoul to a provincial area in order to relieve congestion and hyper-centralization. And almost inevitably, it seemed, his presidency lost its public support, coming to an end amidst a general sense of unease from stagnant job growth and, ironically, increasing bifurcation of the population according to wealth.

President Lee Myung-bak, former head of Hyundai Construction and mayor of Seoul, promised bold steps to provide "relief" from the policies pushed by ten years of liberal rule when he won the election in 2007. He also called for a sobering reassessment of the Sunshine Policy regarding North Korea and vowed to achieve rates of economic growth that would harken back to the Park Chung Hee era—without the dictatorship, of course. The judgment on his two main promises for change—one economic, the other diplomatic—awaits to be written. In fact, the most notable event involving his administration originated from his predecessor: the shocking suicide of Roh Moo-hyun in May 2009 amidst intensifying investigations by government prosecutors into suspicions of bribery during his presidency. As if by fate, the other main pillar of recent liberal politics, former president Kim Dae Jung, passed away three months later. The long-term response of South Korean society and polity to this extraordinary turn of events promises to color significantly the historical legacy of the new millennium's first decade.

Sources and Further Readings

GENERAL HISTORIES AND SOURCE COMPILATIONS

Cumings, Bruce. *Korea's Place in the Sun: A Modern History*. New York: W. W. Norton, 1997.

Haboush, JaHyun Kim (ed.). *Epistolary Korea: Letters from the Communicative Space of the Chosŏn, 1392–1910*. New York: Columbia University Press, 2009.

Kim, Djun-Kil. *The History of Korea*. Westport, CT: Greenwood Press, 2005.

Lee, Ki-baek. *A New History of Korea*. Edward W. Wagner, with Edward J. Shultz, tr. Cambridge, MA: Harvard University Press, 1984.

Lee, Peter H. (ed.). *A History of Korean Literature*. Cambridge: Cambridge University Press, 2003.

Lee, Peter, Theodore DeBary, Yŏngho Ch'oe, and Hugh H. W. Kang (eds). *Sources of Korean Tradition, Vols 1–2*. New York: Columbia University Press, 1996, 2000.

Peterson, Mark. *A Brief History of Korea*. New York: Facts on File, 2010.

Pratt, Keith. *Everlasting Flower: A History of Korea*. London: Reaktion Books, 2007.

Pratt, Keith and Richard Rutt, with additional material by James Hoare. *Korea: A Historical and Cultural Dictionary*. Richmond, Surrey, UK: Curzon, 1999.

Robinson, Michael E. *Korea's Twentieth-Century Odyssey*. Honolulu: University of Hawai'i Press, 2007.

Seth, Michael. *A Concise History of Korea: From the Neolithic Period through the Nineteenth Century*. Lanham, MD: Rowman & Littlefield Publishers, 2006.

1 KOGURYŎ AND ANCIENT KOREA

Barnes, Gina. *State Formation in Korea: Historical and Archaeological Perspectives*. Richmond: Routledge Curzon, 2001.

Byington, Mark (ed.). *Early Korea: Reconsidering Early Korean History Through Archaeology*. Honolulu: University of Hawaii Press, 2008.

National Museum of Korea. *Goguryeo Tomb Murals – Replicas in the National Museum of Korea*. Seoul: National Museum of Korea, 2007.

Jeon, Ho-tae. *Koguryo: The Origin of Korean Power and Pride*. Seoul: Northeast History Foundation, 2007.

Nelson, Sarah. *The Archaeology of Korea*. Cambridge, UK: Cambridge University Press, 1993.

2 QUEEN SŎNDŎK AND SILLA'S UNIFICATION OF KOREA

Best, Jonathan. *A History of the Early Korean Kingdom of Paekche, Together with an Annotated Translation of The Paekche Annals of the Samguk Sagi*. Cambridge, MA: Harvard University Asia Center, 2007.

Lee, Kidong. "The Indigenous Religions of Silla: Their Diversity and Durability." *Korean Studies* 28 (2005): 49–74.

Mintz, Grafton (ed.), Ha, Tae-Hung (tr.). *Samguk Yusa: Legends and History of the Three Kingdoms of Ancient Korea*. Seoul: Silla Pagoda, 2008.

McBride, Richard D., II. "Pak Ch'anghwa and the *Hwarang segi* Manuscripts." *Journal of Korean Studies* 13:1 (Fall 2008): 57–88.

Nha, Il-Seong. "Silla's Cheomseongdae." *Korea Journal* 41:4 (Winter 2001): 269–81.

Park, Hyun-Sook. "Baekje's Relationship with Japan in the 6th Century." *International Journal of Korean History* 11 (December 2007): 97–115.

3 THE UNIFIED SILLA KINGDOM

Ennin. *Diary: The Record of a Pilgrimage to China in Search of the Law*. Edwin O. Reischauer, tr. New York: Ronald Press Co., 1955.

McBride, Richard D., II. *Domesticating the Dharma: Buddhist Cults and the Hwaom Synthesis in Silla Korea*. Honolulu: University of Hawaii Press, 2007.

Reischauer, Edwin O. *Ennin's Travels in Tang China*. New York: Ronald Press Co., 1955.

Wŏnhyo. *Cultivating Original Enlightenment: Wohnyo's Exposition of the Vajrasamadhi-Sutra (Kumgang Sammaegyong Non)*. Robert E. Buswell Jr., tr. Honolulu: University of Hawai'i Press, 2007.

4   FOUNDING OF THE KORYŎ DYNASTY

Duncan, John. "Koguryŏ in Koryŏ and Chosŏn Historical Memory." *Journal of Inner and East Asian Studies* 1 (2004).

Ledyard, Gari. "Yin and Yang in the China-Manchuria-Korea Triangle." In Morris Rossabi, ed. *China Among Equals: The Middle Kingdom and Its Neighbors, 10th–14th Centuries*. Berkeley: University of California Press, 1983.

Ro, Myoung-ho. "Perception and Policy of the Koryŏ Ruling Class toward the People of Parhae." *Seoul Journal of Korean Studies* 13 (2000): 125–42.

Rogers, Michael C. "National Consciousness in Medieval Korea: The Impact of Liao and Chin on Koryŏ." In Morris Rossabi (ed.). *China Among Equals: The Middle Kingdom and Its Neighbors, 10th–14th Centuries*. Berkeley: University of California Press, 1983.

5   RELIGION AND REGIONALISM IN THE KORYŎ ORDER

Breuker, Remco E. "Koryŏ as an Independent Realm: The Emperor's Clothes?" *Korean Studies* 27 (2004): 48–84.

Chinul. *The Korean Approach to Zen: The Collected Works of Chinul*. Robert E. Buswell, tr. Honolulu: University of Hawai'i Press, 1983.

Lancaster, Lewis R., Kikun Suh, and Chai-shin Yu (eds). *Buddhism in Koryŏ: A Royal Religion*. Berkeley, CA: Institute of East Asian Studies, 1996.

Shultz, Edward J. "An Introduction to the *Samguk Sagi*." *Korean Studies* 28 (2005): 1–13.

Vermeersch, Sem. *The Power of the Buddhas: The Politics of Buddhism during the Koryŏ Dynasty (918–1392)*. Cambridge, MA: Harvard University Asia Center, 2008.

6   THE MONGOL OVERLORD PERIOD

Shultz, Edward J. *Generals and Scholars: Military Rule in Medieval Korea.* Honolulu: University of Hawai'i Press, 2000.

Yun, Peter I. "Popularization of Mongol Language and Culture in the Late Koryo Period." *International Journal of Korean History* 10 (December 2006): 25–41.

Robinson, David M. *Empire's Twilight: Northeast Asia under the Mongols.* Cambridge, MA: Harvard Asia Center, 2009.

7   KORYŎ-CHOSŎN TRANSITION

Ch'oe, Yong-ho. *The Civil Examinations and the Social Structure in Early Yi Dynasty Korea, 1392–1600.* Seoul: Korean Research Center, 1987.

Duncan, John B. *The Origins of the Chosŏn Dynasty.* Seattle: University of Washington Press, 2000.

Wagner, Edward W. *The Literati Purges: Political Conflict in Early Yi Korea.* Cambridge, MA: Harvard University Press, 1974.

de Bary, Wm. Theodore, and JaHyun Kim Haboush (eds). *The Rise of Neo-Confucianism in Korea.* New York: Columbia University Press, 1986.

8   CONFUCIANISM AND THE FAMILY IN THE EARLY CHOSŎN DYNASTY

Chung, Edward Y. J. *The Korean Neo-Confucianism of Yi T'oegye and Yi Yulgok: A Reappraisal of the "Four-Seven Thesis" and Its Practical Implications for Self-Cultivation.* Albany, NY: SUNY Press, 1995.

Deuchler, Martina. *The Confucian Transformation of Korea: A Study of Society and Ideology.* Cambridge, MA: Harvard University, Council on East Asian Studies, 1992.

Lee, Hai-soon. *The Poetic World of Classic Korean Women Writers.* Won-Jae Hur, tr. Seoul: Ewha Womans University Press, 2005.

Ro, Young-chan. *The Korean Neo-Confucianism of Yi Yulgok.* Albany, NY: SUNY Press, 1989.

Yi Hwang. *To Become a Sage: The Ten Diagrams on Sage Learning.* Michael C. Kalton, tr. New York: Columbia University Press, 1988.

9   THE GREAT INVASIONS, 1592–1636

Ha, Tae-hung (tr.), and Sohn Pow-key (ed.). *Imjin Changch'o: Admiral Yi Sun-sin's Memorials to Court.* Seoul: Yonsei University Press, 1981.

Ledyard, Gari. "Confucianism and War: The Korean Security Crisis of 1598." *The Journal of Korean Studies* 6 (1988–89): 81–119.

Lewis, James B. *Frontier Contact between Chosŏn Korea and Tokugawa Japan.* London: Routledge Curzon, 2003.

Swope, Kenneth M. *A Dragon's Head and a Serpent's Tail: Ming China and the First Great East Asian War, 1592–1598.* Norman, OK: University of Oklahoma Press, 2009.

Yu Sŏng-nyong. *The Book of Corrections: Reflections on the National Crisis During the Japanese Invasion of Korea, 1592–1598.* Choi Byonghyon, tr. Berkeley, CA: Institute of East Asian Studies, 2002.

10   IDEOLOGY, FAMILY, AND NATIONHOOD IN THE MID-CHOSŎN ERA

Chi, Sung-jong. "The Study of Social Status Groups in the Chosŏn Period." *The Review of Korean Studies* 4:2 (December 2001): 243–63.

Duncan, John B. "Proto-nationalism in Premodern Korea." In Sang-Oak Lee and Duk-Soo Park (eds). *Perspectives on Korea.* Sydney: Wild Peony, 1998.

Kim Haboush, Jahyun and Martina Deuchler (eds). *Culture and the State in Late Chosŏn Korea.* Cambridge, MA: Harvard University Asia Center, 1999.

Park, Chan E. "Sukchong's Triangle: The Politics of Passion." *Korean Studies* 19 (1995): 83–103.

Park, Eugene Y. *Between Dreams and Reality: The Military Examination in Late Chosŏn Korea, 1600–1894.* Cambridge, MA: Harvard University Asia Center, 2007.

Peterson, Mark. *Korean Adoption and Inheritance: Case Studies in the Creation of a Classic Confucian Society.* Ithaca, NY: Cornell University East Asian Program, 1996.

Setton, Mark. "Factional Politics and Philosophical Development in the Late Chosŏn." *Journal of Korean Studies* 8 (1992): 37–79.

Song, Ki-joong. *The Study of Foreign Languages in the Chosŏn Dynasty.* Seoul: Jimoondang, 2000.

11 INTELLECTUAL OPENING IN THE LATE EIGHTEENTH CENTURY

Jun, Seong Ho, James B. Lewis, and Kang Han-Rog. "Korean Expansion and Decline from the Seventeenth to the Nineteenth Century: A View Suggested by Adam Smith." *Journal of Economic History* 68:1 (March 2008): 244–82.

Haboush, JaHyun Kim. *The Confucian Kingship in Korea: Yŏngjo and the Politics of Sagacity.* New York: Columbia University Press, 2001.

Haboush, JaHyun Kim (ed. and tr.). *The Memoirs of Lady Hyegyong: The Autobiographical Writings of a Crown Princess of Eighteenth-Century Korea.* Berkeley: University of California Press, 1996.

Ledyard, Gari. "Hong Taeyong and His Peking Memoir." *Korean Studies* 6 (1982): 63–103.

Palais, James. *Confucian Statecraft and Korean Institutions: Yu Hyŏngwŏn and the Late Chosŏn Dynasty.* Seattle: University of Washington Press, 1996.

12 POPULAR CULTURE IN THE LATE CHOSŎN ERA

Haboush, JaHyun Kim. "Rescoring the Universal in a Korean Mode: Eighteenth-Century Korean Culture." In Hongnam Kim (ed.). *Korean Arts of the Eighteenth Century: Splendor and Simplicity.* New York: The Asia Society Galleries, 1993.

Jungmann, Burglind. *Painters as Envoys: Korean Inspiration in Eighteenth-Century Japanese Nanga.* Princeton, NJ: Princeton University Press, 2004.

Pettid, Michael J. "Sexual Identity in Chosŏn Period Literature: Humorous Accounts of Forbidden Passion." *The Review of Korean Studies* 4:1 (June 2001): 61–85.

Pihl, Marshall R. *The Korean Singer of Tales.* Cambridge, MA: Council on East Asian Studies, 1994.

Shima, Mutsuhiko. "In Quest of Social Recognition: A Retrospective View on the Development of Korean Lineage Organization." *Harvard Journal of Asiatic Studies* 50:1 (June 1990): 87–129.

13 NINETEENTH-CENTURY UNREST

Chung, Chai-Sik. *A Korean Confucian Encounter with the Modern World: Yi Hang-No and the West*. Berkeley: Institute of East Asian Studies, 1995.

Deuchler, Martina. *Confucian Gentlemen and Barbarian Envoys: The Opening of Korea, 1875–1885*. Seattle: University of Washington Press, 1977.

Karlsson, Anders. "Challenging the Dynasty: Popular Protest, *Chŏnggamnok* and the Ideology of the Hong Kyŏngnae Rebellion." *International Journal of Korean History* 2 (2001): 255–77.

Kim, Sun Joo. *Marginality and Subversion in Korea: The Hong Kyongnae Rebellion of 1812*. Seattle: University of Washington Press, 2007.

Palais, James B. *Politics and Policy in Traditional Korea*. Seattle: University of Washington Press, 1991.

14 1894, A FATEFUL YEAR

Eckert, Carter. "Korea's Transition to Modernity: A Will to Greatness." In Merle Goldman and Andrew Gordon (eds). *Historical Perspectives on Contemporary East Asia*, pp. 119–54. Cambridge, MA: Harvard University Press, 2000.

Hwang, Kyung Moon. *Beyond Birth: Social Status in the Emergence of Modern Korea*. Cambridge, MA: Harvard Asia Center, 2004.

Lew, Young Ick. "The Conservative Character of the 1894 Tonghak Peasant Uprising: A Reappraisal with Emphasis on Chŏn Pong-jun's Background and Motivation." *The Journal of Korean Studies* 7 (1990): 149–80.

Lew, Young Ick. "Yuan Shih-kai's Residency and the Korean Enlightenment Movement, 1885–94." *The Journal of Korean Studies* 5 (1984): 63–108.

Mutsu Munemitsu. *Kenkenroku: A Diplomatic Record of the Sino-Japanese War, 1894–95*. Gordon Mark Berger, ed. and tr. Princeton, NJ: Princeton University Press, 1982.

15 THE GREAT KOREAN EMPIRE

Chandra, Vipan. *Imperialism, Resistance, and Reform in Late Nineteenth-Century Korea: Enlightenment and the Independence Club*. Berkeley: Institute of East Asian Studies, Center for Korean Studies, 1988.

Hwang, Kyung Moon. "Citizenship, Social Equality and Government Reform: Changes in the Household Registration System in Korea, 1894–1910." *Modern Asian Studies* 38:2 (May 2004): 355–88.

Kim, Christine J. "Politics and Pageantry in Protectorate Korea (1905–10): The Imperial Progresses of Sunjong." *The Journal of Asian Studies* 68.3 (2009): 835–59.

Larsen, Kirk W. *Tradition, Treaties, and Trade: Qing Imperialism and Chosŏn Korea, 1850–1910.* Cambridge, MA: Harvard East Asia Center, 2008.

Schmid, Andre. *Korea Between Empires, 1895–1919.* New York: Columbia University Press, 2002.

Son, Min Suh. "Enlightenment and Electrification: The Introduction of Electric Light, Telegraph and Streetcars in Late 19th Century Korea." In Dong-no Kim, John Duncan, and Do-hyung Kim (eds). *Reform and Modernity in the Taehan Empire.* Seoul: Jimoondang, 2006.

16 THE JAPANESE TAKEOVER, 1904–18

Dudden, Alexis. *Japan's Colonization of Korea: Discourse and Power.* Honolulu: University of Hawai'i Press, 2004.

Duus, Peter. *The Abacus and The Sword: The Japanese Penetration of Korea, 1895-1910.* Berkeley: University of California Press, 1995.

Finch, Michael. *Min Yŏng-hwan: A Political Biography.* Honolulu: University of Hawai'i Press, 2002.

Myers, Ramon H. and Mark R. Peattie (eds). *The Japanese Colonial Empire, 1895–1945.* Princeton, NJ: Princeton University Press, 1984.

Rhee, Syngman. *The Spirit of Independence: A Primer on Korean Modernization and Reform.* Honolulu: University of Hawai'i Press, 2001.

Robinson, Michael. "National Identity and the Thought of Sin Ch'aeho: Sadaejuŭi and Chuch'e in History and Politics." *Journal of Korean Studies* 5 (1984): 121–42.

17 THE LONG 1920s

Kim, Yung-Hee. "Creating New Paradigms of Womanhood in Modern Korean Literature: Na Hye-sŏk's 'Kyŏnghŭi.'" *Korean Studies* 26.1 (2002): 1–60.

Robinson, Michael. *Cultural Nationalism in Colonial Korea, 1920–1925*. Seattle: University of Washington Press, 1988.

Hyun, Theresa. *Writing Women in Korea: Translation and Feminism in the Early Twentieth Century*. Honolulu: University of Hawai'i Press, 2004.

Kim, Janice. *To Live to Work: Factory Women in Colonial Korea, 1910–1945*. Stanford, CA: Stanford University Press, 2008.

Wells, Kenneth. *New God, New Nation: Protestants and Self-Reconstruction Nationalism in Korea, 1896–1937*. Honolulu: University of Hawai'i Press, 1991.

Yoo, Theodore Jun. *The Politics of Gender in Colonial Korea: Education, Labor, and Health, 1910–1945*. Berkeley, CA: University of California Press, 2008.

18   NATION, CULTURE, AND EVERYDAY LIFE IN THE LATE COLONIAL PERIOD

Caprio, Mark E. *Japanese Assimilation Policies in Colonial Korea, 1910–1945*. Seattle: University of Washington Press, 2009.

Ch'ae, Man-Sik. *Peace Under Heaven*. Chun Kyung-ja, tr. Armonk, NY: M.E. Sharpe, 1993.

Eckert, Carter J. *Offspring of Empire: The Koch'ang Kims and the Colonial Origins of Korean Capitalism, 1876–1945*. Seattle: University of Washington Press, 1991.

Kim, Chong-un, and Bruce Fulton (trs). *A Ready-Made Life: Early Masters of Korean Fiction*. Honolulu: University of Hawai'i Press, 1998.

Pai, Hyung Il. *Constructing "Korean" Origins: A Critical Review of Archaeology, Historiography, and Racial Myth in Korean State-Formation Theories*. Cambridge, MA: Harvard University Asia Center, 2000.

Park, Soon-Won. *Colonial Industrialization and Labor in Korea: The Onoda Cement Factory*. Cambridge, MA: Harvard University Asia Center, 1999.

Park, Sunyoung. *On the Eve of the Uprising and Other Stories from Colonial Korea*. Ithaca, NY: Cornell East Asia Program, 2010.

Shin, Gi-Wook Shin and Michael Robinson (eds). *Colonial Modernity in Korea*. Cambridge, MA: Harvard University Asia Center, 1999.

Yom Sang-seop. *Three Generations*. Yu Young-nan, tr. Brooklyn, NY: Archipelago Books, 2005.

19 WARTIME MOBILIZATION, 1938–45

Allen, Chizuko. "Northeast Asia Centered Around Korea: Ch'oe Namsŏn's View of History." *Journal of Asian Studies* 49 (1990): 787–806.

Eckert, Carter J. "Total War, Industrialization, and Social Change in Late Colonial Korea." In Peter Duus, R. H. Myers, and M. R. Peattie (eds). *The Japanese Wartime Empire, 1931–1945*. Princeton, NJ: Princeton University Press, 1996.

Howard, Keith. *True Stories of the Korean Comfort Women*. London: Cassell, 1995.

Kang, Hildi. *Under the Black Umbrella: Voices from Colonial Korea, 1910–1945*. Ithaca, NY: Cornell University Press, 2001.

Lee, Ann Sung-hi. *Yi Kwang-su and Modern Korean Literature: Mujong*. Ithaca, NY: Cornell East Asia Program, 2005.

Park, Hyun Ok. *Two Dreams in One Bed: Empire, Social Life, and the Origins of the North Korean Revolution in Manchuria*. Durham, NC: Duke University Press, 2005.

Palmer, Brandon. "Imperial Japan's Preparations to Conscript Koreans as Soldiers, 1942–1945." *Korean Studies* 31 (2007): 63–78.

Shin, Gi-Wook. *Peasant Protest and Social Change in Colonial Korea*. Seattle: University of Washington Press, 1996.

20 THE LIBERATION PERIOD, 1945–50

Cheong, Sung-hwa. *The Politics of Anti-Japanese Sentiment in Korea: Japanese-South Korea Relations Under American Occupation, 1945–1952*. New York: Greenwood Press, 1991.

Clark, Donald N. *Living Dangerously in Korea: The Western Experience, 1900–1950*. Norwalk, CT: Eastbridge, 2003.

Cumings, Bruce. *The Origins of the Korean War*, 2 vols. Princeton: Princeton University Press, 1981, 1990.

Oh, Bonnie B. C. (ed.). *Korea under the American Military Government, 1945–1948*. Westport, CT: Greenwood, 2002.

Weathersby, Kathryn. *Soviet Aims in Korea and the Origins of the Korean War, 1945–1950: New Evidence from Russian Archives*. Working paper no. 8, Cold War International History Project. Washington DC Woodrow Wilson Center, 1993.

21 THE KOREAN WAR

Appleman, Roy A. *Disaster in Korea: The Chinese Confront MacArthur.* College Station, TX: Texas A & M University Press, 1989.

Bateman, Robert L. *No Gun Ri: A Military History of the Korean War Incident.* Mechanicsburg, PA: Stackpole Books, 2002.

Halberstam, David. *The Coldest Winter: America and the Korean War.* New York: Hyperion, 2007.

Jin, Jingyi. "A Historical Review of the Return to Korea of Korean Soldiers in the Chinese Army." *Social Sciences in China* 27:4 (Winter 2006): 72–85.

Kim, Hak-joon. "The Korean War and China: The Sino-North Korean Relations Before the Chinese Intervention in the Korean War." *Journal of Social Sciences and Humanities* 59 (June 1984): 1–90.

Lee, Chae-Jin (ed). *The Korean War: 40-Year Perspectives.* Claremont, CA: The Keck Center for International and Strategic Studies, 1991.

Stueck, William. *Rethinking the Korean War: A New Diplomatic and Strategic History.* Princeton, NJ: Princeton University Press, 2002.

Tucker, Spencer C. *The Encyclopedia of the Korean War*, 3 vols. New York: ABC-CLIO, 2010.

22 EARLY NORTH KOREA

Armstrong, Charles K. *The North Korean Revolution, 1945–1950.* Ithaca, New York: Cornell University Press, 2003.

Cathcart, Adam, and Charles Kraus. "Peripheral Influence: The Sinuiju Student Incident of 1945 and the Impact of Soviet Occupation in North Korea." *The Journal of Korean Studies* 13:1 (Fall 2008): 1–28.

David-West, Alzo. "Marxism, Stalinism, and the Juche Speech of 1955: On the Theoretical De-Stalinization of North Korea." *The Review of Korean Studies* 10:3 (September 2007): 127–52.

Kim, Gwang-Oon. "The Making of the North Korean State." *The Journal of Korean Studies* 12:1 (Fall 2007): 15–42.

Lankov, Andrei N. *Crisis in North Korea: The Failure of De-Stalinization, 1956.* Honolulu: University of Hawai'i Press, 2004.

Lankov, Andrei N. *From Stalin to Kim Il Sung: The Formation of North Korea, 1945–1960.* New Brunswick, NJ: Rutgers University Press, 2002.

Myers, Brian R. *Han Sŏrya and North Korean Literature: The Failure of Socialist Realism in the DPRK.* Ithaca, NY: Cornell East Asia Series, 1994.

Suh, Dae-Sook. *Kim Il Sung: The North Korean Leader.* New York: Columbia University Press, 1995.

23   1960s SOUTH KOREA

Cha, Victor D. "Bridging the Gap: The Strategic Context of the 1965 Korea–Japan Normalization Treaty." *Korean Studies* 20 (1996): 123–60.

Han, Sungjoo. *The Failure of Democracy in South Korea.* Berkeley, CA: University of California Press, 1974.

Kirk, Donald. *Korean Dynasty: Hyundai and Chung Ju Yung.* Armonk, NY: M.E. Sharpe, 1997.

Nam, Hwasook. *Building Ships, Building a Nation: Korea's Democratic Unionism under Park Chung Hee.* Seattle: University of Washington Press, 2009.

Park Chung Hee. *Our Nation's Path: Ideology of Social Reconstruction.* Seoul: Dong-a Publishing Company, 1969.

Steers, Richard M. *Made in Korea: Chung Ju Yung and the Rise of Hyundai.* New York: Routledge, 1991.

24   CULTURE AND POLITICS IN 1970s SOUTH KOREA

Pihl, Marshall R., Bruce Fulton, and Ju-Chan Fulton (trs). *Land of Exile: Contemporary Korean Fiction.* Armonk, NY: M.E. Sharpe, 1992.

Kim Chi-ha. *Cry of the People and Other Poems.* Hayama, Japan: Autumn Press, 1974.

Kim Chi-ha. *The Gold Crowned Jesus and Other Writings.* Maryknoll, NY: Orbis Books, 1978.

Kim, Eun Mee. *Big Business, Strong State: Collusion and Conflict in South Korean Developments, 1960–1990.* Albany, NY: SUNY Press, 1997.

Moon, Seungsook. *Militarized Modernity and Gendered Citizenship in South Korea.* Durham, NC: Duke University Press, 2005.

Oberdorfer, Don. *The Two Koreas: A Contemporary History.* New York: Basic Books, 2002.

Pak, Kyŏng-ni. *Land: A Novel.* London: Kegan Paul International, 1996.

25   MONUMENTAL LIFE IN NORTH KOREA

Chinoy, Mike. *Meltdown: The Inside Story of the North Korean Nuclear Crisis*. New York: St. Martin's Griffin, 2009.

Cumings, Bruce. *North Korea: Another Country*. New York: The New Press, 2004.

Kihl, Young Whan and Hong Nack Kim (eds). *North Korea: The Politics of Regime Survival*. Armonk, NY: M.E. Sharpe, 2005.

Oh, Kongdan and Ralph C. Hassig. *North Korea through the Looking Glass*. Washington DC: Brookings Institution Press, 2000.

Quinones, C. Kenneth and Joseph Tragert. *The Complete Idiot's Guide to Understanding North Korea*. New York: Alpha, 2004.

Ryang, Sonia (ed.). *North Korea: Toward a Better Understanding*. Lanham, MD: Lexington Books, 2008.

Yu, Chong-Ae. "The Rise and Demise of Industrial Agriculture in North Korea." *The Journal of Korean Studies* 12:1 (Fall 2007): 75–110.

26   SOUTH KOREAN DEMOCRATIZATION

Abelmann, Nancy. *Echoes of the Past, Epics of Dissent: A South Korean Social Movement*. Berkeley, CA: University of California Press, 1996.

Kim, Sunhyuk. *The Politics of Democratization in Korea: The Role of Civil Society*. Pittsburgh, PA: University of Pittsburgh Press, 2001.

Lee, Namhee. *The Making of Minjung: Democracy and the Politics of Representation in South Korea*. Ithaca, NY: Cornell University Press, 2009.

Shin, Gi-Wook and Kyung Moon Hwang (eds). *Contentious Kwangju: The May 18 Uprising in Korea's Past and Present*. Lanham, MD: Rowman & Littlefield, 2003.

Lee, Jae-Eui, Kap Su Seol, and Nick Mamatas. *Kwangju Diary: Beyond Death, Beyond the Darkness of the Age*. Los Angeles: UCLA Asia Institute, 1999.

27   SOUTH KOREA IN THE NEW MILLENNIUM

Abelmann, Nancy. *The Melodrama of Mobility: Women, Talk, and Class in Contemporary South Korea*. Honolulu: University of Hawai'i Press, 2003.

Huat, Chua Beng and Koichi Iwabuchi (eds). *East Asian Pop Culture: Analysing the Korean Wave*. Hong Kong: Hong Kong University Press, 2008.

Kendall, Laurel. *Under Construction: The Gendering of Modernity, Class, and Consumption in the Republic of Korea*. Honolulu: University of Hawai'i Press, 2001.

Kim, Jasper. *Crisis and Change: South Korea in a Post-1997 New Era*. Seoul: Ewha Womans University Press, 2006.

Russell, Mark James. *Pop Goes Korea: Behind the Revolution in Movies, Music, and Internet Culture*. Berkeley, CA: Stone Bridge Press, 2009.

Index

Printed and bound in the United States of America